To David
who have ha
of Scotland
Haste ye back. Hazel

WELSH ORIGINS OF SCOTTISH PLACE-NAMES

Welsh Origins of Scottish Place-names

William Oxenham

ISBN: 0-86381-957-5

Cover design: Sian Parri

First published in 2005 by
Gwasg Carreg Gwalch, 12 Iard yr Orsaf, Llanrwst,
Wales LL26 0EH.

01492 642031   01492 641502
books@carreg-gwalch.co.uk
Web site: www.carreg-gwalch.co.uk

To my wife

CATHERINE

without whose support, encouragement, patience and assistance this book would never have been started let alone finished!

Preface

'If you have not found it, you cannot know where it is, you can only surmise, which is not the same thing'

The Cadfael Chronicles, The Pilgrim of Hate

It ought first to be explained what the description *'Welsh Origins'* in the title of this book implies. There are some who might consider it more appropriate to select a title employing descriptions such as Brythonic, Brittonic, Cumbric, Cymric or British to describe the languages which gave rise to the P-Celtic place-names of Scotland in earlier times. However, almost nothing is known of these ancient 'lost' languages and the only proven satisfactory way of giving any meaning to Scottish place-names thought to have originated in any of them is to relate the individual names to the surviving P-Celtic languages of the British Isles and France. These are Welsh, Cornish and Breton, of these three both Cornish and Breton have declined – Cornish vanished completely at one time and is now in use as a resurrected form.

On the other hand Welsh has survived intact and it is this language which has been very successfully used, in all previous authoritative works on Scottish place-names, to aid the interpretation of Scotland's P-Celtic place-names. This book accepts and extends this principle, taking as it's basic premise the factual statement that at one time the only language spoken and understood throughout the whole of what is now known as Scotland was an archaic form of the language now spoken in present day Wales. It then makes the very reasonable assumption that, with some relatively few exceptions which are explained later, all the place-names then existing in Scotland would have been founded in that early form of the Welsh language.

This being so, it is the aim of this volume to take a representative list of present-day Scottish place-names and subject each of them to further scrutiny with the particular objective of discovering and determining any evidence, hint, or possibility that it once originated in the P-Celtic 'old Welsh' languages of the Scotland of times long ago. It pursues this objective by drawing on the resources contained within the works of established authors in this field such as W.J. Watson, J.B. Johnston, W.F.H. Nicolaisen, Stuart Harris and others. It makes no categorical assertions about any selected place-name but rather puts forward suggested 'Welsh' interpretations, invariably based on the evidence of the earliest available Records, and compares these with the interpretations and opinions of Watson, Johnston, Harries *et al.* In the chapter, 'Place-names of Scotland', it will be seen that Welsh interpretations are given first and these are then compared with interpretations already documented, primarily in the works of Watson and Johnston, but also sometimes elsewhere. Readers are left to judge for themselves between the possibilities and probabilities presented: other chapters are written in similar fashion. Watson and Johnston are recognised as two of the original founts of knowledge on the subject of Scottish place-names and there are but few interpretations available in the works of other authors which cannot also be found amongst those contained in either Watson's *The History of the Celtic Place-Names of Scotland* or in Johnston's *Place-Names of Scotland*. The importance of these two works of reference can be gauged by the fact that even today they are still found to be in print more than 70 years after they were first published! It is noteworthy that amongst the examples of place-names which *they* see as having such a 'Welsh' origin are; Edinburgh, Glasgow, Aberdeen, Applecross, Perth, Stirling, Lanark, Peebles, Kelso and Melrose. Both of these authors refer to the P-Celtic elements they quote in their interpretations as 'Welsh' and only very occasionally use the descriptions Brythonic, Brittonic, British, Cumbric or Pictish when they are unable to find suitable words in Welsh Dictionaries and are forced to resort to linguistically contrived retro-reconstructions (based on Welsh)) of lost-language words. The use of the adjective *'Welsh'* (in inverted commas) in this book can therefore be quite legitimately applied to embrace all those P-Celtic languages variously described as Brythonic, Brittonic, Cumbric, Cymric, British or Pictish which were spoken in those far off days when Scotland was known only as *Caledonia*. It is for this reason, and to maintain consistency with Watson and Johnston that this book is titled *'Welsh' Origins of Scottish Place-Names.* Being myself more of an enthusiastic amateur rather than a dedicated professional in this field it is my hope that for this reason the general reader will find it more accessible than might otherwise have been the case; it is also my hope that although it contains relatively little original material the more knowledgeable toponymist will still find it useful inasmuch as it brings together in one volume all the available relevant attributions from the recognised authorities on this subject – and this sometimes makes for interesting comparisons!

In this book it is made quite plain that no matter what reasoned arguments are put forward in support of various place-name interpretations, no matter how clever the detective work, and no matter what linguistic or other knowledge is applied to the problem, none of us in this day and age can possibly *know* what these obscure names from our distant past actually were, and what their real meaning was, at the time they were first formed and then used by our ancestors, we *'can only surmise, which is not the same thing'*!

Contents

Chapter 1

Introduction

'Take heart, nothing is ever quite what it seems'

Cadfael Chronicles, The Virgin in the Ice

That there are place-names in Scotland which can legitimately be described as 'Cymro-Caledonian' or 'Welsh-Scottish' is no longer a matter of dispute; these place-names are however of some antiquity and can be considered to have originated at times which could be anything from 1,000 to 2,500 years ago. Many of these names have survived in forms which, although distorted, still retain sufficient traces of their earliest ancestry to allow their original forms and meanings to be discerned with an acceptable degree of confidence. In one or two remarkable instances this can be achieved with exceptional ease – the place-name **Perth** is today pronounced and spelled in Scotland, in precisely the same way as the word *perth* is pronounced in present day Wales and as it is spelled in any modern Welsh dictionary. In other cases Welsh origins are less apparent and a 'reasoned inference' is perhaps all that can be achieved. The purpose of this book is to take a general selection of Scottish place-names, identify any possible Welsh roots they are said to have had or are thought to have had and thereby illuminate a somewhat neglected aspect of early Scottish history: i.e. the underlying Welsh dimension not only to the pre-Roman, Roman and Dark-Age eras of that history but also to make the point that this dimension is still relevant to the Scotland of the 21st century.

The content of this volume, as has been said before, relies heavily on the published work of others, foremost among which is W.J. Watson's *The History of the Celtic Place-names of Scotland,* often affectionately referred to as 'CPNS'. Published in 1926, but based on work first initiated in 1916, this is a truly magisterial work of great scholarship and erudition and has been an essential starting point and reference for all subsequent authors, researchers and students of Scottish toponymy. The depth and breadth of Watson's coverage of his subject is truly astonishing, even today after almost a century his is the first work resorted to for any serious study. It remains a 'mine of information' but as in all 'mines' the precious metal is hidden underground and has to be dug out nugget-by-nugget, with some considerable effort! This book has assiduously 'mined' Watson's legacy, but it has to be admitted that much is still left unrecovered. A pioneer in the study of Scottish place-names and someone who probably did more than anyone else to *popularise* the study of of this Subject was J.B. Johnston, his *Place-names of Scotland* published in 1934 was based on some earlier works of 1892 onwards which he updated extensively after the publication of Watson's 'magnum opus'. Nowadays the primary value of his work lies in the early records which he so painstakingly collected and although his interpretations and a few of his early records are no longer considered to be built on secure foundations some of the least likely are often quoted in the works of more modern authors. This book makes extensive use of Johnston's Early Records but balances his interpretations against those of Watson and against other suggestions of Welsh origins. A work of great scholarship is *Scottish Place-Names* by W.F.H. Nicolaisen (2001). Rather more modern, and also very useful, is *Scotland's Place-names* by David Dorward (1995). As a detailed study of a particular individual area *Place-names of Edinburgh* by Stuart Harris (1999) is another monumental work which does for the place-names of Edinburgh what Watson and Johnston did for those of Scotland as a whole. Each of these five authors has a very individual approach to his subject. Watson, as a native speaker of the language, naturally dwells on the Gaelic connotations of any given name but it has to be remembered that his work is a '*History*' of the Celtic place-names of Scotland and it is not always clear in his dissertations whether he is making a definite attribution or simply discussing various alternative historic derivations from an array of ancient languages, including the older forms of the Irish-Gaelic, and Scots-Gaelic, 'Q-Celtic' languages, or the older forms of the Gaulish, Brythonic, Cumbric, etc. 'P-Celtic' languages and other early forms of Welsh and Pictish. There is however no questioning that Watson approached his subject with anything other than total professional impartiality, and he was palpably upset when it was suggested by Dr E.G. Gwynn (*Scottish Place-Name Papers*) that, if anything, he was being overly 'pro-British' (i.e. pro-Welsh). Johnston, despite a deserved criticism that when in doubt he conjured up rather too many fanciful Gaelic attributions, is a particular favourite of mine, not only is his obvious enthusiasm highly infectious but he also researched his subject deeply and his work is the source of many of the early place-name records in this book. Nicolaisen's approach is rather more geographical and broadly based; he selects certain key word-elements defined as being 'Gaelic' or 'Scandinavian' or 'Early English' or 'P-Celtic: Pictish or Cumbric' and then by researching the geographical distribution of these names he assesses the degree of influence various peoples and their languages had on the place-name map of Scotland. Unfortunately, but perhaps naturally, he does from the viewpoint of this particular book make very few quotable interpretations that are not already to be found in Watson or Johnston, so his contribution to the background research of this book is not made as obvious as maybe it ought to be. Dorward, very helpfully, lists most of the word elements found in Nicolaisen and elsewhere and explains them in some detail, an approach which is followed herein with much expanded references to the Welsh elements. Interestingly, Dorward himself states that he is intentionally 'perverse' in describing names of 'Welsh' origin as 'Brittonic' or 'Cumbric'; but in this respect he is no different to any of the others. Stuart Harris, in common with the other four authors, consistently employs the description *British,* but in common with everyone else quite obviously derives most of his *'British'* word-elements from modern *Welsh* dictionaries. I am however indebted to this author for the following encouraging statement, which accords well with the fundamental ethos of this book.

> *Lastly when the circumstances are given their proper weight, the realistic view of any Celtic name in the area* (i.e. Edinburgh and District) *is surely to presume it to be British, unless there is some particular and special reason for taking it to be Gaelic; and on this basis nearly nine out of ten of the Celtic names are either certainly or probably British in origin.*
>
> Stuart Harris

All five of the above works are indispensable sources of information and I take pleasure in acknowledging my debt to the authors as without their research, expertise and dedication this volume could not and would not have been written. In writing it I have in effect 'scavenged' through all these five references, plus various others, collected together into this volume all the names said or seen to have an apparent Brittonic, Cumbric or Welsh connection, listed them, reviewed any past interpretations and then reassessed them with particular emphasis on any possibility of them displaying any evidence or indication of a P-Celtic Welsh origin. Modern Welsh dictionaries and updated modern knowledge, including what is now known of contemporary and historical place-names in Wales itself, has eased and benefited this task. The difficulty in attributing a definite 'Brythonic' or 'Cumbric' root to any given placename is the lack of any existing 'Brythonic' or 'Cumbric' literature apart from a few words and scraps of sentences handed down to us by Roman scribes or on Romanno-British coinage. All we know for certain is that these two ancient languages are closely related to Modern Welsh. (see Chapter 6). Therefore, in this book, no attempt will be made to explain Scottish place-names in terms of supposed Brythonic or Cumbric roots, the nearest we will get to guessing what these roots may have been is to relate what evidence still exists to the present day Lexicon, Literature and History of the Modern Welsh language together with it's associated Dictionaries, Gazetteers of place-names and linguistic idiosyncrasies. This is not a new idea, the precedent for such a procedure has already been set in the works of Watson, Johnston, Nicolaisen, Harris, Dorward and all others who have followed in their footsteps. It can be said, quite fairly that this book has undertaken a purposefully blinkered 'Cymro-Centric' study of Scottish place-names which has placed greater emphasis on suggesting possible Welsh roots in contrast to some others in the past who have perhaps placed greater emphasis on suggesting possible Gaelic roots. It is hoped, that in comparison with the much publicized Irish-related Heritage of the Western Highlands and Islands and the apparent Hiberno-Centric approach of some previous publications, this book with it's different way of viewing, and illuminating, these ancient names will have the effect of establishing some awareness of, and perhaps stimulating some interest in, the underlying but neglected Welsh-related Heritage of *all* Scotland, particularly the Lowlands.

Chapter 2

Origins & Ancestry

'Truth, like the burgeoning of a bulb under the soil, however deeply sown, will make it's way to the light'

Cadfael Chronicles, 'The Potter's Field'

To many people the claim that place-names which are essentially 'Welsh' in character are to be found almost everywhere in Scotland comes as something of a surprise and is met with a certain amount of disbelief! So why are such names to be found in Scotland and why can they be described as 'British' or 'Welsh'? The description *British Isles* first appeared in historical records somewhere around 400 BC and applied to all the islands in the group including the two that are now known as 'Great Britain' and 'Ireland'. When the Romans arrived in this Island some 2000 years ago they called the inhabitants 'British', but when the Angles and Saxons came some half a millennium later they called *the very same people* 'Welsh'! Thereafter the terms 'British' or 'Welsh' were synonymous and were used interchangeably until in the year 1707 the Parliaments of England and Scotland were united to form the first Parliament of 'Great Britain'. Overnight the term *British* changed from its original meaning and came to mean a 'Citizen of Great Britain'; later still it changed again and nowadays it is understood to mean a 'Citizen of the United Kingdom of Great Britain & Northern Ireland'. Thus place names, found anywhere in England, Scotland or Wales, which survive from Roman or pre-Roman times and have their roots in the Brythonic language can legitimately be referred to as 'Brythonic' in it's original sense of it being the language of the Britons during those early years. Unfortunately, very few people today will claim to have a subjective understanding or clear comprehension of anything described as *Brythonic* yet they can immediately understand and relate to a language described as 'very early Welsh' – which is exactly what Brythonic was. That is why in this book language descriptions such as *British, Brythonic, Cumbric, Cymric* or *Pictish* will, although pedantically correct, be avoided wherever possible in favour of the simpler and more universally understood description *Welsh.* To get some idea of why there are P-Celtic Welsh place-names in today's Scotland it is necessary to go back to the history of Roman times and even earlier. The last ice age ended about 9000 BC and before that there were no identifiable places and therefore no place-names. As the ice retreated the first settlers arrived, these were hunter-gatherers of 'no fixed abode', as we say today, and had no fixed settlements worthy of a name. Landmarks and other topographical features were however of the utmost importance to them and foremost among these were the major Rivers which were undoubtedly given names in the languages prevailing at that time, but most of whose meanings are now lost to us today. Many of the rivers in the British Isles still bear names which are unexplainable in terms of those languages for which we have historical knowledge and it can be reasonably assumed that these names are therefore from pre-Celtic times and are the oldest and least understood of all our surviving place-names. The earliest names for which we have credible explanations are those which have their origin in the Celtic languages which arrived in these Islands together with the technologies that sparked off the end of the Bronze Age and the beginning of the Iron Age. Only two Celtic languages were introduced at that time; *P-Celtic* was the language of the Brittonic Celts and *Q-Celtic* was the language of the Goidelic Celts. Today we know those of Goidelic origins as 'Irish' and those of Brittonic origins as 'Welsh'.

Watson quotes the 8th century historian Nennius (referring to the population of these Islands at the time of the Roman invasions):

> *' . . . the Britons at first filled the whole Island with their children from the sea of Icht to the sea of Orcs. i.e. from the English Channel to the far north.'*

Note: *Sea of Icht* = The Solent; *Sea of Orcs* = The Pentland Firth. Watson himself has this to say:

> *As I have already pointed out, the evidence at our disposal goes to show that at the time of the Roman occupation the language current all over Britain was Celtic of the P-group, that is to say, Old British, represented now by Welsh.*

Thus, according to Watson, at the time of which Nennius spoke the whole of Great Britain, including Scotland would have been populated exclusively by people who spoke a form of very early Welsh and therefore *all* of the place names then existing in Scotland would, with few exceptions, have had their origin in that language. It is the purpose of this book to consider how many of these names have survived and how many of today's 'Scottish' place-names can be traced back to a possible origin in an 'Archaic', 'Early' or 'Old' Welsh Language. It will do this by following the example of Watson, Johnston, Nicolaisen and others who invariably base their P-Celtic interpretations on words still to be found in modern Welsh Dictionaries. The justification for adopting this method seems to be the very simple fact 'that it works'! Since this book aims only to be an introduction to the subject the treatment will necessarily be simplistic and broadly based, for example it will be assumed that the Welsh place names of Scotland came into being in the same way and at about the same time as those now existing in present day Wales, thus a study of Welsh place names will assist the process of deciphering their Scottish equivalents. Also, when I first became interested in this subject some 15 years or so ago I very quickly became aware that almost all the Welsh word-elements found in Scottish place names and identified as such by Watson, Johnston etc. can still be found either in modern Welsh dictionaries or else in the place names of Wales itself – interestingly this evidence from *Scottish* place names supports the belief of some academics that the *Welsh* language has not changed very much since the days when Scottish and Welsh place names were first recorded in the Middle Ages! Conveniently then the attribution of relevant Scottish place-names will, in this book, be interpreted in terms of word-elements found in modern Welsh dictionaries and in various publications devoted to the place-names of Wales. In this respect it differs not a lot from the methods used in all other books dealing with Scottish place-names!

But, many will ask, how *important* are these Welsh place names of Scotland? They are certainly not of any lesser importance nor of any greater importance than the English, Gaelic or Norse place names but some idea of their *significance* can be gauged by the fact that at this present time one quarter of Scotland's population live within the three major cities of Scotland and all three of these cities, i.e. Edinburgh, Glasgow & Aberdeen, have names which are undeniably of Welsh origin. Moreover at least two thirds of

Scotland's population live either in these three cities or within Local Authority areas having names such as Lanarkshire, Renfrewshire, Perthshire, Peebleshire, Stirlingshire, Dumfriesshire, Aberdeenshire and the Lothians which are also of Welsh origin. These figures may perhaps be criticized as an exercise in 'selective statistics' but they nevertheless are more than sufficient to make the point that in Scotland, Welsh place-names not only exist but are also the names of places and localities which feature prominently in the pages of Scottish History:

Given then that such names are not uncommon in present day Scotland, how old are they and how have they survived the ravages of time? It is now thought that the Welsh language survived in areas south of the Forth Clyde line until about the 13th or 14th century, mainly in those areas of Ayrshire, Lanarkshire and Renfrewshire known in history as the home of the 'Strathclyde Britons' or the 'Strathclyde Welsh', but also in the Central Borders region south of Edinburgh. The earliest 'Scottish' poetry was written in Scotland by the North-British (Northern-Welsh) poet 'Aneurin' sometime around the 7th century AD, it was called *'Y Gododdin'* and was written in the Welsh language of his day to both celebrate the heroism of the Gododdin and to bewail their defeat at the ill fated battle of Catraeth. P-Celtic Welsh Languages would therefore have been spoken in Scotland continuously from at least the early Iron Age, certainly up to the 7th century, and then in decline up to the 13/14th century. In this case it may be thought that the oldest Welsh place-names, i.e. before 550 AD, would be *Brythonic* in form, that the youngest would be in the form of what the pedants call *Middle Welsh* (circa 1135-1300 AD) or *Modern Welsh* (1300 AD onwards) and that in the middle would be names either in the form of *Primitive Welsh* (circa 550-775 AD) or *Old Welsh* (circa 775-1135 AD). Maybe not! As the language changed into it's later forms so, it seems, did most of the names change with it, these did not assume their first recorded form until they were written down, and this form would have been in one of the later forms of Welsh – not the earliest! The majority of these names were recorded either shortly before or shortly after the time of the Domesday Book i.e. circa 1050-1250 AD and would have been in a form relevant to that time period i.e. bridging *Middle Welsh* and *Modern Welsh* – hence the usefulness of modern Welsh dictionaries! It will be seen later that the accepted interpretations of actual place-names do in fact accord with this presumption – which the following quotation supports.

> Scotland's Story – Part 3 (1999): *'Britons are the ancestors no one seems to have heard about. They were Christians, spoke Welsh, worshipped at Govan, and ruled from Carlisle to Glasgow for 600 years. They are the nearest thing we (Scots) have to a 'native' people.'*

At this point there will I am sure be some readers who will be thinking to themselves 'What about the Picts!' – Well what about them? The Picts have for decades been the subject of considerable argument and conjecture, so much so that I think I can do no better than simply quote some authorities on this subject :-

> David Dorward – 'Scotland's Place-names' (1995): *'The concept of P-Celtic is not an easy one to grasp, and since it might seem a trifle perverse to refer to certain Scottish place-names as having a Welsh or Cumbric origin, the term used in this book to describe the language of the Picts and Strathclyde Britons is Brittonic'*

> W.J. Watson – 'The History of the Celtic Place-names of Scotland' (1926): *'Regarding the Picts, it is important to keep in view that while all Picts were Cruithnigh, i.e. Britons, all Cruithnigh were not Picts.'*

and : ' . . . *a 'Brython', a Briton, a Welshman; . . .* '

Dr Thomas Owen Clancy – The Triumph Tree (1998): *'The Picts . . . shared the same political and cultural space, the same language and the same ethnicity . . . as their fellow Britons to the south of them.'*

There you have it! – the *Picts* were in all essentials *Britons*, and therefore in all essentials *Welsh*! Or at the very least sufficiently 'Welsh' for the word-elements seen in the place-names of the Pictish heartlands to be adjudged by reference to words found in Welsh dictionaries and by comparison with word-elements found in the place-names of Wales itself. In other words 'Pictish' place-names will be treated no differently from others elsewhere in the Lowlands said to be 'Brittonic', 'Brythonic', or 'Cumbric'. The success or otherwise of this approach may in turn serve as an additional indication as to how 'Welsh' the Picts were, or else how 'Welsh' they were not! As Addendum A to this book I have included an Hypothesis which argues forcefully that the Pictish Stone 'Hilton of Cadboll' has strong associations with Welsh Folklore as contained within that collection of ancient Welsh Folk Tales known as 'The Mabinogion'.

Chapter 3

Death and Resurrection

'What is gone may return.
The roads lead always two ways,
hither as well as yonder'

Cadfael Chronicles, 'The Pilgrim of Hate'

In the days before the coming of the Romans, when the inhabitants of Scotland spoke a language described today as Brythonic or Cumbric, the language of the Goidelic Celts in Ireland was then what is described today as *Archaic Irish*. Why the language of the Brittonic Celts should then, 'perversely', be described as *Brythonic* and not *Archaic Welsh* would seem to be one of history's many little mysteries! This book is aimed at the average reader who, like me, wishes to keep things simple and thus avoid the complicated nuances of specialist academia. So to keep things simple for me and readily understandable for anyone else the descriptions 'Brythonic', 'Cumbric' etc. etc., where they appear in other works of reference, will in this book be removed and replaced, but only where appropriate, by the description 'Welsh', or perhaps Early Welsh, Old Welsh, Archaic Welsh or 'Whatever-Welsh'.

As the language in Scotland progressed in stages correspondingly similar to Archaic Welsh, Primitive Welsh, Old Welsh, Middle Welsh and Modern Welsh the original place-names would have undergone significant changes but these changes would have been relatively minor compared to the changes which would have occurred after the language went into decline and eventually died out. Since the language must have died out at different times in different parts of Scotland the development of the language would, depending on the particular area, have been arrested at various times within the period from 500-1300 AD and this means that we can probably expect to find in Scotland examples of place-names whose development was frozen at various stages in the sequence Primitive Welsh – Old Welsh – Middle Welsh – Modern Welsh. In the subsequent battle for survival it can be expected that the earliest Primitive Welsh and Old Welsh names stood the least chance of retaining some semblance of their original form, whilst the later Middle Welsh/Modern Welsh names stood the best chance of doing so.

This could explain why the majority of surviving names particularly those in the more southern and eastern areas of Scotland can be explained in terms of words and word-elements found in today's Welsh Dictionaries – especially those dictionaries which include obsolete or old forms of some Welsh words. It may be thought as stretching credibility to equate the Welsh spoken in Scotland in those early times to the language spoken in Wales today, after all Hadrian's Wall had cut off the northern Welsh (i.e. the 'North Britons' of Scotland) from the Welsh of the rest of Britain for the 300 years between the 2nd and 5th centuries AD and the Angles and Saxons had thereafter continued to drive wedges between these northern and western regions. It could perhaps be expected that in these circumstances the language would have developed differently in those two areas and therefore diverged significantly; so why the apparent correlation between the language spoken in southern Scotland at that time and the language spoken in Wales today? One possible reason could be the 'Oral Tradition' of the Celts whereby the Bards and Shamans (story tellers) of that time wandered far and wide to relate and pass on the myths and legends of their ancestors. The strict rhythms and scansion of P-Celtic poetry, transferred by word of mouth, has perhaps conserved the language significantly better than anything written down in prose. It is true even today that the local pronunciation of a place-name is very often a better guide to it's original form than what is to be found in many written records. We also have to take notice of the historical links between Southern Scotland and Wales. In the 5th century a North British Chieftain, by name of Cunedda, together with fellow members of his war band left southern Scotland and established themselves as rulers of northern Wales and, since the language of an area in those days tended to be that of it's ruling class, the language of northern Wales might then have been influenced by that of the followers and family of Cunedda and this language would at that time have been the Welsh language of Southern Scotland. This would have been reinforced in the 7th century when the survivors of the battle of Catraeth, including the bard Aneurin, fled to North Wales. Aneurin's great epic poem *'Y Gododdin'* which although originating in the language of 7th century Southern Scotland but only written down in the 13th/14th centuries is still intelligible to any fluent speaker of modern Welsh.

From the times when the language died out, area by area, the toponymical Welsh names of Scotland were subjected to influence and change from many quarters; they would have entered a veritable minefield of etymological disruption. Names were handed down from one century to the next either by word of mouth or by being written down in historical records of one sort or another. The Romans who were the first to record place-names in the British Isles also 'Latinised' them! This process was continued to some extent by British and Irish monks whose written language was also Latin; then in the wake of Saint Columba came an inrush of Gaelic speaking 'lesser' saints and scribes whose natural tendency was to 'Gaelicize' – or perhaps more accurately 'Ersify' them; their language at that time was of course more Irish-Gaelic than Scots-Gaelic. The number of place-names recorded in these times was perforce relatively few as also were the number recorded by early Anglo-Saxon chroniclers such as Bede. Most recorded names appear after the coming of the Normans in 1066, and some first records go back only as far as the Late Middle Ages. We can expect therefore to find that the majority of surviving Welsh names are from about or shortly after 1000 AD i.e. from the Middle Welsh and Modern Welsh periods. Before 1000 AD we can expect to have to try to disentangle Welsh names from their Latin and Irish-Gaelic distortions. All written records of Welsh place-names could not have been written down without first having been transferred to a mediaeval scribe by word of mouth in a language of which the scribe had perhaps little or no knowledge. Written records would also have suffered from spelling anomalies which differed according to the whims and fancies of individual scribes – there were no Oxford English Dictionaries in those days! Neither were there any printing presses; books had to be copied painstakingly by hand mostly in the scriptoriums attached to monasteries. Obviously some copies were better than others and some corruption was inevitable, even the type of script employed by one scribe was not necessarily the same as that employed by another! The wear and tear of ages would also have taken their toll, slovenly speech habits, misheard articulations, the attempts by scribes to make sense of a name using a language different from that in which it was formed all contributed to alter the original, sometimes into unrecognizable forms. Even when written down, names were still under threat from future researchers who following the mistaken spellings then proceeded to pronounce the names in these mistaken forms thus adding confusion to confusion. An idea of how this could have taken place can be seen in the American attempt to simplify English spelling, for example by replacing *'-our'* word endings with *'-or'* word endings, thus *colour* became *color* and the original English pronunciation which somewhat reflects it's origin in the French *coleur* is, in America, now pronounced more like the word *collar* i.e. the mistaken pronunciation has followed on from the change in spelling. Fortunately in Scotland there are several instances where the vernacular pronunciation has remained true to form even though the name itself suffered quite a few misspellings, for example the name 'Corstorphine' is known from early spellings as 'Crostorfin'(1130), 'Crorstorfin'(1140) and 'Corstorphyne'(1508). Today's pronunciation however is still as per 'Cors-Tor-Ffin', meaning *Marsh* (Cors), *Rock Outcrop* or *Rocky Hill* (Tor), *Boundary* (Ffin), the accent is as expected in a P-Celtic name on the penultimate syllable, the 'o' in Tor.

Before 1000 AD we can expect to to have to try to disentangle Welsh names from their Latin and Irish-Gaelic distortions. Trying to work backward through these veneers of Latinisation and Gaelicisation is like trying to strip off Victorian and Georgian wallpapers and mediaeval colour washes from a wall to reveal the precious original Dark Age murals hidden underneath – more often than not an impossible task.

One of the difficulties involved in disentangling original names from Gaelic alteration, addition or replacement is the question of 'How Irish is Scots Gaelic?' – and also 'How Welsh is it?'. There are a number of words in Scots-Gaelic dictionaries for which there are no equivalents in Irish-Gaelic dictionaries but for which, apart from the differing alphabets, suitable matches can be found in Welsh dictionaries. Watson euphemistically describes these as being 'borrowed – from Welsh'. He could equally well have described the Scots-Gaelic words as being 'borrowed – from Irish-Gaelic' – but probably assumed this as being quite obvious! The truth appears to be that Scots-Gaelic is basically an Irish language incorporating some few topographical Welsh words in the same way that English is basically a German language incorporating some words of Latin, Greek and French etc., the difference being that English, Latin and French have much the same alphabets so that the words 'borrowed' into English are easily recognised as such. The Irish alphabet however differs significantly from that of the Welsh and the English so that in present day Scots-Gaelic the task of recognition and attribution becomes rather more difficult.

There are many names which are described as 'hybrids' meaning that they are partly Welsh and partly Scots-Gaelic. Since Welsh can be considered the 'Senior' language of all Scotland it is entirely fair to assume that any 'hybrid' containing a word element of Welsh origin would once have been formed wholly of Welsh word elements. The chronology of the languages is such that whereas an original Welsh name could suffer subsequent partial alteration by the replacement of one Welsh element by a later Gaelic synonym the reverse is not true; an original Gaelic name could not suffer subsequent change from a Language known to have preceded it. There is therefore no apparent mechanism whereby a Welsh word element can replace a Gaelic element in a name originating wholly in the Gaelic language. This process of partial replacement can be seen in more modern times and an example can be found in the Welsh place-names of Patagonia: these were first allocated by the Welsh colonists who settled in Argentina in the middle of the 19th century. They gave the name 'Porth Madryn' to the place where they first landed in Patagonia but now when the indigenous Spanish language of the rest of Argentina is taking over the place-name has been changed to 'Puerto Madryn'. The retention of the last element 'Madryn' remains as an indication that the name was once wholly Welsh. When dealing with the hybrid names in this book there are times when some attempt will, where appropriate, be made to back translate the Gaelic element in a hybrid name into a corresponding Welsh element and thereby arrive at what it is hoped will be a credible reconstruction of a wholly Welsh original. In the case of the Patagonian name Puerto Madryn, the back-translation of Spanish *puerto* = 'port' into its Welsh synonym *porth* = 'port' shows how valid this exercise can sometimes be.

Chapter 4

'The Welsh'

'She had always thought of the Welsh with fear and distrust, as uncouth savages; and suddenly here was this trim and personable young man whose cheeks flamed at meeting her gaze, She thought of him much'

Cadfael Chronicles, 'Dead Man's Ransom'

The Welsh Language is one of the three oldest of all surviving European languages and as such it has inherited peculiarities all of it's own which may appear strange to anyone brought up to speak one of the much later languages, such as English whose evolution owes such a lot to the two Classical languages – Greek and Latin. One little peculiarity is that plurals are not as commonly formed in a standard fashion, as is usually the case in English by simply sticking an 's' or an 'es' on the end of a word; instead the word can, and often does, change form significantly, as with the English singular *goose* and it's plural *geese.* For example the plural of *pabell* (tent) is *pebyll* (tents), but the plural of *bedwen* (birch tree) is *bedw* (birch trees) and the plural of *merch* (girl) is *merched* (girls). There is no single common rule – for each word the singular and the plural have to be learned separately! Another little peculiarity results from what might be described as the development of Welsh as a 'lyrical' language and although there are some who, citing the case of Llanfairpwllgwyngyllgogerychwyrndrobwllllan tisiliogogogoch, may disagree, there are no 'tongue-twisters' as such in Welsh conversational language. If the juxtaposition of one word next to another causes an embarrassing impediment to the flow of language then the beginning of a word will be changed depending on what word precedes it. Much the same thing occurs in the English language where 'a Apple' is transposed into 'an Apple'. The difference being that in English the ending of the word preceding the article is changed whereas in Welsh the change is made to the beginning of the word succeeding the article and the changes differ according to the grammatical circumstances in which the word finds itself. The word *'pen'* for example can be found in the forms *'ben'*, *'mhen'* and *'phen'*. This is known as *mutation,* there are three sets of mutation – *'Soft' ('Lenitive'), 'Nasal',* and *'Spirant'*. Any one word may therefore have up to four different beginnings, the first being its normal *'Radical'* beginning and the other three mutated beginnings being dependent on the particular qualifying word which precedes it, not only that but each word can have a different form depending on whether it is singular or plural, masculine or feminine. Fortunately the last two sets of mutations *'nasal'* and *'spirant'* are only rarely encountered in place-names, and in any case the strict rules of Modern Welsh were probably not always observed in the days when place-names first came into being, nor in the days when they were first recorded. All this adds greatly to the fascination and frustration of trying to perceive and identify any possible P-Celtic Welsh origins in existing Scottish place-names!

Mutation

The mutation most likely to be encountered in Scottish place-names is 'Lenition', or 'Radical-to-Soft Aspiration' – as in the following table:

Radical		to	Soft
b	>	f	bychan > fychan, bechan > fechan
c	>	g	carn > garn
d	>	dd	du > ddu
g	>	-	glais > lais
ll	>	l	llan > lan
m	>	f	maes > faes
p	>	b	pen > ben
rh	>	r	rhos > ros
t	>	d	trum > drum

Pronunciation

Letter	Pronunciation
'a'	as in p*a*t
'â'	as in p*ar*
'b'	as in *b*at
'c'	as in *c*at
'ch'	as *ch* in Scottish lo*ch*
'd'	as in *d*og
'dd'	as *th* in shea*th*e
'e'	(a) as in b*e*t
	(b) as *ae* in sund*ae*
'f'	as *v* in *v*iaduct
'ff'	as *ff* in o*ff*er
'g'	as in *g*arden
'ng'	as *ng* in si*ng*ing
'h'	as in *h*ub
'i'	(a) as in p*i*n
	(b) as *ee* in *ee*l

'l'	as in *l*i*l*t
'll'	if you don't already know how to pronounce this – then you don't know! Fortunately in Scottish place-names you don't *have* to know, as all 'll's' are either by aspiration or default reduced already to a single 'l'.
'm'	as in *m*ug
'n'	as in *n*ot
'o'	(a) as in g*o*t
	(b) as *oa* in gl*oa*t
'p'	as in *p*u*p*
'r'	as in *r*agged – but 'trilled'
'rh'	as *rh* in *rh*eum – but with the 'r' again trilled
's'	as in *s*un
't'	as in *t*ug
'u'	(a) as *i* in *i*nch
	(b) as *u* in f*u*ll
'w'	(a) as *u* in f*u*ll
	(b) as *oo* in w*oo*l, or as *u* in French *u*ne
'y'	(a) as *i* in p*i*n
	(b) as *ee* in *ee*l
	(c) as *u* in s*u*n

Suffixes

1. Diminutive Endings

-ach	*Mawdd* (a River in N. Wales) and *Mawddach* 'the Little Mawdd' – a tributary. *-ach* survives unchanged as a diminutive in Scots Gaelic
-an	*carreg* (rock); *carregan* (little rock)
-cyn	*bryn* 'hill', *bryncyn* 'little hill'
-cen	*ffoll* 'bag', *ffolcen* 'little bag'
-ell	*traeth* 'beach, *traethell* 'little beach'
-ig	*afon* 'river' *afonig* 'little river

-os	*plant* 'children', *plantos* 'little children'
-yn	*bachgen* 'boy', *bachgennyn* 'little boy'
-og	*cloch* 'bell', *clochog* 'little bell'

-awc, -awg, -oc, are old forms of *-og*. Interestingly; *-awc* was adopted into Scottish Gaelic placenames in the form *-ag* and into Scots-Gaelic in general as *-ach*. See below:

> Quote: *'The ending* -ag *serves in Gaelic as the diminutive suffix feminine . . . It is a curious fact that this suffix which has attained so great a vogue in Gaelic, is not of Gaelic origin but borrowed from Welsh* -awc, *now* -og, *representing the early* -acos *which appears in Gaelic as* -ach'.
>
> (W.J. Watson)

2. Possessive Endings (of a named person)

-iog	*Brycheiniog* (lands or possessions of *Brychan)*
-ion	*Ceredigion* (lands or possessions of *Ceredig)*
-ydd	*Meirionydd* (lands or possessions of *Meirion)*

3. Adjectival Endings

-iog	*or* (margin), *oriog* (marginal)
-aidd	*gwlad* (country), *gwladaidd* (countrified)
-eid	– is an older form of *aidd*
-us	*grym* (power), *grymus* (powerful)

The following adjectival endings when applied to the name of a plant or tree in the context of a particular placename imply an 'abundance' of that plant, present at that place.

-og	e.g. *eirin* (plum), *eirinog* (plummy, plummish place)
-or	e.g. *mawn* (peat), *mawnor* (peaty place)

-os e.g. *rhig* (heather), *Rhigos* (heathery place)
-as e.g. *bedw* (birch trees), *bedwas* (place full of birch trees)
-ais = Pictish form of *as* (see' Kinnettles' place-name entry)

4. Abstract Endings

-ed transforms a noun into an abstract noun e.g. *mig* 'bog' into *miged* 'bogginess' or 'bog-like qualities'
-et an older form of *-ed*

Prefixes

Usually form an easily recognizable and identifiable element wherever they occur in Scottish place-names and as such can justifiably be treated in the same way as other word elements. There is not the same complexity as there is with suffixes. The following are some which may find an application in place-names.

ach- (in place-names only) = near to-, nearby-
eil- = second-, secondary-
gor-, *gwar-* = over-, super-
lled- = half-, rather-
rhy- = very-, too-
tra- = over-, excessive-
try- = through-

Word-elements

The following is a selection of the Welsh word elements most commonly found in Scottish place-names; a number of these are discussed in rather more detail in David Dorward's book *Scotland's Place-names* but the Ordnance Survey booklet *Place names on maps of Scotland & Wales* completely ignores them – even though it was supposedly updated in 1995!

aber 'confluence of rivers', 'mouth of a river', 'river estuary'. Older forms – *obar, odber, apor, aper* appear in shortened forms as *arb,* e.g. Arbroath (Aber Brothoc), Arbuthnott (Aber Buthenot) and *abr,* e.g. Abriachan (Abir Hacyn); also as *apor,* e.g. Applecross (Apor Crosan).

aber is a classic case of an original Welsh element sometimes being replaced by a straight Gaelic equivalent. Watson has this to say on the subject:

> *'Thus British 'obar' had no chance against Gaelic 'inbhear', for both had exactly the same meaning'* (CPNS p.390)
>
> and
>
> *' . . . it is safe to say Gaelic 'inbhear' in many place-names took the place of British 'aber'.'* (CPNS p.459)

On present day maps of Scotland *'inbhear'* appears in the form *'inver'* or *'inner'*. If we attend closely to what Watson is telling us it is quite clear that, as *'inver'* or *'inner'* came, as he says, to *'replace aber'* then it is likely that names now seen to begin with *inver* or *inner* would at one time have begun with *aber*. This would be especially true of those significant estuaries where *inver* or *inner* is coupled with a river name seen to be of Welsh or pre-Welsh origin. On this assumption 'Inverness', for example, would in all probability have once been 'Aberness', 'Inveralmond' have once been 'Aberaman', 'Innerleithen' have once been 'Aberleithan', etc., etc., etc.

afon = 'river'

allt In southern Wales dialect the meaning is 'a wooded slope' and in northern Wales dialect it is 'a hillside' but in Scotland the same word *allt* in Scots-Gaelic has the meaning 'a stream'. Since there is no such word as *allt* in the Irish-Gaelic Dictionary it is fair to assume that Scots-Gaelic inherited the word from the Welsh language which preceded it. In which case it is possible to suppose an original more complex meaning like 'wooded-hillside-along-a-stream' from which the three other truncated meanings could logically derive. If so then one would expect at least some of the Welsh place-names containing *allt* to be located alongside a river or stream. Whether this be true or not is something which is not within the investigative scope of this present volume.

ardd This is an older Welsh word which has two related meanings, (1) as a noun = 'hill', or (2) as an adjective = 'high'. A similar Scots-Gaelic word *ard* = 'high', 'lofty'.

bar Two meanings (1) = 'top', 'summit': (2) = 'tuft', 'bunch'. A similar Scots- Gaelic word is *barr* = 'top'.

beili Three related meanings (1) = 'yard', in the sense of 'a yard of ground' or enclosed area surrounding a steading or dwelling place (e.g. backyard + front yard = Yard), (2) = 'court', in the sense 'courtyard', (3) = 'mound'. A similar Scots-Gaelic word *baile* = 'farm', 'steading', 'village', 'town'.

bre three meanings (1) a noun = 'hill', 'mount', 'peak', (2) an adjective = 'high', (3) 'little hill, 'low hill' (1688). Similar words are Scots-Gaelic *braigh* and Scots *brae.* Both = 'hill'(upper face of).

bychan, buchan, bechan = 'little', 'small'

caer In Wales this has come to mean 'castle' but in Scotland the meaning seems to be not so grand and is more like 'fortlet', 'temporary camp' or at the most 'fortress'. As in Wales it seems to date from Roman, or immediately post-Roman, times and is often found in both Scottish and Welsh place-names in the form 'car'.

caled = 'hard', 'hardy', 'severe', 'harsh'. This word appears in a host of Scottish river-names and elsewhere but it's exact meaning in relation to place-names is difficult to decipher.

careg, carreg = 'stone', 'rock'

cam = 'bent', 'crooked'

camas = 'bay', 'river-bend'. Scots-Gaelic *camus* = 'bay'

cardden = Has two meanings; (1) a 'thicket', 'brake', 'copse'; (2) a 'fort' (probably 'stockaded').

carn = 'heap', 'heap of stones', 'burial mound', adopted into Scots as *cairn.*
Note: in some dialects of Welsh the 'a' is pronounced as the 'a' in 'pale' rather than the 'a' in 'pal', e.g. 'Aberdare' = *aberdair,* not *aberdarr*. Hence *cairn* from *carn*.

cil = 'recess', 'corner', 'nook', 'refuge', 'retreat' or 'cove' or 'source' of a stream. Possibly adopted into Scots-Gaelic as *'cill'* and as such found in Scottish place-names mostly in the form 'Kil' and with the particular meanings firstly 'Cell' (i.e. a 'refuge' or 'retreat' of a holy-man, a saint), secondly 'Church', and then 'churchyard, burial-ground'. Irish-Gaelic *cuil* = 'corner, nook'. The distribution of names beginning with 'Kil-' is concentrated in Western areas running up from the South West to the North West with a branch running up Loch Ness to Inverness. It has much the same meanings as the Welsh *llan* and like *llan* is mostly followed by the name of a 'saint', or 'holy man'. It is noticeable that in the South West it is numerous in those territories inhabited by the people traditionally referred to as the 'Strathclyde Welsh' and it is it's use in these areas which perhaps explains why there are so few *llan* names to be found in Scotland, the alternative *cil* being the preferred description. This would imply that at least some of these *cil* names were generated by Welsh speaking people (the Strathclyde Welsh?) and not Gaelic speaking incomers. This suggestion makes sense when it is remembered that the 'saints' in question were Irish monks come to spread the gospel amongst the heathen, indigenous Welsh-speaking inhabitants and were not wasting their time preaching to already Christianised fellow Gaels. Johnston lists 100 names starting with 'Kil' and though he, Watson, Nicolaisen and others display a natural inclination to favour a Gaelic origin for the Scots element 'kil', and therefore a Gaelic interpretation for the whole name, there seems every reason to examine each name on it's individual merit and consider the possibility of an alternative interpretation based on Welsh *cil*. There is in Wales at least one precedent for this meaning of 'cil' in the place-name Cilsant (Powys) = 'refuge, retreat, of the Saint'. (*The Uses of Place-Names*: p115). There are also a number of other Welsh place-names beginning with *cil*: e.g. Cilgerran (Geraint), Cilcennin (Cennyn), Cilgeti-Kilgetty (Ceti), Cilcain (Cain), Cilwendeg (Gwen teg), Cilmeri (Merin); all thought to be either named after Saints or else have some connection with a Saint.

coed = 'wood', 'forest', 'trees'. Appears in older forms as *coet, ceit, cait, cat, cet, chet, kethe,* and finally, today as *keith.*

craig = 'crag', 'rock'. A similar word in Scots is *craig* = 'crag', 'rock', 'cliff'. In Scots-Gaelic *creag* has the same meaning, but there is no equivalent in Irish-Gaelic.

croes, crwys = 'cross', 'across', 'crossroads', 'crucifix'

crom, crwm = 'bending', 'bowed', 'curved'

din = 'fort', 'hill-fort', 'fortified hill'

> *'British 'din' can seldom now be distinguished from Gaelic 'dun' (hill); for instance Dunpelder was certainly 'Din-' before it became 'Dun-' though the former never appears on record.'*
>
> Watson

A similar appreciation can be extended to other Scottish 'dun' category place-names. The two forms *din* and *dun* exist synonymously in Scottish place-names and it is not always easy to differentiate the latter from the Gaelic *dun* meaning 'hill'. An associated Welsh word is *dinas* meaning a 'fortified hill settlement'. In some few place-names the beginnings of both words are sometimes dialectically changed from 'd' to 't'. In Wales and Scotland there are several word-elements used to describe various types of 'defended settlements'. In chronological order these are *din* – *dinas,* – *caer* – *castle.* Briefly a *din* is an 'iron-age hillfort', a *dinas* is a 'fortified iron-age hill settlement', *caer* is a 'fortification' of some sort not necessarily on a hill (see *caer*) and *castle* is usually a substantial mediaeval fortress or Scottish Baronial residence. In Wales the situation is a little confused as several iron-age 'dins' or 'dinases' have at some time later been thought sufficiently impressive to warrant being upgraded to *castell* status. e.g. Castell Dinas Bran = 'the castle on the iron-age hill settlement of the Crow'. In Scotland we have 'Carstairs' the earliest record of which is in 1172 as 'Casteltarras', a form possibly upgraded subsequently from an original 'Caertarras'.

dol = 'meadow'. Welsh Dictionaries show this word with a circumflex over the 'o' thus lengthening it's sound and this may explain why in Scotland it frequently appears in place-names as *dal.* An older meaning is 'ring' or 'loop' so possibly the entire meaning could be a 'ringed, or fenced meadow'.

dŵr, dwfr = 'water' usually in the form of a stream or small river. The word has been adopted into Scots-Gaelic as *dobhar* and into Scots as *dour,* thus any Scottish placename containing an element such as 'dower', 'dour' or 'dobhar' must be examined closely to identify the possibility of a Welsh origin.

trum, drum = a 'ridge'. A similar word in Scots-Gaelic is *druim* meaning the same thing. There seems to be no equivalent in Irish-Gaelic.

eglwys = 'church' – see *llan*. This Welsh element is found in Scottish, Welsh and English place-names throughout mainland Britain; as the Scots-Gaelic *eaglais*, as the Scots *eagles* or *eccles* and in England again as *eccles*. It is chronologically the oldest 'church' name, apart perhaps from *cil* when used in this sense, and which in Wales came to be displaced by *llan* and in Scotland by 'kirk'. e.g. In Wales we have 'Eglwysnewydd' in 1340, turning to 'Llannewydd alias Newchurch' in 1786 and now simply 'Newchurch' today. In Scotland we have 'Egglesbreth' in 1120, 'Eglesbryth' in 1268 becoming 'Falkirk' today; all deriving from an original *eglwys brith* meaning 'speckled or spotted church'.

fala This is the lenited form of *bala* = 'efflux', or in place-names = 'place where river flows from lake'. The village of Fala in the Borders is just downstream from the place where the stream leaves Fala Flow Loch.

ffin = 'boundary' or 'limit'. Boundaries were very important to Clans and Factions in early Scotland and were marked in various ways, sometimes with reference to natural features. It may be expected therefore that a number of *ffin* type 'boundary' names could be found in Scotland. Unfortunately the situation is complicated by the existence of the Gaelic word *fionn* said to mean 'white' or 'fair'. Thus 'Finglais' of Glen Finglais could mean either Gaelic *Fionn Ghlais* = 'white stream' or Welsh *Ffin Glais* = 'boundary stream'.

ffordd = 'route' in a very general sense i.e. a 'way' of any kind' e.g. a 'highway', pathway', 'roadway', 'seaway', 'railway', etc.

garth Has three meanings, – (1) = 'enclosed place', 'garden', (2) = 'hill', 'ridge', (3) = 'promontory' (1688), as in Penarth (*pen y garth).*

garw Has three meanings, (1) = 'coarse', 'harsh', 'rugged', (2) = 'torrent' in the sense of a 'rough' or 'harsh' stream, (3) = 'roughness'. Scots-Gaelic *garbh* = 'rough, thick, rugged'; 'harsh'; 'brawny'.

glais/glas In it's old sense it is found in place-names as = 'stream'. But other meanings are as a colour = 'blue', grey', 'green', and also = 'green' in the sense of being 'young', 'raw'. In place-names this element very often appears in lenited form as *lais* or *las.*

glyn = 'valley' – usually with a stream running through it. Similar words are Scots-Gaelic *gleann* and Scots *glen.*

gofan = 'a smith' i.e. a 'Blacksmith', 'Silversmith' etc. – alternatively = 'a Smith's' i.e. *gof* – a 'Forge'.

llannerch = 'glade' – in a wood. Appears in Scottish place-names as 'Lanark', 'Lanrig', 'Lanrick', 'Laneryk', and suchlike.

llan / lan In the place-names of Wales it seems that the element *llan* in it's meaning of 'church' did not come into general use until after the middle of the 6th century AD. Before that the word for church was *eglwys* and *llan* then had it's older more general meaning of 'a place', 'a yard' (1688) which later became attached to some early Christians with the particular meaning 'place or enclosure, of a holy man, or saint'. This could have been anything from a simple monastic cell to a religious site such as a burial place or a meeting place, either of which might have included a building of some sort – ie a 'church' or suchlike. In Scotland the '*ll*' pronunciation seems to have disappeared at quite an early stage and the double '*ll*' reduced to a single '*l*'. The only hint that it might ever have existed in Scotland is the placename 'Lhanbryde' near Elgin and this only by the vernacular pronunciation. As in Wales *'llan'* or *'lan'* is usually but not always followed by the name of the appropriate Saint, or holy man. In Scottish place-names *'lan'* is sometimes seen in the forms 'lang' or 'long'.

llefn, llyfn = 'even', 'smooth', 'sleek', 'unruffled'?

llumon = 'beacon', 'peak', 'chimney'. Appears in Scottish place-names as 'lomond', possibly from *llumon* with the suffix *-ed* giving *llumoned* meaning 'having the qualities of a chimney, beacon, or peak'. A similar Scots word is 'lum' meaning 'chimney'.

llwch = 'lake'. This is an older Welsh word which appears mainly in place-names where it has the meanings, (1) = 'pool', 'bog', 'swampy-ground', (2) = 'fishponds', (3) 'standing water' (1688). It may be the origin of Scots 'loch', although for some reason Watson seems to think it is the other way round!

llyn = 'lake'

maes = 'flat ground' or 'flat field', appears also in its older forms *ma* and *mai* and in their mutated forms *faes, fa, and fai* and again in a corrupted form as *moss,* e.g. Mossffenon (Peebles), Mesffennon 1296: = *maes ffynnon* = 'flat ground, or field, by the well'; Ogilvie (Angus) = *uchel fai*: 'high flat ground', Ogilface (Banffs) = *uchel faes:* 'high flat ground'.

march = 'horse', 'stallion'

mawr = 'great', 'large', 'big', 'high'. In Scottish placename records it is sometimes found corrupted in the forms *mor* and *muir* and is easily confused with Welsh *môr* = 'sea' and Scots *muir* = 'moor'. Similar words are *mor* in Gaelic and *more* in Scots, the meaning being the same = 'big'.

melin = 'mill'

melyn = 'yellow'

moel Two related meanings – (1) = 'bare', 'bald', 'barren', (2) = 'bare-topped-hill'.

mig / mign = 'bog', 'quagmire' or simply 'mire'(1688), As a name element it appears to be restricted to the East side of Scotland but is found all the way from Sutherland in the north to the Borders in the south, i.e. the heartlands of the Picts and North Britons. Examples are: Midmar (Aberdeens), older Migmar = *mig mar* (bog of Mar), Midstrath (Aboyne), Migstrath 1170 = *mig ystrad* (quagmire in the flat-bottomed valley), Craigie Meg (Glen Prosen) = *craigiau mig* (crags by the bog), Migvie = *mig fai* (bog on the flat ground) and Dalmigavie = *dol mig y fai* (bog meadow on the flat ground), Meckfen, Meggefen 1230 = *mig faen* (bog by the standing stone), Meigle (old Migdele, Mygille) = *mig dol* (bog meadow) or *mig le* (bog place), Strathmiglo (old Stradmigeloch) = *ystrad mig y llwch* (flat bottomed valley with a boggy lake). Interestingly, Craig Meggen (Aberdeens) = *craig mign* (crag by the bog). *Mign* might also, just possibly, be the root of Scots 'midden'?

moch = 'swine', 'pigs' / *mochyn* = 'a pig', 'a swine'.

mynydd Two related meanings – (1) = 'prominent hill', 'expanse of high ground' – (2) = 'area of rough moorland pasture not necessarily on high ground'. The pronunciation is 'munnith' where the final *-th* is as in 'the' and not as in 'pith'. It is a prime element in Scottish place-names where it is found in a number of guises = 'mounth', 'mount', 'mont', 'month', 'mond', 'mund', 'munt', 'minit', 'monaidh', and variations thereof. Relics of *mynydd* are rare to the North and West of a line running down from Loch Ness from Inverness to Fort William but are prevalent in the area to the South and East of it. Foremost among the survivors is 'The Mounth', a name by which a large area including Cairngorm is still known. A similar Welsh word is *mwnt* = 'mound', 'mount'.

pefr = 'fair', 'radiant', 'beautiful'. Becomes *peffer* by metathesis.

pen This seems to be an all purpose word starting off with the simple meaning 'head' then gathering further similar meanings, firstly as 'top', 'end' then 'far-end', 'headland' and then 'head', 'arch', 'chief', 'main', 'supreme'. The number of Scottish hills and mountains described as 'Ben' (the mutated form of *pen*) are too numerous to list but most of them have a qualifying Gaelic element which may or may not be a straight Gaelic interpretation of a Welsh original. Ben Lomond of course is an exception which retains it's derivation from Welsh *y-pen-llumon*. Otherwise we have in Scotland *Pennan* = little 'headland', *Penpont* = 'far-end' of bridge, and *Penvenna* = 'chief', 'principal' (i.e. most-important) – Stones.

perth = 'bush', 'brake', 'hedge'

peth = 'thing', 'article', 'part' 'quantity of'. Thought to be the origin of 'Pictish' 'pett', 'pet', 'pit' meaning a 'part share of'.

prys = 'copse', 'grove', 'covert', 'brushwood'.

pwll ='pool', 'puddle', 'pit'. An older form is said to be *pol* which is found in old English as *pol,* in Scots as *pow* and possibly in Scots-Gaelic as *poll.* It is also said:

> *that **pol** must have been a British word meaning 'stream' or 'flowing water'* . . . which has *'survived in modern Scots in the form pow, having the sense of 'sluggish stream', often referring to a burn which moves slowly through peaty ground'.*
> In South West Scotland *'the term **pol** occurs so frequently*

that we are forced to conclude that in this instance it was the standard word for a small or medium sized stream (not necessarily slow-moving)' (*The Uses of Place-names* p.59).

See Polwarth, Polmaise, Polmont etc.

rhath Different dictionaries give different meanings: (1) = 'a mound', (2) = 'cleared-land', 'a plain'. Irish Gaelic *rath,* which is also the mutated form of Welsh *rhath,* has the meaning 'fort'. See 'Ratho'.

rhic, ric = 'gap', 'pass'

rhig, rig = 'gap', 'pass', 'groove' Similar words are Scots *rig, rigg* = 'ridge between furrows'.

rhych = 'furrow', 'trench'

rhudd = 'red', 'ruddy', 'crimson'. Similar word = Gaelic *ruadh* = 'red'.

tarw = 'bull'. Similar Gaelic word is *tarbh* = 'bull'.

tir = 'land', 'earth', 'ground', 'territory'. Scots-Gaelic *tir* = 'land', 'shore'.

tor Welsh dictionaries give *tor* = 'heap, mound, belly, bulge', but in Welsh and Cornish place-names *tor* in it's sense of 'a heap' seems to take on the specialised, perhaps older, meaning of a 'rocky-hill' or 'hill-with-rock-outcrops' or simply 'rock-outcrops', these meanings being somewhat reflective of the Welsh verb *tori, torri* = to 'break, cut, rupture, fracture'.

traeth = 'beach', also 'a flat tract of sand or silt' any where – even in hilly country, e.g. *traeth-y-mynydd* = 'mountain beach', in the Brecon Beacons.

tre / tref = a 'steading', e.g. 'farmstead' or 'homestead'. In Scottish place-names it is sometimes found as 'tra' and sometimes in a metathesised form as 'ter'.

ty = 'house'.

uch = 'above', 'over', 'upper'.

uchder] = a 'height', 'highness', 'loftiness', 'altitude'.
uchdwr]
uchedd]

uchel = Two meanings: (1) = 'high', 'lofty', 'towering', (2) = 'loud'. Appears in Scottish placename records variously as – 'Ochil', 'Ogil', 'Ogle' and suchlike.

uwch = 'higher', 'upper'

wysg = 'stream', 'current', 'track', 'forward-bias'.

ynys = 'meadow', 'water-meadow', 'island'. Similar words in Scots are *inch* and *innis*.

Quote: *Of the two Gaelic names for 'island', innis and eilean, the former is native (Welsh ynys), the latter is is borrowed from Norse ey-land* W.J. Watson.

ystrad = 'wide flat bottomed valley'. A similar word in Scots is *strath*. This, according to Watson, is not to be confused with the Irish-Gaelic *srath* which in Irish place-names has the meaning of ' . . . *level, soft, meadowland or holm – often swampy and sometimes inundated – along the banks of a river or lake, . . . a strath differs from a Glen in being as a rule wider and perhaps always smoother. In this usage, as well as in other aspects of river nomenclature, Scotland goes with Wales rather than with Ireland.'*. It seems clear then that Scottish *strath* is derived as a corruption of Welsh *ystrad* – meaning 'wide flat-bottomed valley' and indeed this assumption is borne out by the earliest records of some 'Strath-' names which contain the element 'ystrad' either as itself or in an only slightly corrupted form as 'Strad', or 'Strat', e.g. see 'Strathearn'.

Chapter 5

Scots-Gaelic & Scots-dialect

'Where there is no certainty the mind must turn to the light and not the shadow'

Cadfael Chronicles, 'The Potter's Field'

The earliest records of Welsh place-names in Britain are probably the Latinised versions, based on Archaic Welsh (Brythonic) originals, which were recorded by the Romans. There are no written Welsh records of life in these early ages prior to the ancient tales contained in the Red Book of Hergest written sometime in the 12th century and those in the Black Book of Carmarthen written in the mid 13th century. After the Romans left, the arrival of English speaking incomers into Eastern Scotland and the arrival of Irish Gaelic speaking incomers into Western Scotland brought new threats to the Welsh place-names of Scotland in the form of Anglicized and Gaelicized adaptations of the originals. In each case the names were either transcribed phonetically into the English or Gaelic languages using the appropriate alphabets and word forms existing at that time or else they were translated into those languages by scribes some of whom may have had but little, if any, knowledge of

Welsh. Not surprisingly there must have been many mistranslations and mistranscriptions! In addition there was a tendency for Welsh words to be absorbed into Irish Gaelic as it evolved into Scots Gaelic. These words could be considered as 'Gaelic – adopted from Welsh' or alternatively as 'Welsh – taken into Gaelic' but in either case it leaves the toponymist with the problem of trying to decide whether a particular placename, formed wholly or partly of adopted words is Welsh in origin – or Gaelic in origin – or what.

Phonetic translations into English are fairly easy to decipher e.g. the two hamlets of *Trebrun* and *Trabrown* in the Lothians are clearly mistranscriptions of an original *Tre Bren* = the 'steading by the tree'. Paradoxically straight translations into Gaelic are more difficult – even controversial! *Buchaille Etive Mor* for instance poses the question – is it an original Gaelic name? – or is it a simple translation into Gaelic of a more ancient Welsh name *Bugail Etif Mawr*? Both have somewhat the same meaning although the Welsh version would favour 'herdsman of great etive' whilst the Gaelic version would favour 'great shepherd of etive'. Or is it an example of two Welsh word elements, *Bugail,* and *Mawr* being adopted into Gaelic as *Buchaille,* and *Mor* together with the word *Etif* which is not explainable in either language. Less difficult but more annoying are the silly mistranslations into Gaelic which arise primarily because of the affinity between the two Celtic languages. Edinburgh is a classic case of a phonetic transcription from Welsh *Din Eidyn* into the English spelling *Dunedene,* followed by a part translation into English as *Edinburgh* and then at some later time a totally misconceived mistranslation into Gaelic as *Dùn Eideann.* Originally *Din Eidyn* = 'hill-fort of Eidyn', where Eidyn was either the name of a region or else a title or personal name derived from that region. This, it seems, was phonetically transcribed variously as *Dunedene* and *Dunedin,* then part translated into *Edinburgh,* where the

English *burgh* has much the same meaning as the Welsh *Din* which it replaces, but where a phonetic translation of *Eidyn* is retained in the form of *Edin*. Thus the modern 'Edinburgh' still means 'Fort of Eidyn', not so the Gaelic mistranslation *Dun Eiddean* which has the meaning of 'hill slope' or 'hill hill'. It would seem that this last interpretation evolved from the false expedient of trying to match Gaelic word elements to similar looking Welsh word elements without any thought of matching the meaning! Ironically the modern Welsh name for Edinburgh is *Caeredin,* meaning 'castle of edin', which is a partial back translation into Welsh of an English word which is itself a part translation cum phonetic transcription of an original Welsh name! A case of what-goes-around-comes-around I suppose?

Gaelic Pronunciation:

Letter	Pronunciation
'e'	(a) as in get
	(b) as *a* in p*a*y
'i'	as *ee* in peep
'u'	as *oo* in wool
'n'	(a) as *n* in *n*inny
	(b) as *ng* in thi*ng*
'bh'	as *v* in vim
'mh'	ditto
'ch'	as in lo*ch*
'dh'	as in *ugh*
'gh'	ditto
'dhe'	as *y* in *y*ou
'dhi'	ditto
'ghe'	ditto
'ghi'	ditto
'fh	(a) silent
	(b) as *h* in *h*ello

'ph' as *f* in *f*luffy
'sh' as *h* in *h*ello
'th' ditto

otherwise all remaining vowels and consonants are as in English, except that the consonants 'j', 'k', 'q', 'v', 'w', 'x', 'y', 'z' do not exist as part of the Gaelic alphabet.

Note: The above is intended as a guide to the pronunciation of the Gaelic names and words to be found in this book; but it is only an approximation. There are apparently three main dialects of Modern Irish-Gaelic which differ considerably from one another, so much so that there is presently no accepted standard Irish-Gaelic pronunciation in Ireland itself, and what Gaelic pronunciation was at the time Scots-Gaelic began to diverge from Irish-Gaelic must surely be a matter for some considerable conjecture. The pronunciation of 'Old-Gaelic' names as identified by Johnston and Watson must therefore be treated with some circumspection and in order to maintain the validity of the comparisons made between the Gaelic interpretations given by these two authors the spellings of such Gaelic interpretations will, in this book, be as they appear in the works of Watson or Johnston even though these spellings may not always be in accordance with modern practice. In addition any accents placed above letters in Gaelic words will be those of Watson or Johnston and again may not be in accordance with modern practice. There are sounds in the Gaelic alphabet which cannot be reproduced by reference to the Welsh or English alphabets and any attempt by a non-Gaelic speaker to interpret the changes in phonetics effected by these accents is bound to end in disaster! For the purposes of this book, which concentrates wholly on the P-Celtic aspects of place-names, Gaelic elements are of interest only for comparison purposes and the subtleties of Gaelic pronunciation are best ignored.

Scots-Gaelic and Scots word-elements found in Scotland's place-names

allt Said to have originally meant 'rocky-valley' but now in the Scots-Gaelic dictionary as 'stream', 'brook', 'river with precipitous sides'. It is not found in my Irish-Gaelic dictionary and the presumption is that it was adopted from Welsh *allt.*

ard In Irish-Gaelic *aird* = a 'compass point'; *airde* = 'height', 'altitude', *ard* = 'height', 'high-part'. In Scots-Gaelic *ard* = 'high', 'lofty'; 'supreme', 'tall'; *aird* = 'compass-point'; *airde* = 'height', 'stature'. In Scottish place-names the usual spelling is *ard* and the meaning is 'high-place', 'promontory'. All these similar meaning word-elements have to be compared with Welsh *ardd* = 'height'; 'high', especially in it's aspirated form *ard,* and especially when assessing a place-name such as Airdrie where the second element appears to be Welsh *dre, dref* = 'steading'.

auchter This Scottish place-name element is not found in this form in my Scots-Gaelic dictionary. It's origin is contested between Irish-Gaelic *uachtar* = 'top', 'upper-part'. Scots-Gaelic *uachdar* = 'surface', 'top', and Welsh *uchder, uchdwr* = 'height', and *uwch tir* = 'upper land'. As an example Auchtermuchty, said to mean 'high-ground of the pig-rearing', is not easily explainable from the Gaelic, but follows naturally from Welsh *uwch tir moch ty* = 'upper land of the pig house', 'Auchter' names appear to be confined to the Highland fringes and the Lowlands where Welsh (or Pictish) influence can be expected to be dominant.

avon River-names are probably the most ancient topographical place-names we have, and it seems that *avon* as it appears in Scotland could be Irish-Gaelic *abhainn,* Scots-Gaelic *abhainn,* Welsh *afon,* or some pre-Celtic equivalent, all having the same meaning 'river'. In Scotland it is, being by definition 'ancient', far more likely to have pre-Celtic or Welsh roots than Gaelic.

bal As found in place-names this element is usually assumed to be from Scots-Gaelic *baile* pronouncd 'balla' = 'town, village'. A similar Welsh word is *beili* (pronounced 'beilee') = 'court', 'yard', 'outlet', 'mound'; it also has the meaning of 'bailey' as defined in English as the 'outer walls of a mediaeval castle and also any court within them'. This latter meaning obviously does not apply to the early place-names of Scotland and in Irish-Gaelic the nearest word *balla* = 'a wall' also seems to have this later meaning. The usual meaning of *beili* is 'yard' in the sense of an enclosed space almost always surrounding or attached to some habitable building, it is not a word found in Welsh place-names but that does not necessarily mean that it cannot appear in Scottish place-names, where Scots-Gaelic *baile* is seen to be nearer in meaning to Welsh *beili* than it is to Irish *balla.*

barr Scots-Gaelic *barr* = 'top'; 'point', 'tip', 'end', 'extremity'. Welsh *bar* = 'top', 'summit'. Irish-Gaelic *bar* = 'tip', 'top', 'summit', 'upper-part'.

ben Scots-Gaelic *beinn* = a 'mountain', 'hill', 'pinnacle'. Welsh *ben* = aspirated form of *pen* which in this context has the meaning 'top', 'head'. In Wales it rarely applies to hills or mountains except in the adjectival sense 'top-of'. There seems to be no equivalent in modern Irish-Gaelic, only a reference to an 'Early Irish *benn* = a peak ', which appears to be entirely absent from Irish place-names. The suspicion then is that Scottish *ben* was adopted, with but slightly changed meaning, from Welsh *ben.*

brae This is essentially a Scots-dialect word meaning 'a steepish-slope', 'the brow of a hill', 'upland, mountainous area'. Welsh *bre* (of almost identical pronunciation) = 'hill', 'highland', 'peak', 'high'. Scots-Gaelic *braighe* and *braghad* sound somewhat the same but are of different meaning and Norse *bra* may explain some Shetland place-names, but Scots *brae* is most probably inherited from Welsh *bre*.

cathair In the Scots-Gaelic dictionary the meaning is given as = 'city', but in place-name attributions it has often been said to compare with Welsh *caer* given in the Welsh dictionary as = 'fort', 'wall', 'castle', 'citadel', but which in Scottish place-names seems to be confined to a meaning = 'fortlet', 'lesser-fort' or 'fort-place'.

cairn A Scots inheritance from Welsh *carn* = 'burial-mound, 'tumulus', 'heap', 'heap-of-stones', which then passed from Scots into English as 'cairn'.

cambus Scots-Gaelic *camas* = 'a bay', 'a creek'. Welsh *camas*, plural *cemmaes* = 'a bay', 'a river-bend'. Apparently no equivalent in modern Irish-Gaelic but again a reference to 'Early-Irish' *cammas* = 'bay', 'river-bend'.

carrick Scots-Gaelic *carraig, carig* = 'rock', 'cliff', 'headland'. Welsh *careg, ceryg, carreg, cerrig* = 'a stone', 'a rock'. Irish-Gaelic *carraig* = 'rock', 'boulder'.

craig A Scots inheritance from Welsh *craig* = 'crag', 'rock'. Scots-Gaelic *creag* may be from the same source.

crom Scots-Gaelic *crom* = 'to bend', 'to descend', 'bent', 'crooked'. Welsh *crwm, crom* = 'bent', 'crooked', 'bending'.

cul / cuil Scots-Gaelic *cul* = 'the-back-of-' anything! Scots-Gaelic *cuil* = 'corner, recess, nook, niche'. Welsh *cil* = 'back', 'recess', 'corner', 'nook', 'retreat'. There appears to be no Irish-Gaelic equivalent so perhaps this is another Scots-Gaelic inheritance from the Welsh. It does for example occur in the place-name Coultrie, said by some to be Scots-Gaelic *cul tref* = 'back place', but quite obviously Welsh *cil tre* = 'back, steading' or 'corner, steading', where the present

Welsh pronunciation 'keel' has been Scottified to 'kool'.

dal This appears in Scots-Gaelic as *dail* = 'field', 'plain', 'dale', and it seems generally agreed that it is an inheritance from Welsh *dol* = 'a meadow', 'a dale'; although English *dale* and Old Norse *dalr* are sometimes also found in this same guise 'dal'.

dour Scots-Gaelic *dobhar* inherited from Welsh *dŵr, dwfr* = 'water', a word that in place-names usually means 'water' in the sense of a stream or river. No apparent equivalent in Irish-Gaelic.

drum Scots-Gaelic *druim* = 'back', 'keel', 'ridge'. Welsh *trum* aspirated to *drum* = 'back', 'ridge', 'summit'. Irish-Gaelic *droim* = 'back', 'ridge', 'depression'. With forms and meanings being so similar in all three Celtic languages it is not surprising that almost any Scottish place-name containing this element can be explained equally in both Welsh and Gaelic. For example Tyndrum is in Welsh *tyn drum* = 'croft on the ridge', whilst in Gaelic it is *tigh an druim* = 'house on the ridge'.

dun Scots-Gaelic *dun* = 'fort', 'fortress', 'castle', 'fortification', 'heap'. Welsh *din* = 'hill-fort', fortress', 'camp'. Irish-Gaelic *dun* = 'fort', 'fortress'. In Scottish place-names *din* is often found in the form *dun* which is often interpreted as 'Gaelic *dun* = hill'. This last can be seen to be a misnomer as the only source of the element 'hill' is from the Welsh definition of *din* = 'hill-fort' where in the course of time the element 'fort' was dropped-off, possibly because the original 'hill-fort' became ruinous and such a description was no longer relevant.

eccles Scots-Gaelic *eaglais* = 'church', 'temple'. Irish-Gaelic *eaglais* = 'church'. Welsh *eglwys* = 'church'. All of these are from Latin *eclesia* = 'church' and the problem in Scottish place-names is to decide between a possible origin in the Gaelic or in the Welsh? Sometimes this is easy, for example Ecclefechan = *eglwys fechan* = 'little church', a Gaelic interpretation such as Eaglais Fechin (of uncertain meaning) doesn't really come close!

edin This element as it appears in the name Edinburgh is still uncertain of meaning and is the subject of much confused thinking. That 'Edinburgh' originated as the Welsh *din eidyn* is no longer disputed, neither is the fact that it lies within an area that went straight from speaking Welsh to speaking English – with no intervening period of Gaelic. Any Gaelic interpretation that now exists has therefore to be regarded as contrived.

fas Dorward describes this as a 'Brittonic term which did not pass into Gaelic' and meaning 'a stance, a pitch, a spot, where a drover might rest his beasts overnight'. It does however appear in my Scots-Gaelic dictionary as *fas* = 'unoccupied', 'uncultivated', 'void'. The origin seems to be from Welsh *faes* = 'open-field', 'plain' which in Welsh place-names usually applies to a piece of flat, 'empty', ground.

gart Scots-Gaelic *garradh* = 'an enclosure', 'garden', 'fence', 'yard'. Welsh *garth* = 'enclosure', 'garden', 'buttress', 'ridge'. There appears to be no sensible equivalent in Irish-Gaelic. Dorward cites Old Norse *gardr,* Brittonic *garth,* Gaelic *garradh,* and Old English *geard* all with the meaning 'yard', 'garden', and all with an input to Scottish place-names. The biggest cluster of *gart* names is, according to Dorward, around Glasgow, an area in which one can expect P-Celtic Welsh names to prevail over Q-Celtic Irish ones. There is also the 'dictionary evidence' as above to indicate that Scots-Gaelic *garradh* is, in any case, an inheritance from Welsh *garth*. Thus Garscadden = 'herring-yard' is said by Dorward to be 'pure Gaelic', but is much more likely to be Welsh *garth sgadan* = 'herrings enclosure', or perhaps more amusingly *gardd sgadan* = 'herrings garden' perhaps in the same sense as 'beer-garden'?

glas (colour) Scots-Gaelic *glas* = 'pale', 'wan', 'grey', 'green-grass'. Welsh *glas* = 'blue', 'pale', 'grey', 'green', 'raw'. Irish-Gaelic *glas* = 'green-plant', 'grey', 'blue-grey', 'raw'.

glas (other) Welsh *glais* = 'stream'. This is also found aspirated to *lais,* or *las.* Dorward cites the example of Douglas = Brittonic *du glas* = 'black stream', he then cites its antonym as Finglas = Gaelic *fionn ghlais* = 'white stream'. There is a problem with this interpretation, I can find *ghlais* neither in my Scots-Gaelic dictionary nor in my Irish-Gaelic dictionary and it would seem that this is one of those cases, mentioned by Watson, where a non-Gaelic word (*glais*) is 'dressed' in Gaelic garb by the simple expedient of respelling it using the Gaelic alphabet, hence *ghlais.* Thus Finglas, instead of being the Gaelic-Welsh hybrid *fionn glais* is far more likely to be the wholly Welsh *ffin glais, ffinglas, ffinlas* = 'boundary stream'.

glen Scots-Gaelic *gleann* = 'valley', 'dell', 'dale'. Welsh *glyn* = 'valley'. Irish-Gaelic *gleann* = 'valley'. Again, three elements of similar form and matching meaning with the same difficulty in deciding on an attribution. The only guide is that the older a name is the more likely it is to have originated in an older form of Welsh.

gordon It is, says Dorward, 'thought to come from the Brittonic words *gor dun* meaning "great fort".' Welsh *gor din* has the same meaning, in Scotland *din* and *dun* are interchangeable but *din* is probably the older form; *gor-* is a Welsh 'enhancing' prefix, adding 'importance' to what follows.

inch This a Scots dialect word derived from Welsh *ynys* = 'meadow', 'water-meadow', 'island', as also is Scots-Gaelic *innis*.

inver This, in the Scots-Gaelic form *inbhir*, is the equivalent of Welsh *aber* = 'river-mouth', 'confluence', 'estuary'. In several place-names the early records show that an original *aber* was, at sometime, replaced by a later *inver*. In Irish-Gaelic *inbhear* has the same meaning. In Scotland it is probable that most *inver* names started life as *aber* names, confluences and river-mouths were significant topographical features and as such were sure to have had names prior to the incoming of the Gaelic language.

kil A highly controversial name as Scots-Gaelic *ceall, cill* = 'church', 'churchyard', 'monastic cell' is confronted head-on by Welsh *cil* = 'refuge', 'retreat', 'corner', 'nook'. Most Kil names are followed by the name of a local 'saint', a practice which is found also in Wales in the name Cilsant = 'refuge', 'retreat' of the Saint. The bottom line is that it cannot be taken for granted that all 'Kil-' names derive from Scots-Gaelic *cill*.

kin This is a straightforward corruption of Scots-Gaelic *ceann* = 'head', 'point', 'end', 'headland', 'chief'. In meaning Welsh *pen* is it's exact equivalent and in the early records of some place-names *ceann* (or *cen)* is shown as displacing an earlier Welsh *pen*, Watson was of the opinion that this was not unusual and that a number of Pen- names probably suffered a similar displacement but for these there are no records as evidence one way or the other.

lanark Welsh llannerch, *lanerch* = 'glade', 'clearing','open-space', 'plain' in a wood. Sometimes metathesised to Lanrick, Lanrig, Lanric.

leven Welsh *llefn, lefn: llyfn, lyfn* = 'even', 'smooth', 'sleek'.

Dorward gives the example of Loch Leven, Kinross, of which, he says, 'a Brittonic origin is much more probable than a Gaelic one', the out dated derivation from Gaelic *leamhan* = 'elm-tree', 'looks rather like an example of the tendency to find a Gaelic origin at all costs.'

linn Scots-Gaelic *linne* = 'pool'. Irish-Gaelic *linn* = 'pool'. Welsh *llyn, lyn* = 'lake'. Seems easy then! Any 'linn' name applying to anything bigger than a 'pool' must by definition be of Welsh origin?

loch Scots-Gaelic *loch* = 'lake', 'sea inlet'. Irish-Gaelic *loch* = 'lake', 'lough'. Welsh *llwch, lwch* = 'lake' (dictionary), but in Welsh place-names it has the meanings 'pool', 'bog', 'swampy-ground'. Very difficult now to prise Welsh origins out of the plethora of Scottish 'Loch' names.

long Scots-Gaelic *long* = 'ship'. Welsh *llong, long* = 'ship'. Irish-Gaelic *long* = 'ship'. English *long* = 'long'. Scots-dialect *lang* = 'long', 'tall', 'high'. Unfortunately 'long', appearing as an element in place-names only very rarely means 'ship' and seldom means 'long', it is more often a corruption of an earlier 'lang' which itself derives from Welsh *llan, lan* with it's usual meanings of 'church', 'burial-ground', or simply 'Christian site' – of some sort. An example is the name Longmorn, pronounced 'langmorr'n', which originated as *llan morgan* = 'church, or refuge, of Morgan the holy man'. Similarly Longniddrie was once on record as Langnudre, and Longformacus was at one time Langeford Makhous.

maol Scots-Gaelic *maol* = 'bald', 'bare', 'blunt', 'high-rounded-headland'. Welsh *moel* = 'bald', 'bare', 'barren', 'bare-topped-hill'. Irish-Gaelic *maol* = 'bald', 'blunt'. Old Norse *muli* = 'headland'. It would seem that Scots-Gaelic *maol* has combined all the meanings given for the others except for Welsh 'bare-topped-hill'.

marc Scots-Gaelic *marc* = 'horse', 'steed'. Welsh *march* = 'horse', 'stallion'. Irish-Gaelic = no equivalent! It seems therefore that Scots-Gaelic *marc* is an inheritance from Welsh *march*.

may Scots-Gaelic *magh* = 'field', 'plain'. Welsh *maes, mai, ma* = 'field', 'open-field', 'plain', 'square'. Irish-Gaelic (nearest equivalent) *machaire* = 'field', 'plain', 'level-ground'. Dorward takes as an example the name 'Cambus o' May' which he derives from Scots-Gaelic *camas a mhaigh* = 'bend of the plain'. Interestingly the equivalent in Welsh is *camas-y-mai* = 'river-bend in the open-field, plain'. The village Cambus o' May is, Dorward says, by a bend on the river Dee.

meall Scots-Gaelic *meall* = 'a mass', 'a heavy shower, bank of clouds, mist, fog', 'lump, knob, bunch'. Irish-Gaelic *meall* = 'ball', 'globe', 'protruberance', 'lump'. None of the above meanings seem particularly suited to the element *meall* as it appears in Scottish place-names and one is left with the lingering suspicion that here *meall* is but another case of a Welsh word, in this instance *moel*, being roughly re-spelled using the Gaelic alphabet but retaining its Welsh meaning when applied to Scottish place-name construction.

monadh The source of this word is summed up very nicely by Dorward – '*Monadh* appears to be Brittonic in origin, and has it's equivalent in Welsh *mynydd*.' As such it is found in Scottish place-names in various forms such as – 'mounth', 'mount', 'mont', 'month', 'mond', 'mund', 'munt', 'minit', and the like.

more Scots-Gaelic *mor* = 'great', 'great-size', 'tall', 'important'. Welsh *mawr* = 'big', 'great', 'high', 'large'. Irish-Gaelic *mor* = 'big', 'large', 'main', 'senior'. Welsh *mor* = 'sea', 'ocean'. Also see *muir* below.

muir Scots-Gaelic *muir* = 'sea', 'ocean', 'wave'. Welsh *mor* = 'sea', 'ocean'. Irish-Gaelic *muir* = 'sea'. Scots *muir* = 'moor', 'rough-heathery-land', 'a common'. English *moor* = 'moor'. The very blurred boundaries and crossed meanings between *more, muir, mor* and *mawr* make it difficult to assess some names such as Dalmore; is it 'meadow on the moor'?, or 'big meadow'? or 'meadow by the sea'? or 'senior', i.e. most-important, meadow'? Obviously the topographical situation will greatly help to decide which meaning is most likely and the fact that the first element Dal- is Welsh *dol* = 'meadow' will limit the choice in this case to that between *dol mor* = 'meadow by the sea' and *dol mawr* = 'big meadow'. If however Dalmore takes it's name from a big meadow by the sea then the final attribution has to remain unresolved.

nemed An ancient name relating to sites of pagan worship which Dorward connects to Old-Irish *nemed* = 'sanctuary' but which, he says, does not appear in the Gaelic dictionary. Others take a different view – G.W.S Barrow (*The Uses of Place-Names*) states: 'It is almost by definition likely to be P-Celtic, *neued* (Gaulish *nemeton*) = 'sacred grove, sanctuary', even though the Q-Celtic cognate (Gaelic *neimhidh*) must lie behind some of our modern reflexes e.g. Nevie, Nevay'. Some Welsh words of related meaning to P-Celtic *neued* are *nef* = 'heaven', *nefwy* = 'heaven', *nefol* = 'heavenly, celestial', *nefed* = 'heavenliness', *nefyn* = 'little-heaven'.

ochil As Dorward says: 'The Brittonic word *uchel* means "high" . . . ', and it's wide distribution throughout Scotland 'serves as a reminder of the extent to which the Brittonic language was spoken in Scotland in pre-Gaelic times'. It, *uchel*, passed into Gaelic in the form *uasle* meaning 'of high birth'. Welsh *uchel* = 'high', 'lofty', 'towering', 'loud'.

pan Said to be a Brittonic word related to Welsh *pant* = 'valley', 'dent', 'hollow', 'depression', 'low-place'. There is however no need to presume upon an earlier Brittonic *pan* to explain Scottish place-names such as Panmure = *pant mawr*. Linguistically the close juxtaposition of 't' to 'm' in the combination *pantmawr* almost ensures that in ordinary speech the 't' is eliminated to give a more easily pronounced *panmawr*, from which Panmure.

peffer Welsh *pefr* = 'bright', 'shining'.

pen Welsh *pen* = 'head', 'far-end', 'headland', 'chief'. A very widely distributed element which suffered in many instances from being usurped by the later Gaelic *cen, ceann* of similar meaning. It is a fair guess that a number of place-names now beginning with 'Ken', 'Kin', or 'Can', will have had the element *pen* as a precursor.

pit This, again, is a highly controversial element said to be related to and have somewhat the same meaning as Welsh *peth* = 'part-of', 'quantity-of', 'thing', 'article'. Occurs almost exclusively in those areas in Eastern Scotland above the Firth of Forth which are generally regarded as the heartlands of the 'Picts' and for that reason is defined as being a 'Pictish' word-element. The accompanying element is almost always attributed to Gaelic and on this account it is considered that Pit- names came to be generated at the time that P-Celtic was giving way to Q-Celtic Gaelic. As always there are anomalies, Johnston identified the village of Pity Me, south of Jedburgh and in England, as Welsh *peth-y-medd;* yet it is very probably a Pit- name. Pitmilly (Crail) attributed to *pit* plus Gaelic *muileann, muillin* = 'croft with the mill' is based on the recorded Putmullin of 1211 and is just as likely to be from Welsh *peth melin* = the 'part by the mill', the 'part' alluded to being a 'piece of land'. Pitgaveny (Elgin) was Bothnguanan in 1100, Bothgouane in 1251 and Bothgauenan in 1251, it is not recorded as a 'Pit-' name until Pittarie in 1662. It can be argued that the early Both- names derive from *bwythyn* = 'cottage' and *bwth* = 'hut'. Pitkeathly (Bridge of Earn) was Pethkathilin in 1225 and Petcathle in 1461, clearly demonstrating the change from *peth* in 1225 to *pet* in 1461 and to *pit* today. The second element is obscure but may, Watson thinks, be a personal name Cathalan.

poll Dorward describes this as a Gaelic word – which it is, but the element, as it appears in Scottish place-names, is more likely to derive from Welsh *pwll* = 'pool', 'puddle', 'pit'. Or from an older 'British' word *pol* = 'stream', 'flowing-water'.

preas Scots-Gaelic *preas* = 'bush', 'shrub,' 'thicket'. Welsh *prys* = 'copse', 'grove', 'covert', 'brushwood'. Irish-Gaelic = no apparent equivalent. Scottish-Gaelic *preas* is therefore an inheritance from Welsh. Some have said it is of Pictish origin but Dorward refers to it as being originally a Brittonic word.

rath Scots-Gaelic *rath* (pronounced ra) = 'fortress', 'residence'. Irish Gaelic *rath* = 'ring-fort'. Welsh *rhath, rath* = 'mound', 'cleared-spot', 'plain', but in Welsh place-names T. James *(Uses of Place-Names)* suggests looking at *rath* as an element uncertainly related to *rhath,* and with a meaning more akin to Gaelic *rath* = 'fort'. According to Dorward *rath* names were once common in Pictish areas but few have survived. It's absence from the Gaelic heartlands in the west would favour a Welsh origin, possibly as a word that retained it's original meaning amongst the Picts but lost it in Wales itself. See Ratho.

rig Scots dialect *rig* = 'ridge', 'spine', 'hill-crest', 'long strip of land'. Welsh *rhych* = 'furrow', 'groove', 'trench'. Two very different meanings for similar looking words, Johnston considers Restalrig (Edinburgh) is Welsh *llys tal rhych* = 'hall, mansion on the lofty-ridge', but 'hall, mansion at the front-end of the furrow' is more in accordance with the dictionary definitions.

ross Scots Gaelic *ros* = 'a promontory', 'a wooded-promontory'. Irish Gaelic *ros* = 'a wooded-headland'. Welsh *rhos, ros* = 'moor', 'plain', 'coarse-highland'. 'In Scottish place-names it is not always possible to say which of the languages is relevant and which meaning is correct.' (Dorward)

strath Scots Gaelic *strath* is not found in my dictionary. Scots *strath* = 'broad, flat, river-valley'. Watson is of the opinion that it derives from Welsh *ystrad* = 'vale', 'flat-vale', = 'broad, flat-bottomed valley' (in Welsh place-names).

tarff Scots Gaelic *tarbh* = 'a bull'. Welsh *tarw* = 'bull'. Irish Gaelic *tarbh* = 'bull'. River or stream names are the oldest of all place-names and are often accepted as being pre-Celtic of unknown meaning so where these elements apply to stream names and are seen to have a possible meaning then the supposition has to be that the origin is P-Celtic Welsh rather than Q-Celtic Irish.

teine Scots Gaelic *teine* = 'fire'. Welsh *tan, tannau* = 'fire', 'fires'. Irish Gaelic *tine* = 'fire'.

tigh Scots Gaelic *tigh* = 'house'. Welsh *tŷ* = 'house'. Irish Gaelic *teach* = 'house'. Note that the Scots Gaelic *tigh* is nearer in both spelling and pronunciation to Welsh *tŷ* than it is to Irish *teach.*

tilly Scots Gaelic *tulach* = 'knoll'. Welsh *tyle* = 'hill', 'ascent', e.g. Tillicoultry = *tyle cul tre* = 'hill at back of the steading'.

tir Scots Gaelic *tir* = 'land', 'shore'. Welsh *tir* = 'land', 'earth', 'ground', 'territory'. Irish Gaelic *tir* = 'land', 'country'.

traigh Scots Gaelic *traigh* = 'to ebb, dry-up', *traighad* = 'shore,' 'strand', 'sand-beach'. Welsh *traeth* = 'beach'. Irish Gaelic *tra* = 'beach', 'strand'.

tref Welsh *tref* = 'steading'. Place-names incorporating *tref* '. . . are nearly all to be found within the boundaries of the old kingdom of Strathclyde, the remainder in Pictland.

Chapter 6

Brittonic, Brythonic, British and Cumbric

'As for what you have lost, it is lost only to this world'

Cadfael Chronicles, 'The Rose Rent'

This chapter will be the shortest in the book for the simple reason that so little is known about these languages that there is little to relate other than to place them in a proper context relative to the Welsh languages to which they are connected.

Glanville Price (*Languages in Britain and Ireland*) defines 'British' as being a noun and as being the name of the Language spoken by the Britons of Roman and pre-Roman times. 'Brittonic' and 'Brythonic' he categorizes as adjectives in the sense that Welsh, Cornish and Breton, all derived from 'British', can then be described synonymously as Brittonic or Brythonic languages. This is a useful classification which was not however that adopted by earlier authors such as Watson and Johnston. As the early 'Britons' had no written language the only surviving clues to their spoken language are just a few references to place-names and personal names to be found in Latin texts of Roman times. They, naturally, were very much corrupted, almost always displaying obtrusive Latin suffixes such as *'-a'* or *'-us'*.

The language known as Cumbric is thought to have been that development of 'Brythonic' last spoken in what is now Cumbria and which is thought to have died out sometime around the 12th century. The evidence for the existence of this language is restricted to only three words; *mercheta, galnes / galnys,* and *kelchyn* occurring in a circa 11th century Latin legal text and which are thought to correspond to Welsh *merch* = 'daughter', *galanas* = 'blood-line' and *cylch* = 'circuit'. Whether or not these mere three words are sufficient evidence to establish 'Cumbric' as a separate language from Brittonic / Brythonic / British (or even Welsh!) is perhaps doubtful, especially if we relate *mercheta* to Welsh *merchet* = 'girliness' (but with an intrusive Latin *'a'* stuck on the end) and relate *kelchyn* to Welsh *cylchyn* = 'small circuit'.

It has to be admitted that present day perceptions of any P-Celtic languages prior to the 6th century are nebulous in the extreme and it is something of an anomaly when authors such as Watson, Johnston and others gaily define word elements in Scottish place-names as being British, Brittonic, Brythonic or Cumbric when there are no historical records to substantiate such claims and particularly when the word elements they then quote as 'British', 'Brythonic' or 'Cumbric' are obviously taken straight from modern Welsh Dictionaries. It is for this reason that words appearing in this book which are still found in Welsh dictionaries are described as 'Welsh' and not as anything else. Any elements ascribed by the various other writers to the earlier Languages seem only to have been the result of 'retrospective linguistic reconstruction' – hardly an exact science!

Chapter 7

River names

'The day will come when all will be made plain.
Then shall we know as now we trust'

Cadfael Chronicles, 'The Raven in the Foregate'

As has been said before River names are probably the oldest of all topographical place-names and if pre-Celtic or very early P-Celtic (Archaic Welsh?) names have survived anywhere in Scotland then it is in the names of the Rivers that we should expect to see them. Watson devotes all of two chapters and over fifty pages to the consideration of these ancient names and I am pleased to acknowledge that the entire content of this chapter is based almost solely on his findings, dissertations and attributions. But where Watson sometimes derives meanings from the present day Gaelic names that many of these rivers, especially the smallest and least significant ones, now bear it is noteworthy that a number of these can equally well be explained in terms of equivalent Welsh constructions and where this is the case a suitable Welsh interpretation is suggested. In some instances it can be seen that the Gaelic name is formed from Welsh word elements that have subsequently been adopted into the Scots-Gaelic language; the river Tarf for example takes its name from *tarw* (bull) which was taken in to Scots-Gaelic as *tarbh*. Almost all the great rivers of Scotland however are to be found not in the Gaelic heartlands of the Western Seaboard but either in the Lowlands or in the Pictish North East and nearly all of their names seem to have retained at least some evidence of, or connection with, their Welsh origins.

Alder Burn (Ben Alder) – from *allt dwr* = 'hillside stream' plus a superfluous Scots *burn* = 'stream'.

Almond (Perthshire, Linlithgow) – Both names originate in an early Celtic *Ambona* which, in similar fashion to *Abona,* translates into modern Welsh as *Amon* or *Aman*. The second element in the name of Cramond on the river Almond near Edinburgh may be a corruption of *almond* or it may possibly be a reflection of the older *amon*. In Wales there are a Cwmaman and an Aberaman at Aberdare where the rivers Dare and Aman join the Cynon. The meanings of *Ambona, Abona* are obscure but studies of Welsh toponymy suggest that *Aman* derives from *Amanw* or *Amanwy*, these being the names of some river Goddess and are associated with the word *Banw* = 'pig, piglet' or simply a 'woman'. It is suggested that the 'pig' meaning is descriptive of a stream 'rooting' or 'boring' its way along its river bed. This compares with river name *Twrch* as found elsewhere.

Abhainn Poibhlidh (Ross) – Watson's discussion of this Gaelic name seems at first to be somewhat confusing. It is, he says, – 'for *Abhainn Poible* = 'river of the tent', from *poball,* borrowed from Latin *papilio* = a butterfly'. He then relates the name to *Achadh Poible* (Inverness) = 'field of the tent'. This last connection seemed strange to me but Watson, as usual, is right and the key to these apparently conflicting statements is that Latin *papilio* is actually the root of the

English word *pavilion* which is one of the meanings given for the Welsh word *pabell* (plural *pebyll)* = 'a tent', 'a pavilion'. This compares with Scots-Gaelic (also Irish-Gaelic) *puball* = 'a tent', so the root of both these Celtic words would also be Latin *papilio*. The element *pabell* is also found in the place-names Peebles (Peebleshire), Papple (East Lothian) and Cairnpapple (West Lothian). Also, Watson's Gaelic *Achadh Poible* (Inverness) is actually named 'Achpopuli' and is listed by G.W.S. Barrow ('The Uses of Place-Names') as a P-Celtic *pebyll* name. In which case *abhainn poiblidh* probably originated similarly as *afon pebyll* = 'river of tents'. It is intriguing to speculate as to the meaning hidden within the phrase 'river of tents'; superficially it makes little sense and neither by themselves do 'Peebles', 'Papple' or 'Cairnpapple'. Individually we can imagine Peebles to be an 'encampment of tents' and Papple to have been one 'tent' on it's own, but Cairnpapple aks 'cairn of the tent' stretches credibility. If however we make the imaginative assumptions that 'tents' is shorthand for 'tent-people' and that this is possibly a reference to the pre-Celtic indigenous inhabitants of Scotland then *abhainn poibhlidh (afon pebyll)* is immediately explainable as = 'the river of the tent-people', as also is Cairnpapple as the = 'cairn of the tent-man' – who would most definitely have been pre-Celtic! Interestingly Scots-Gaelic *pobull* = 'people', 'a community', 'a congregation', and *poibleach* = 'people'; but whether or not this is relevant I do not know. It has been said that Watson in his study of place-names had the advantage of being brought up as a native Gaelic speaker and was therefore able to obtain the local Gaelic name for a feature directly from local Gaelic speakers. This particular name *abhainn poibhlidh, abhainn poible* perhaps highlights the disadvantages of this apparent advantage; it is probable that Watson was given the names by a local Gael and it may be that a Gaelic name given by a local Gaelic speaker may not be as reliable a source of information as to it's origin than that given by the locally accepted Scots or English rendition and certainly not as reliable as any early written records that might exist.

Banvie (Perthshire) – *banw* = 'a sow'

Bran (Strathbran, Ross) – *bran* = 'a crow'. **Strathbran** would have been *ystrad bran* = 'valley of the crow'.

Brothock Water (Arbroath) – Welsh *brothog, brothoc* = 'tumultuous.' Passed into Scots-Gaelic as *brothag* = 'boiling'.

Caddon Water (a tributary of the Tweed), **Cadan** (Kinloch Rannoch) – both from early Celtic *Catona* = 'a goddess of war'. Development into Welsh drops the *-a-* and changes the *-t-* to *-d-* giving *Cadon* or *Cadan.* The Welsh word *cad* = 'battle' is from the same source.

Calder (a common river or stream throughout Scotland) – *caled dŵr* = 'hard water'. The name appears in Scots-Gaelic form as *Caladar* or *Chaladair.*

Cander (Lanarks) – Candouer 1150, *can dwr* = 'white water'.

Cawdor – In Scots-Gaelic this stream name is known as *allt chaladair* said locally to mean 'hard stream', but this is obviously taken from *caled dŵr* which is of the same meaning. See Calder and also Cawdor as place-names.

Clyde – Watson identifies this as the river referred to by Tacitus as *Clota* – which in Old Welsh *'becomes Clut later Clud, whence the English form Clyde . . . Like many other river names, Clota is really the name of the river goddess, meaning "the washer, the strongly flowing one" or such.'* This explanation seems to assume that the present name is taken from Romanno British *Clota* translated through Old Welsh *Clut* and *Clud* and later into English as *Clyde.* But as one of the great rivers of Scotland the name of the Clyde will almost certainly have predated the coming of the Romans whose grip on Scotland was at all times somewhat tenuous! It is possible therefore that Tacitus' *Clota* was an interpretation of an existing P-Celtic or pre-Celtic name, also since the Romans were fond of tagging an 'a' or an 'us' onto Celtic names (e.g. Buddig into Boudicca, Caradoc into Caractacus) it is possible that *Clota* would have derived from *Clut* rather than the other way round. *Clud* in modern Welsh is *Clyd-* meaning 'sheltered, sheltering', a very apt description of the Clyde Estuary but probably not of the Clyde river that feeds into it.

Conon (Ross) – may derive from *Conona* meaning 'goddess of hounds' in which case it would be cognate with the river *Cynon* at Aberdare and Abercynon, S. Wales.

Conghlais (Banff, Argyll) – *cwn glais* = 'dog stream', see 'Glais'.

Daer (a tributary of the Clyde) – cognate with 'dare' as in Aberdare Wales, from *dar* = 'oak trees', it is pronounced 'dare' in the local South Wales dialect.

Dee – From British *Deua* meaning 'Great Goddess' – see entry for Aberdeen.

Devon (Perthshire) – Probably from early 'British' *Dubona* or *Dobona* whose exact meaning is somewhat obscure but which may be 'black goddess' or such like. On development into Welsh the *-a-* is dropped and the *-b-* aspirates to *-f-* thus giving *dufon* or *dofon* – from which the anglicized Devon.

Dobhar – is the name or part name element of many small streams or rivulets in Scotland. It is a survival in Scots-Gaelic of Welsh *dŵr* = 'water' which is seen in Scottish place-names as *dour, -der,* as well as in it's Gaelic dress as *dobhar, dobhair.*

Don –The name of the Goddess *Don,* the 'Mother Goddess' of ancient Europe – see entry for Aberdeen.

Doon – derives from the same roots as Don – see Aberdeen.

Douglas, Dubhghlais, Dhubhghlais (several, dispersed throughout Scotland) – *du glas, du glais* = 'black, or dark stream or ditch' see 'Glais'.

Esk (Lothian, Kincardine, Forfar) – The name of all three is related to that of the Welsh 'Usk' which is thought to be from *wysg,* an older Welsh name for 'water' which in it's plural form *wysgau* or *wysgi* meaning 'waters' and pronounced 'wusgay' or 'wusgee' may also be the source of the Scots word 'whisky' – possibly via the intervening Gaelic *uisge,* meaning 'water' and pronounced 'ooshka'.

Finlas, Finglas, Fionnghlais (Loch Lomond, Brig o' Turk, Loch Doon respectively) – *Ffin glais* = 'boundary stream, boundary ditch' see 'Glais'.

Forth – Ptolemy's name for the Forth was *Boderia* later *Bodotria* (Tacitus), which names survive today as the second element in Aberbothrie on the north bank of the Forth estuary. Watson attributes this to Gaelic *boidhre* = 'the deaf one', 'the silent one' but then adds: 'This is one of the many instances in which a British name has either been taken over direct into Gaelic or translated during the period of transition from British to Gaelic'. By this he seems to be intimating that the derivation may be from the Welsh word *byddar* = 'deaf'. This however cannot be the source of the present name the derivation of which remains obscure. If however the assumption is made that an important river and estuary such as this must have had a name from very early times then consideration has to be given to the Welsh *Ffordd* the meaning of which is 'way' in it's widest sense i.e. a road*way,* path*way* sea*way* etc. etc. the last of which aptly describes the Forth Estuary. There are other equally wild guesses including Norse (*fiord*) and Gaelic (*foithre*). What is certain is that the estuary *would* have had a name, whatever it was, prior to the coming of either the Norse Vikings or the Irish Gaels.

Glais (Ross, Inverness) – *glais* = 'stream, rivulet, ditch'. Appears as an element in other river names either as *Glas* or in the aspirated forms *'lais* and *'las*. In Scots-Gaelic dress it becomes *ghlais*.

Glaster (Inverness) – *glas dŵr* = 'green, blue, water', or alternatively *glas tir* = 'green land'.

Gloy (Lochaber) – Watson says this appears to be an old British name taken into Gaelic. Therefore from Welsh *gloyw* = 'bright, shining-one'.

Gowrie (Perthshire) – *gofer* = 'a rill', 'a streamlet'.

Irvine (Ayrshire) – Watson considers this to be cognate with that of the river *Irfon* in Ceredigion but the early records, *Yrewyn* 1258, and *Irwyn* 1296, suggest the possibility of a different interpretation such as *hir waen* = 'long moorland-pasture' stream.

Jed (Roxburgh) – from Welsh *gwdd* = 'that which twists and turns', the *dd* being hardened into *d* and the *g* being softened into *j*.

Kelty (Perthshire, Stirlingshire, Fife) – Watson derives the name from Gaelic *Cailtidh*, the 'reduced' form of an earlier Gaelic *Caladar*, itself from an even earlier Welsh *caled-dŵr* = 'hard water'.

Labhar (Perthshire) – Although this name is given here in it's Scots-Gaelic form, as it appears on maps of the area, no such word is found in Irish Dictionaries, the supposition must therefore be that it's origin is in the earlier Welsh language of Scotland. Watson suggests Welsh *Llafar* meaning 'the noisy one', a title also attributed to the second element in the name of Aberlour in Banffshire and whereas there are several river names containing *llafar* in Wales there are no equivalents in Ireland. The English spelling of the name is Lawers. Other *llafar* names are **Llabharag** (= *llafarach* or *llafarog*) 'the little loud one' in Ross and another enters Loch Laggan.

Lavern/Levern (Renfrewshire) = Laberane 1539, **Laveran** (Loch Lomond) = Laueran/Inner-laveran 1225, **Louran** (a burn in Wigtownshire) – Watson considers all three derive from the goddess name *Labarona* meaning 'the loud one' which is reflected in the Welsh word *Llafar* = 'loud' and *Llafaran* = 'little-loud-one'.

Leader (Lauderdale) – relates to the river Leder, a tributary of the Conwy in Wales, whose meaning is obscure but may be from *lled dŵr* where *lled* has two meanings, either 'breadth' or 'death', *dŵr* = 'water'. Therefore either 'water of breadth' or 'water of death'.

Water of Leith (Edinburgh) – *llaith.* This has two meanings, firstly an adjective = 'damp, moist, soft', secondly a noun = 'death'. Therefore either 'soft, moist stream' or 'stream of death'.

Lossie (Moray) – *llysiau* (pronounced 'lussee eye') = 'herbs', or perhaps *llysiaidd* = 'herby, herbaceous'. Today's Gaelic name is *Lossa* = 'herbaceous'. This being a significant river in the East of Scotland precedence must be given to the Welsh interpretation.

Lugar / Lugdour (Ayrshire) – The first version may come directly from early Celtic *Loucara / Loucaros* = 'the bright one', alternatively the second version may be from a later Welsh *Llug dŵr* = 'bright water'.

Luggie (a tributary of the Kelvin) – relates to rivers *Llugwy* in Merionethshire and Anglesey; *Llug wy* is a 'goddess' name meaning 'the bright one'.

Mossat (Aberdeenshire) – *mwset* = 'having stale or stinking characteristics'. Passed into Scots-Gaelic as *mosach, musach* = 'nasty'.

Morar (Inverness) – early forms are Mordhobhar, Moreovyr, Morowore: These *'are doubtless old British names taken over into Gaelic'* (WJW). Therefore probably from *môr dŵr* = 'sea stream' or *mor dŵr, mawr dŵr* = 'big stream'. The former meaning is the more likely as the river Morar is only some 100 yds long from it's source in Loch Morar to it's entry into the sea. If Watson is right then the Loch would have taken it's name from the stream.

Nant (Taynuilt) – The stream runs through the valley 'Glen Nant' and empties into Loch Awe. There seems no reason to consider this as anything other than a survival of Welsh *glyn nant* = 'valley with a stream', but Watson hazards a guess at a Gaelic *abhainn neannt* = 'river of nettles'.

Nethan (Lanarkshire) – from the early Celtic river goddess name *Nectona* meaning 'pure one' which when translated into early Welsh dropped the *-a-* and had the *-ct-* transformed into -th- thus becoming *Nethon* or alternatively *Nethan.*

Nevis (Inverness) – *nef* = 'heaven', then *nefus* (pronounced 'nevis') meaning 'heavenly' or 'the heavenly one'. Obviously then a goddess-type river name. – see also Ben Nevis as a place-name.

Oykel – *uchel* = 'high'.

Paphrie (Forfar) – Possibly *pefr* in a the diminutive form *pefryn,* with the change of ending *-yn* to *-ie* giving *pefrie* then Paphrie = 'little bright stream'; see 'Peffer', and 'Peffery'.

Peffer (two brooks of this name in Haddington, E. Lothian) – *pefr* = 'radiant', 'sparkling'.

Peffer (part of the Braid burn, Edinburgh) – same as above.

Peffery (Strathpeffer, Ross) – May be for *pefryn* = the 'little-peffer' i.e. the 'little sparkling one'. Metathesis plus *-yn* to *-y* conversion would then give Pefery and so Peffery. Note: the 'native name' for Dingwall is Scots-Gaelic *Inbhir Pheofharan* probably from an original *aber pefryn.*

Polintarf (Peebleshire) – Probably from *pwyllyn tarw* = 'little pool on the bull river'.

Quair (Peebles) – From *gwyr,* a slightly corrupted form of *gwyrdd* = 'green'.

Spey (Moray) – Watson (paraphrased): 'Spey means "hawthorn stream" the British equivalent of Gaelic *Allt na Sgitheach* – and relates to Welsh *ysbyddad* = hawthorn'.
Note: This is not a difficult match and Watson's reasoning leading to this interpretation is quite intricate. I cannot say I fully understood it and it may simply be that 'Spey' is a pre-Celtic term whose meaning we have to accept as being irretrievably lost.

Spean (Inverness) – diminutive of 'Spey'.

Tarbhan (Loch Lyon) – *tarwan* = 'little-bull'.

Tanner (Selkirkshire), **Tanar** (Aberdeenshire) – Both from *Tanaros,* a British thunder-god, equivalent to the Roman thunder-god Jupiter. The same god appears under the title *Taranis* which is reflected in the name of the river *Tarrenig* in Wales.

Tarff (Fort Augustus, Inverness) – probably preserved in full from an older Welsh name through the intervening Scots-Gaelic *tarbh* itself a survival in Gaelic of Welsh *tarw* =

'bull.' There are other rivers of this name in Galloway, Atholl and Forfar.

Tay – is related to the Welsh *Tawe* and both are derived from an early P-Celtic word meaning 'peaceful' or 'placid' as does *tawel* in modern Welsh.

Treig (Lochaber) – Watson – It may be connected with Welsh *trànc* = 'end, cessation, death' which if taken over into Gaelic would become *trec,* later *Treag.*
– It possibly relates better to Welsh *treiglad* = 'wanderer, wandering' or *treiglo* 'to trickle'.

Turk (Brig o' Turk Callander) – Watson – Wales has several rivers called the *twrch,* Brig o' Turk is not an instance; the water is the Finglas and my Gaelic authorities for that district disclaimed any Gaelic origin for Brig o' Turk.
– However a Welsh interpretation of Finglas, variously spelt as Finglais, Finlais and Finlas, would be *Ffin glais-glas, -lais, -las* meaning 'boundary ditch', or 'boundary stream', leaving open the question of the name of the stream itself which might (just might!) have been *twrch.*

Ythan (Aberdeenshire) – from the early river goddess name *Iectona* meaning the 'talking one' developing (similarly to *Nethan)* into *Iethon, Iethan.* The same name occurs in Mid Wales as the river *Ieithon* of Radnor and Shropshire.

Chapter 8

Place-names

'Words, words, I don't doubt they were spoken,
but words can be interpreted in many ways,
and even a small doubt cast can alter the image'

Cadfael Chronicles, 'The Heretic's Apprentice'

In the arena of placename interpretation 'possibilities' are the only 'facts', 'probabilities' are only 'opinions' and 'certainties' are nonexistent! This is particularly true of Scottish place-names where the mix of languages is probably more intertwined than in any other component part of the British Isles. The only degree of 'certainty' present is that the 'uncertainty' of any Welsh interpretation is always equalled by the 'uncertainty' of any Gaelic, Norse or Anglo-Saxon interpretation – but since it can be considered that Welsh is, or was, the 'senior' language of Scotland any Welsh interpretation ought therefore to be accorded some modicum of preference. The uncertainties themselves become apparent as soon as we try to determine the evidence upon which we have to base our reasoned conclusions regarding the origins and meaning of particular place-names. In most cases the basic data amount to little more than the following:

* early records – more often than not written down by Lowland Scots scribes using the English alphabet and English phonetic spelling. The earliest records usually, but not always, being the most reliable.

* the present day name.

* the present day pronunciation.

* any Gaelic attribution – but this last is, within the context of this book, only of consequence when it is demonstrably connectable to a Welsh original; note also that when any Gaelic attribution is said to have been that obtained from 'a local Gaelic speaker' then this source is probably the least reliable of all. If a Gaelic speaker is asked the name of a place then if at all possible he will give it one in his native tongue. Thus if the place had no Gaelic name before the request was made it would very probably have had one after! Watson had this to say of the 'Gaelic' place-names of the region around Grantown on Spey: ' . . . *the present Gaelic tradition of this district is unreliable being often merely a reproduction of anglicized forms'*. This stricture applies equally to other regions. Watson does not enlarge upon his statement but the question which has to be asked is – What were these the Anglicized forms of? Watson dismisses any Gaelic interpretation as 'unreliable' so what he is really inferring is that the 'forms' which he refers to as 'anglicized' can in reality only be the written down, or spoken, forms of Welsh originals.

The attribution of possible Welsh roots to the names included in this chapter will be predicated on the following assumptions:

* At one time, prior to the coming of the Gaels, the Anglo-Saxons and the Norsemen, all the place-names which

then existed in Scotland originated in some early form of the Welsh language variously described as P-Celtic, Brythonic or Cumbric. There were no Gaelic, no Norse and no English place-names at that time. Gaelic names began to appear in the West Islands and Highlands from about 500 AD, Anglian names in the Eastern Border areas from about 650 AD and Norse names in the Northern Isles and extreme North East from about 700 to 900 AD.

* Most of the surviving names of Welsh origin can be expected to consist of word elements from Middle Welsh or Modern Welsh with only a few from Old Welsh, Primitive Welsh or 'Archaic Welsh' (Brythonic). It appears however that when 'locked-into' place-names the old Welsh word elements exhibited great tenacity and this might explain why so many of them have survived intact and can still be found in modern Welsh dictionaries, irrespective of any local changes in the Welsh language which may have occurred in the meantime.

* In the case of a compound, or hybrid, name containing a Welsh element in association with an element from Gaelic or English or Norse it will initially be assumed that the name was once entirely Welsh and that the non-Welsh element is but a translation of some original Welsh synonym. In the absence of any valid argument to the contrary, or until decided otherwise, the name will be assessed on this basis.

The above rules can be compared to the 'self evident truths' and 'theoretical propositions' encountered in mathematics. The former requires no formal proof but the latter, which is the case with most Scottish place-names, has to be proven either by logical argument or by a process known as 'reductio ad absurdum'. In this the proposition is assumed to be true, but if any logical argument based on this assumption results in an absurd conclusion then the original assumption is itself deemed absurd. Conversely if the logical arguments result in sound conclusions then the original proposition can, in the absence of any evidence to the contrary, be deemed sound. It will be seen that most of the structural word elements forming the place-names included in this chapter can be attributed to words found in modern Welsh dictionaries and that the interpretations based on these attributions are never less than possible, almost always plausible and sometimes even probable, all this reflects positively on the original propositions.

In the catalogue of place-names contained within this chapter and elsewhere in this book it is noteworthy that the *-ie* or *-y* endings of present day names are seen to have developed from original *-yn, -in, -en, -an* or suchlike endings as exhibited in the earliest records. Similarly endings in *-o* or *-ock* are seen to have developed from earlier endings in *-ach, -och, -oc* or *-og*. According to Roibeard O' Maolalaigh (The 'Uses of Place-Names' p.33) – *'it was G.F. Black (Surnames of Scotland 1946) who first suggested that the '-ie' suffix in certain Scottish place-names represented the weakened or unstressed form of another common diminutive place-name ending '-in'. Black however, offers no explanation for the diminutive suffix '-in' and it is unclear whether he took it to be a Gaelic or or a Scots element'* O'Maolalaigh supports Black's hypothesis and suggests, with some difficulty, that the ending *-ie* derives from an Irish-Gaelic diminutive *-in / -ein* seen only in some few place-names in Ireland itself. There is no such difficulty however if we assume that the ending derives, under the influence of Scots, from any of the Welsh diminutives *-yn, -in, -cyn, or -an*. The development of the placename Rosemarkie exemplifies the possibility of it's *-ie* ending deriving from the Welsh diminutive suffix '*-yn*'.

e.g. **Rosemarkie** (*rhos marchyn* = 'little-horse moor'). – was earlier Rosemarkin (1190), Rosmarkyn (1257) and Rosemarky (1510): the change of ending from *-yn* to *-y* occurring between 1257 and 1510.

Similarly, **Craigie** (*craigyn* = 'little-crag'). was earlier Cragin (1178), Cragyn (1266), Cragyn (1296), and Cragy (1296-1693).

O'Maolalaigh notes that most '-ie' endings are to be found in East Aberdeenshire, Fife, Stirlingshire and West Lothian. It is perhaps no coincidence these are some of the heartlands of P-Celtic Scotland where it can be expected that at least some place-names will have retained evidence of original P-Celtic diminutives. The change to an *-ie* ending is not always associated with diminutives, any *-yn, -in, -en,* or even *-an* ending can sometimes be susceptible to this change. There are over 20 entries in this chapter where the explanation involves a reference to the conversion of the P-Celtic diminutive suffixes *-yn, -in, -en, -an* at the end of an early place-name record into a later Scots diminutive ending *-ie,* as postulated by Roibeard O'Maolalaigh. For all these entries due acknowledgement is made here to both Roibeard O'Maolalaigh and George Fraser Black who first noticed and then provided an explanation for this conversion.

As is the case for *-ie* endings there are a significant number of place-names whose earliest endings in *-ach* are seen later to change to *'o'*. This phenomenon is discussed by O'Maolaigh and also by Nicolaisen, but only from a Q-Celtic point of view and in relation to Scots-Gaelic *-ach* endings. There are of course *-ach* endings to P-Celtic Welsh words, including an *-ach* diminutive. Amongst the sample names provided by Nicolaisen is the placename Aberlemno for which the early records give Aberlevinach (1202&1220), Aberlemenach (1220), Abberlennoche (1320), Aberlemno (1466&1553) and Abbyrlemnoch (1488). Here the first element is Welsh *aber* which is a sure indication that at one time the name would have been wholly Welsh. With this in mind it is possible to look at the 1202, 1220, and 1488 names and see the second element as *mynach* = 'monk', shown also in it's mutated form *fynach as* 'vinach'. The middle element might be *lle* = 'place', 'steading', giving *aber le mynach* or *aber le fynach* = 'confluence at the steading of the monk'. One interesting aspect of this interpretation is that *-ach* in this case is not a diminutive but an intrinsic part of the word *mynach*. Another example, this time with a possible diminutive ending, is Balerno, given by various authorities as Scots-Gaelic *baile airneach* = 'sloe tree steading' or *bal eornach* = 'barley farm'. Early records are, Balernoch (1280), Balernaugh (1289), Balernaghe (1296) and Balerno (1461). As an alternative to the Gaelic interpretations it is possible to interpret these early spellings as Welsh *beili eirinog (or eirinawc or eirinawg)* = 'enclosure of little plum trees', making it quite apparent that when place-names which display endings like *-ie* or *-y* and like *-o, -ock, -och* or *-ach* are encountered then a Welsh origin cannot be totally discounted and should be considered.

As has been said before the intent in this chapter is to settle upon a list of selected Scottish place-names for which early records are readily available and for which it is possible to postulate a Welsh interpretation for each placename therein, thereby indicating it's likely origin in the old Welsh language of Scotland, and which in turn can be compared with existing interpretations derived from the work of Johnston, Watson and others. Fortunately it is possible to select such a list from the catalogue of names contained in J.B. Johnston's 'Place-names of Scotland'. Johnston's list is itself arbitrary and our selection of names from it is even more arbitrary but the result is that the final cut is, fortuitously, broadly representative of a wide range of Scottish place-names, as a whole, without being in any way exhaustive or comprehensive – it is but a sample!. For each name the first entry contains the placename itself together with it's earliest records from Johnston's *'Place-names of Scotland'*, plus any other records from Watson's *'History of the Celtic Place-names of Scotland'*. The second entry is the preferred Welsh suggestion, the next entries quote any relevant interpretations, conflicting or otherwise, from the various authorities listed in the bibliography, usually beginning with those of Johnston (whose list, with but few exceptions, it is) and then, of course, Watson as the ultimate authority. The last entry is a 'Note' embracing any background information and general comment thought to be relevant to this individual entry. Abbreviations will be avoided wherever possible except perhaps for the occasional use of 'WJW' for William J. Watson, 'JBJ' for James B. Johnston, 'OM' for Roibeard O'Maolalaigh, 'NI' for W.H.F.N. Nicolaisen, 'DD' for David Dorward and 'DR' for David Ross. Although the Welsh place-names of Scotland may not nowadays be as numerous as they once were it is still true to say that what they lack in numbers they more than make up for in significance. Almost all the prominent place-names in Scottish history have retained at least some traces of their Welsh ancestry – Edinburgh, Glasgow, Aberdeen, Falkirk, Bannockburn, Perth, Loch Lomond, Lanark, Gleneagles, Cawdor are but a few examples. In addition to listing the particular Welsh attributions of Watson, Johnston, Nicolaisen and others this chapter is devoted to newly assessing as many other Scottish place-names as can be reasonably connected with their Welsh roots and as can be conveniently included in a modest introductory volume such as this is.

In the following pages entries will be found in the format exemplified below:

Soutra (Fala) – 1160 Soltre, 1455 Sowtra, 1461 Soltra
sal tre = 'steading of the ill, frail, poor'
* Johnston – Perhaps British *sul tra, sul tre* = 'watch- tower' literally 'outlook-tower', from Welsh *sulw* = 'a sight,' 'a view'
* Watson – Comments on the founding of a hospital in this area by Malcolm IV in 1164. He gives no suggestion for the first element *sou* but implies the second element *tra* = 'stead'.
* Nicolaisen – Interprets it as Welsh *sulw tref* = 'steading with a wide-view'.
** Today there is definite evidence that there was some form of pre-mediaeval medical activity on this site long before 1164, perhaps extending back as far as Roman, or even pre-Roman times. All of which leads more towards an interpretation such as *sal tre*. In Scotland *tre* is often found in a slightly corrupted form as *tra* which in this case gives *saltra* from which comes Soltra of 1461 in the same way as Soltre of 1160 comes from *saltre*. See Soutra Aisle, following.

In the above example the first entry gives the Placename as it appears today and this is followed by all available early records in chronological order. The next entry gives a Welsh interpretation for the name as thought to have originated in the time of the early Welsh language of Scotland. Below that an entry with a single asterisk * denotes a quotation or synopsis taken from the works of my reference Authors. An entry with a double asterisk ** denotes my own personal comments for which I alone am responsible.

A

Aberarder (Aberdeenshire) – 1451 Aberardoure, 1456 Aberardor, 1645 Abirairdour
aber ardd dwr = 'confluence of the high water'
* Watson – 'confluence of high water' (language unspecified). A stream with the Gaelic name *Allt Ardobhair* meaning 'stream – high-stream' enters Loch Laggan at Aberarder.
* Johnston – Gaelic *aber aird dobhair* = 'confluence of the high water, or stream'.
** Watson states that *dobur* is a name for 'water', common to Gaelic and Welsh, and in Irish Gaelic it means 'dark' as well as 'water'. It was, he says, *'doubtless borrowed from Welsh and figures only very slightly in Irish literature or in Irish stream-names'*.

Aberarder (Strathnairn) – as above

Aberarder (Speyside) – as above

Abercairney (Stratherrick, Perthshire) – 1218 Abercarnich, 1221 Abercharni, 1268 Abircarnyche, Abbircarnich, 1339 Abercarny
aber carnau = 'confluence by the cairns (burial mounds)' or *aber carnyn* = 'confluence by the little cairn' = then *abercarny* (-yn to -y) and finally Abercairney
* Johnston – Gaelic *aber carnach* = 'rocky marsh', no confluence here.
* Watson – places the site at the junction of a small (nameless) burn and the Peffray stream and suggests *aber cardeny, cardnie* = 'copsy mouth', from Welsh *cardden* = 'a copse', or alternatively *aber carnaigh* = 'confluence by place of cairns', from Gaelic *carnaigh, carnach*.

Aberchalder (Invernessshire) – 1238 Abbircaledouer / Aberchalladour

aber caled dŵr = 'confluence of the hard stream'
* Johnston – Probably British, same root as in Callender. The ending is Old Gaelic *dobhar* = 'stream'.
* Watson – The *aber* = 'confluence' is that of the Calder stream, from early British *caleto-dubron* = 'hard-water', in Welsh *caled dŵr.*

Aberchirder (Banffshire) – 1204 Aberkerdour, 1212 Aberkerdouer, 1291 Abirkerdor
aber caer dŵr = 'confluence at the fortlet by the water'
* Johnston – Old Gaelic *aber chiar dobhair* = 'confluence of the dark, or brown, stream'.
* Watson – It is probably from Gaelic *ciardhobhar* = 'swart water' (confluence of).

Abercorn (Lothian) – 720 (Bede) Aebbercurnig, Ebbercurnig, Aeburcurnei, Aeborcurnit 1130 Ebercurn, 1300 Abourcorn, 1335 Abercorn
aber corniog = 'horned confluence' or
aber cornig = 'little-horn confluence'
* Johnston – Probably British or Welsh *aber corniog* = 'horned confluence'.
* Watson – The church and old village are situated upon an angular point below which the Cornie and Midhope burns are united, it is to be compared with Welsh *corniog* = 'horned'.
** If Watson is to be believed then the name will have been taken from that of the stream which Watson refers to as the 'Cornie'. In which case the stream name might be from *cornyn* = 'little horn'-stream which with later conversion of *yn* to *ie* givies 'cornie' and hence Abercornie = 'confluence of the Little Horn stream'.

Abercrombie (Fife, now in the Parish of St Monans) – 1165 Abercrumbi, 1250 Abircrumbyn, 1270 Abbercrumby, 1461 Abircumby

aber crwm bych: 'little curved confluence'. Compare Tenby (Wales) from *din bych* = 'little hill-fort'.
* Johnston – Old Gaelic *crumb,* Gaelic *crom* = 'crooked', therefore 'crooked marsh'.
* Watson – *aber chrombaidh* = 'bent confluence'. This is probably a Gaelic adaptation of a British term of similar meaning.
** Neither Watson nor Johnston make any attempt to account for the *-bie* ending.

Aberdalgie (Perthshire) – 1150 Abirdalgyn, 1215-1221 Aberdalgin, 1348 Aberdalgy
aber dol gyn ='confluence by the wedge- shaped meadow'
* Johnston – Gaelic *aber dealg* = 'confluence of the thorn'.
* Watson – *aber dealg* = ditto.
** *aberdolgyn,* = *aberdolgy* = *aberdalgy* = Aberdalgie (-yn to -y to -ie).

Aberdeen – 1100 Abberdeon, 1114 Aberdon, 1137 Aberden, 1178 Aberdoen
* Johnston – Gaelic *obair dheathain* = 'at the mouth of Dee, or Don'.
* Watson – It is 'Abberdeon' in the book of Deer, now in Gaelic *obar dheathan* = 'mouth of the river Don', here *deon, deathan,* represents Early Celtic *Devona,* a river-goddess name, but 'Don' did not arise from Gaelic *deon, deathan.* In Welsh the word for 'god' is *duw,* for an older hypothetical *dwyw;* in Old Welsh 'Devona' would be 'Duion' and it is some such form that is represented by 'Don'.
** Two rivers, the Dee and the Don, empty into the harbour estuary at Aberdeen about two miles apart from each other. In earlier times there were two separate settlements between them, the original settlement to the north of today's city, and on the south bank of the river Don, was known as Aberdon, later another settlement was formed further south on the north bank of the river Dee. In 1136 King David 1st created

'new' Aberdeen (Aberden?) on the site of this southern settlement and properly this should have been called 'Aberdee'. This anomaly perhaps accounts for the rather schizophrenic history of today's placename, it not knowing whether it was to be Aberdee or Aberdon! The present 'Aberdeen' seems to be an acceptable compromise between the two. As for the names Don and Dee it is certain that these are extremely ancient, the river on the border between England and northern Wales is known to the English as the Dee and to the Welsh as Dyfrdwy, from 'dyfr' (water) and 'dwyw' (goddess), but also known poetically as Dwfr Donwy. It is said that the English name derives from British 'deua' (Great Goddess) and that the goddess in question was 'Don' – the paramount Mother-Goddess of ancient Britain and Europe whose provenance in this Island stretches back to before 15,000 BC. She appears in mediaeval Welsh folklore in different forms and in a variety of names, one of which may have been 'Rhiannon'. Elsewhere there is a river Don in Yorkshire and further afield in Europe her presence is detected in the names of the river Danube in Eastern Europe and the river 'Don' in Russia. (Acknowledgements are due to *www.undiscoveredscotland.co.uk* for it's contribution to the above note.)

Aberdour (Fife) – 1126 Abirdaur, Aberdovar, 1329 Abirdouer, 1336 Abirdowyr
aber dŵr or *aber dwfr*, = 'mouth of the water (ie. stream)'
* Johnston – 'dour' is from Old Gaelic *dobhar, dobboir* therefore *aber dobhar/dobboir* = 'mouth of the water, stream'.
* Watson – From Gaelic-British *dobor*, later *dobhar*, Welsh *dwfr* = 'mouth of the streamlet'.

Aberfeldy (Perthshire) –
* Johnston – Gaelic *obar pheallaidh* Probably not from Palladius, Rome's missionary to Scotland, but from Paldoc or Paldy, disciple of St Ninian.

* Watson – Aberfeldy is in Gaelic *Obar Pheallaidh* = 'confluence of Peallaidh', It is at the confluence of the Moness Burn with the Tay and derives it's name from 'Peallaidh', an ancient water-sprite or river-demon.
** No early records hence much doubt about the second element '-feldy'. Reference to a Saint Paldoc seems indeterminate, more likely is the attribution to some water sprite known as *Pheallaidh* in Gaelic but which could well have once had an original Welsh name to match the first element *aber*. Neither explanation is wholly satisfactory and it may be that the full meaning is irretrievably lost. On the other hand it may be something trivially simple like *aber foel din* = 'confluence by the bare-hill fort', -to *aberfoeldy* (-yn to -y), -to Aberfeldy.

Aberfoyle (Perthshire) – 1481 Abirfull, also an early Irish reference to *'eperpuill'*
Possibly *aber foel* 'confluence by the bare-topped hill', several in that area now but how many in the olden days?
* Johnston – Gaelic *aber phuill* = 'confluence of the streams'. Where *phuill* is the genitive of *poll* = a 'stream' or 'pool'.
* Watson – Gaelic *obar puill* = 'confluence of the 'pow' i.e. a sluggish stream'.
** No denials that the first element is Welsh *aber*. Therefore see entry for *pwll, poll, pol.*

Abergeldie (Aberdeenshire) – 1451 Abergheldy
aber-y-caledyn aspirated to *abergaledyn,* then *abergaledy* and finally Abergeldie (-yn to -y to -ie)
* Johnston – 'Gaelic *Geallaidh*: compare with *geal* = 'clear', fair'. (Presumably Johnston is hinting at *aber geal* = 'confluence of the clear stream'?)
* Watson – 'geldie' is a common stream name, meaning 'white water'.
** The confluence is that of the Geldie burn with the Dee. Watson includes Geldie in his problematicals list of which

he says the explanation seems to be that they came into vogue during a period of linguistic transition; deriving from a method of reducing, and incidentally gaelicizing, old compound names which then led to the formation of names 'on the same model as the old compound names'. Note: The name survives only as that of Abergeldie Castle near Craithes but is more probably the original name of nearby Invergelder where the river Gelder joins the river Dee. 'Gelder' may be a corruption of 'Galder' the mutated form of 'Calder', a common name elsewhere and derived from *Caled dŵr* = 'hard-water'. Similarly 'Galder' would derive from lenited form *(y) galed dŵr* = '(the) hard-water'. Replacing Gaelic 'Inver' by the earlier Welsh 'Aber' gives the full original name of Invergelder as *aber (y) galed dŵr* = 'confluence of the hard water' (cf Aberchalder). Alternatively Abergeldie may have little to do with Invergelder and simply be *aber (y) galedyn* = 'confluence by the hard-fort', which by reduction of *-yn* to *-y* becomes Abergaledy and then Abergheldy; but this suggestion *aber caledyn* is just one of many 'old compound name' possibilities. The one and only record is too late to be of any great help.

Aberlady (Lothian) – 1221 Aberlauedy, 1214/1229 Aberleuedi, 1275 Aberlefdi, 1328 Abirleuedy, 1336 Aberleuedy
aber llefadyn = 'mouth of the little-crying-out stream' see Note below.
* Johnston – Watson's 'mouth of stench' will not do! *aber,* here is 'marsh' and Aberlady = 'marsh of the Virgin Mary'.
* Watson – argues from circumstantial evidence that this name is of wholly Welsh origin and means something like 'stinking river mouth', but concludes that the second element, the word for 'stinking', has either been lost or else has been so mistranslated as to be unrecognisable. The name

does not appear to have derived from that of the local stream which is the 'Peffer' (*pefr*).

** Taking the early records at face value we have the Welsh words *llef* = 'cry', *llefad* = 'a crying-out' and *llefadyn* = a 'little crying-out'. Thus *aber llefadyn* when displaying the *-yn* to *-y* conversion becomes *aberlefady* = 'mouth of the little' crying-out stream'. Which is no more fanciful than what is above.

Aberlemno (Angus) – 1250 Aberlevinach, Aberlemenach, 1320 Abberlennoche, 1553 Aberlemno

aber lle mynach, aspirated to *aberlefynach* = 'river-mouth by the monk's place'

* Johnston – Gaelic *aber leamanach* = 'confluence of the elm stream'.

* Watson – the second part is *lemnach,* later *leamhnach* meaning 'elmish', most probably a Gaelic adaptation of a British name or stream name. The place so called is some distance from the stream Lemno.

** A possibility has to be *aber lle mynach* either as-is or in an aspirated form *aber le fynach* as above, both meaning 'confluence by the place of the Monk' and both displaying conversion of the *-ach* ending to *–o*, e.g. *aberlemyno* Watson's and Johnston's explanations both ignore the '-vinach' element in the earliest 1250 record.

Aberlour (Moray) – 1226 Aberlower, 1275 Aberlogher

aber llafar = 'mouth of the noisy stream' (literally 'the loud, or resounding, one').

Alternatively *aber llawr* = 'confluence of the meek, or lowly, stream'.

* Johnston – Gaelic *aber labhar* = 'loud confluence'.

* Watson – Aberlour is situated, says the Old Stat. account, at the mouth of a noisy burn, the stream was doubtless called *labhar* 'the loud one', Welsh *llafar*.

Abermilk (Dumfries) – 116 Abermelc (Watson)

aber mulawc, aber muloc = 'mouth of the modest little river'
* Johnston – It is 'mouth of the 'milky' river' from Old Irish *melg* = 'milk'.
* Watson – The river Milk itself appears in 1272 as 'Melych'. The meaning of Melc, Milk is obscure; it may stand for Malcia, to be compared with Gaelic *malc* = 'putrefy'.
** Few records and no attributions apart from Johnston's rather desperate attempt at 'mouth of the milky river'. There is however a now obsolescent Welsh word *mul* = 'modest' or 'sad', this combined with the obsolescent suffix 'awc' gives 'mulawc' = 'little', 'bashful' (or 'modest'). The interpretation would then be *aber mulawc* pronounced 'aber mill-ouk', meaning 'mouth of the bashful little river'. cf Abermule (pronounced Aber-mill-e), Denbighshire on the river Mule.

Abernethy (Perths) – c. 970 Aburnethighe, 1097 Abernithici, 1107 Abernethyn, 1461 Abernethi
aber neithion = *aberneithy* = 'river-mouth of Nectona, the pure one', a goddess
* Johnston – *obair neithich* = either 'mouth of the nixie's river', a 'nixie' is a water sprite, or *obar nyth* = 'mouth of the new river' from Welsh *newydd*, Gaelic *nuadh*. but the early forms suggest Gaelic *obar an eitighich* = 'river-mouth at the narrow opening'.
* Watson – see Note below.
** The origins of this name provide very significant insights into the development of place-names in Scotland. It is worth quoting Watson – at length!
'Early Celtic -ct- becomes in Welsh -th-, . . . The river Nethan in Lanarkshire, twelfth century Neithan, is for an early Nectona, 'pure one.' . . . Thus . . . Abernethy near Perth . . . is gaelicized either from Neithon directly or from a British river name from the same root. With it goes Abernethy on Speyside . . . proving that the change of Early Celtic or Old British -ct- into -th- took place not only in Perthshire but also north of the Grampians . . . These

names, Nethy and Ythan **cannot be explained from the Gaelic,** *and they show that they were taken over into Gaelic at a period when Old British had passed into the stage corresponding to Early Welsh.' W.J. Watson*
Translating Watson's derivation into modern Welsh, Abernethy would be *Aber nethion* = 'mouth of the river of the goddess Nectona', cf, river Nedd and the town of Neath in South Wales.

Abertarff (Lochaber)) – 1231 Aberterch c. 1240 Aberterth, 1282 Abertarf
aber tarw = 'mouth of the bull-river'
* Johnston – The second element is the genitive of Gaelic *tarbh* = 'a bull'.
* Watson – in Gaelic it is *obair thairbh* = 'bull's confluence'.
** In Welsh a 'bull' is *tarw,* hence *aber tarw* = 'mouth of the Bull river' – a 'bullish' stream perhaps? But the 1231 record could equally be *aber twrch* = 'mouth of the boar-river'.

Aberuchill (Perths) – 1461 Abbiruchil, 1465 Abbirquill, 1594 Aberurquhill
aber uchel = 'confluence of the high-stream'
* Johnston – The second element, the name of the river, is Gaelic *ruadh choil* = red flood', therefore 'confluence of the red flood'.
* Watson – In Gaelic it is called *obar ruchail* = 'confluence of the red flood', but this local explanation is impossible phonetically. The spelling Aberurquhill suggests it begins with the preposition *ar* = 'on' with possibly Gaelic *coille,* Welsh *celli,* = 'wood', as the second part. Therefore *aber ar celli* or *aber ar cuille* = 'river mouth on the wood'.
** Neither Johnston nor Watson seem to have considered the much simpler explanation *aber uchel* = 'mouth of the high stream' and that the river Ruchil is simply *yr uchel* = 'The high (or loud) stream'. There are other streams with 'high' or 'loud' names.

Aberuthven (Perth) – 1198 Aberruadeuien / Aberrotauin / aberruadeuien, 1199 Aberrotheuin, 1200 Abirruotheven, 1211 Aberrotheuin

aber rhyd-y-maen aspirated to *aber rhydd faen* = 'river-mouth by the stone-ford'

* Johnston – For the second element the old forms strongly point to Gaelic *ruadh abhuinn* = 'red river' or else Pictish or Welsh *rhudd faen* = 'red rock'.

* Watson – The second element *ruthven* is common throughout Scotland and is recorded in a variety of spellings and while we might compare Welsh *rhudd faen* = 'red stone', the name is almost certainly Gaelic *ruadh- mhaighin* = 'red spot', therefore 'confluence at the red spot'.

** The wide distribution of the name Ruthven does not accord with explanations such as ' confluence of the red-rock, red-stone, or red-river'. Both Johnston and Watson hint at a possible Welsh (or Pictish!) interpretation so why not *aber rhyd y faen* = 'confluence at the stone ford', or 'stone ford at the river-mouth', where 'stone ford' probably means 'stepping-stone ford' of which there must have been many distributed throughout Scotland.

Abriachan (Loch Ness) – 1239 Abirhacyn, 1334 Aberbreachy, Abriach

aber hacyn = 'river-mouth in the little-notch'

* Johnston – Gaelic *ob'ritheachan* is doubtful. Perhaps Gaelic *dhitheach* = 'confluence of the beggars'.

* Watson – The site is primarily where the Abriachan burn enters Loch Ness. In Gaelic it is called *obr'itheachan* but this is of uncertain meaning. The stream falls very steeply and the name is probably from Old Irish *bri*, Welsh *bre* = a 'hill'.

** *aber hacyn* = 'river-mouth at the little-notch, (or little-cut)', accords well with the spelling of 1239. The spelling 'Aberbreachy' of 1334 could be an expansion of the original name into *aber bre hacyn* = 'river-mouth, hill, little-notch (or little-cut)' subjected to final *-yn* to *-y* conversion as *aber brehacy*. The other spelling 'Abriach' of 1334 could be a simple truncation of 'Aberbreachy' or it could be a non-diminutive throwback to *aber hac* = 'river-mouth at the notch (or cut)', metathesised into *abrehac* and hence 'Abriach'. Watson describes the stream as 'falling steeply' – perhaps through or from a 'notch'in the hillside?

Achallader (Stirlings) –
ar caled dŵr = 'by the hard water'
* Ross/Mackay – Gaelic *achadh chaladdair* = 'field of the chaladair stream'. Chaladdair is a Scottish-Gaelic stream name anglicized as 'Calder', perhaps from Brythonic *caleto dubron* = 'hard water'.
** Brythonic *caleto dubron* would have passed into Welsh long before Scottish-Gaelic ever came to this area. The supposition must therefore be that the element *challader,* in this name, had it's origin in Welsh *caled dŵr,* – possibly in an earlier form. Achallader then = *arcaledwr.*

Airdrie (Lanarks) –
ardd dre, ardd dref then by assimilation *ardre* = the 'high steading or farmstead'
* Johnston – Probably Gaelic *aird airigh* = 'high hill pasture', but may be site of 577 battle of Arderyth, if so could be Celtic *ard tref* = 'high steading'.
* Watson – Gaelic *ardruigh* = 'high reach, high slope'.
* Ross/Mackay – Gaelic *airde ruighe* = 'high slope or shieling'.
** Johnston's 'Celtic' *ard tref* is actually Welsh!

Airthrey (Stirlings) – same derivation as Airdrie but with unaspirated second element i.e. *ardd tre* = 'high steading, farmstead'.

Allermuir – *ael y mor* = 'seaward brow of the hill', see 'Edinburgh Place-names'.

Almanack Hill (Inch) –
allt mynach = 'wooded hillside (or wooded river valley) of the monk'.
* Johnston – Gaelic *allt manach* = 'monk's glen'.
** *allt* appears in Scots-Gaelic but not in Irish-Gaelic, the implication being that Johnston's 'Gaelic' *allt* must derive from Welsh *allt* anyway.

Alton (Beith) –
alltan = 'little wooded river valley'
* Johnston – Gaelic *alltan*: = 'little burn'.
** See 'Airdrie' for *allt* arguments.

Altrive Burn (Yarrow) – 1587 Eltryve
allt tref = 'wooded-hillside by the farmstead'
* Johnston – Probably Gaelic *allt t'snaimh* = 'stream with the swimming-place'.
* Watson – Probably Scots -Gaelic *alt* = a 'height', later a 'burn', plus *ruighe* = a 'slope'.
** See Airdrie.

Altyre (Elgin) –
allt tir = 'wooded-hillside land'
* Johnston – *allt tir* = 'river land'.
** *tir* is common to Welsh, Irish-Gaelic and Scots-Gaelic but *allt* is common to Welsh and Scots-Gaelic only. See Airdrie.

Annandale (Dumfries) – 1124 Estrahanent, 1152 Stratanant, 1295 Anandresdale
ystrad anau = 'valley of the river Anau, now Annan'
* Johnston – 1124 Estrahent implies Welsh *ystrad* = 'strath, valley'. Dale of Onand-r is an old Norse name found at Great Yarmouth (1198) as Anund.
* Watson – whilst ceding the first element in the old records as Welsh *ystrad*, concentrates on the river name Annan which he relates to an early Celtic 'Anava' which would have developed into Welsh *anau* and which could

then have been Gaelicized into *anann.*
** Thus, according to Watson, Annandale is derived via a very tortuous route from *ystrad anau* where the first element has been anglicized into *dale* and the second element gaelicized into *annan.* The 1124 and 1152 names would indicate *ystrad a nant* 'wide flat-bottomed valley with a stream'. It would seem that the name was later half-translated by exchanging Old English *dale* for Welsh *ystrad* and transposing this, English fashion, to place it after *a nant* thus producing *anantdale* as another possible derivation for Annandale.

Anwoth (Kirkubright) – 1200 Anewith, 1280 Avinethe
* Johnston – First element is Avon = 'river', the second might be British *weth* = 'hill-face'.
** If we take the 1280 element *avin* as *afon* = 'river', then this would be indicative of a Welsh origin and if we take the 1200 element as *newith* = *newydd* then we have *afon newydd* = 'new river' This is no more, nor no less fanciful than Johnston's *afonweth* = 'river hill-face'. I find no trace of *weth* in any of my Welsh Dictionaries. But *gwaeth* = 'harm', *gweith* = 'battle' are perhaps possibilities?

Applecross (Wester Ross) – 673 Aporcrosan, 737 Apuorcrossan, 1080 Applecross, 1510 Appilcroce, 1515 Abilcros
* Johnston – Old Gaelic *apor crossain* = 'mouth of the river Crossan', but this stream name, meaning 'little-cross', is now forgotten.
* Watson – It is in Gaelic *a'Chromraich* = 'sanctuary of St,. Maelrubha'.
** Early Welsh *apor croesan* = 'little-cross river-mouth' or alternatively *apor croesyn* = 'mouth of the river Jester'. The original name of the river at Applecross has, as Johnston says, been lost and it is now known simply as the Applecross River, probably back-titled from the name of the

village; neither is there is any record, or trace, of a 'little-cross'. Johnston's Old Gaelic *apor crossain* is so akin to Welsh *aber croesan* that, not for the first time, I have this faint suspicion that his 'Old-Gaelic' is possibly Early-Welsh in disguise? Equally when Watson refers to a name as 'in Gaelic it is -?' I have come to the conclusion that what he means is that this is the name somehow given to it by present-day Gaelic speakers and that he himself does not necessarily believe that it bears any certain relationship to the original name or to the origins of that original name.

Arbirlot (Arbroath) – 1198 Aberhelot, 1202-1214 Arbirlot, 1210 Abereloth, 1250 Aberelloch, Aberellot, 1323 Abrellot
aber elliot 'mouth of the river Elliot' (river name obscure)
* Johnston – *aber elliot* = 'ford on the river Elliot'.
* Watson – It is at the junction of Elliot Water and Rottenraw burn.
** Johnston's definition of *aber* = 'ford' seems to be based on rather flimsy evidence.

Arbroath (Angus) – 1178 Aberbrothoc, 1189 Aberbrudoc, 1190 Aberbruthoc, 1187-1203 Aberbrodoch, 1300 Abbirbroth
aber brothoc = 'mouth of the little-tumult stream'
* Johnston – It is hybrid Welsh-Gaelic *aber brothach* = 'mouth of the filthy stream'.
* Watson – Probably from *bruth* whence *brothach* = 'boiling', 'eruptive', 'scabby'; therefore hybrid Welsh/Gaelic *aber brothach* = 'mouth of the eruptive stream' or = 'mouth of the scabby stream'.
** Welsh *broth* also *brwth* = 'a stir', a 'tumult', *-oc* is a diminutive ending.

Arbuckle (Renfrew) – 1546 Arbucle, 1560 Arbuchell
ardd bugail = 'height of the herdsman'
* Johnston – Gaelic *ard an buchaille* = 'height of the shepherd'.

** The records although late are nevertheless instructive.

Arbuthnott (Kincardines) – 1242 Aberbothenoth, 1282, 1283 Abirbuthenoth, Aberbuthenot
aber byddinoedd = 'mouth of the Byddinoedd stream' where *byddinoedd* = 'armies, hosts, war bands'. The pronunciation is 'aberbutheenoith', where *dd* is 'dull' and = *th* as in 'the'
* Johnston – Gaelic *abar baothanaich* = 'marsh of the silly fellow'.
* Watson – *aber buadhchag* = 'mouth of the Buadhchag stream' where Gaelic *buadhchag* = 'little-one of virtue'.

Ardentinny (Loch Long) –
ardden tanau = 'little-height of the fires'
* Johnston – Gaelic *ardd na teine* = 'height of the fire'. Apparently fires were lit here as a signal to the ferryman.
* Watson – Ardentinny, old Ardatinny is Gaelic *ard an t-sionnaigh* = 'height of the fox'.

Ardentryve (Oban) –
arddan tref = 'little height by the steading'
* Johnston – Gaelic *an t'snaimh* = 'point of the swimming place' (for cattle).

Ardmillan (Girvan) –
ardd melin = 'height by the mill'
* Johnston – Gaelic *ardd muillean* = 'height by the mill'.

Ardoch (Perths) –
arddawc = 'place of heights' or *ardach* = 'little height'
* Johnston – Gaelic *ardach* = 'high place'.
* Watson – *ardach* = high place'.
** No records, so toss a coin!

Ardow (Mull) –
ardd du = 'dark height'
* Johnston – Gaelic *ard dubh* = 'dark height'.

Ardrossan (Firth of Clyde) – 1375 Ardrossan
ardd rhosan / ard rhosan = 'height of the little-moor'
* Johnston – Gaelic *ard rosan* = 'height of the little cape'.
* Watson – Ardrossan is *aird* = 'cape', plus *rosan* = 'little-cape', so *airdrosan* = 'cape of little-cape', a pleonasm.
** Watson, to my mind, seems to be alittle over-academic here? In any case is *an* a Gaelic, particularly an Irish Gaelic, suffix?

Arran (Firth of Clyde) – 1154 Arran, 1251 Araane, 1294 Aran, 1326 Arran
aran ='alp' (high peaked hill), a 'high place'
aren = a 'kidney'
* Johnston – Welsh *aran* = 'peaked hill' is very appropriate. Otherwise Gaelic *arain* from *ara* = kidney' plus an old locative *-inn*, whence *arainn* = *'at ara'* = 'kidney place', said by some to be 'exactly Arran's shape'.
* Watson – The meaning is unknown so far and the name may be pre-Celtic, but there are several Welsh names which appear similar: *afon Aran* in Radnor; and *Aran Mawddwy, Aran Benllyn,* adjacent hills south-west of Bala.
* Ross/Mackay – The name may indicate 'place of peaked hills' from Cumbric *aran* = 'height, peaked hill'. Irish-Gaelic *arainn* = 'kidney' is only true of Arran when viewed from the mainland looking north!

Artafaillie (Munlochy) – 1526 Ardirfalie, 1590 Arthirfairthlie 1599 Ardafailie
ardd yr faelyn = 'hill of the little-Prince'
* Johnston quotes Watson as postulating a Gaelic *ard tir faillidh* = 'high land of the place of sods' – 'a rather abnormal name' was Johnston's comment!
* Watson – see Johnston above.
** Another possibility is *ardd y faelyn* = 'hill of the little Prince', (*-yn* to *-ie,* conversion), or alternatively *ardd tir faelau* = 'hill land of the Princes' or *ardd tir faelyn* = 'high land of

the little Prince'. The records are rather 'late' to be either reliable or good indicators. I cannot find 'Artafaillie' in Watson's book.

Arthur's Seat –
craggenmarth = 'crag of sadness' see 'Edinburgh Place-names'.

Auchelchanzie (Crieff) –
uchel cuneddydd = 'high (place) belonging to Cunedda'
* Johnston – hybrid British-Gaelic *uchel chanice* = 'height of Kenneth'. Welsh *uchel* = 'high' and Old Irish *Canice,* Gaelic *Coinneach* = 'Kenneth'.
** *cuneddydd* would have to be compressed first to *cuneddy,* final 'dd' drops off easily, then to *cunddy* – from which Chanzie. Cunedda = 'Cunedd, Cinaeth, or Kenneth ', was a North British Chieftain in this area before he emigrated to North Wales where his name is still commemorated in that of the region now known as Gwynedd; from y-Cunedd, aspirated to Gunedd, hence Gwynedd.

Auchenairn (Glasgow)-
* Johnston thinks this is probably a corrupted form of 'Auchencairn'. In which case see 'Auchencairn'.

Auchencairn (Kirkcudbright) – 1305 Aghencarne
achcarn = place – 'near-to the cairn'
* Johnston – Gaelic *achadh an cairn* = 'field with a cairn (a barrow)'.
* Watson – It is 'field of the cairn'.
** The Welsh suggestion here is made with the sole purpose of raising the possibility that Gaelic *ach, achadh* = 'field' could sometimes have displaced an earlier Welsh prefix *ach-* = 'near, nearby, near-to'. In this case an original *achcarn* could have been partially gaelicized to *ach an cairn* with the resulting slight change in meaning. The only hint that this

could have occurred here is the record of 1305 where Welsh *carn* is represented still by the last element '-carne'. Given the name that the place now has Johnston's interpretation is the better fit to the 1305 record.

Auchencloich (Kilmarnock) –
achclog = place – 'near the large-stone'
* Johnston – Gaelic *achad an cloiche* = 'field with the boulder stone'.
** No records but see Auchencairn.

Auchterarder (Perths) – 1200 Eohterardeuar, Vchterdouere, 1295 Eutrearde, Outreart, 1330 Huchtirardor, 1597 Ochterardour
uwch tir ar dŵr, uch tir ar dŵr = 'upper land on the water'
uchder ar dŵr = 'height above the water'
* Johnston – Gaelic *uachdar ard dobhair* = 'upland of the high stream'. Welsh *uchdar* (from *uch*) = 'top, summit', disregard the records of 1295 as 'English bad shots!'
* Watson – Gaelic *dobhar* was doubtless borrowed from Welsh. Auchterarder = 'upland of high water'.
** Welsh *uwch, uch,* as an adjective = 'higher', and as a prefix = 'above, over', *uchder,* as a noun = 'height'.

Auchterderran (Kirkcaldy) –
uwch tir deran, uch tir deran = 'upper land of little oak trees'
uchder deran = 'height of little-oak-trees'
* Johnston – Gaelic *uachdar doirean* = 'upland with the thickets or groves'.

Auchterless (Turriff) – 1300 Ochthrelyss, 1280 Uchterless, 1364 Othyrles
uwch tir Llys, uch tir Llys = 'upper land of the Llys', i.e. 'great-court, mansion'
uchder Llys = 'height, loftiness of the Llys'
* Johnston – Gaelic *uachdar lios* = 'highland with the enclosure'.

Auchtermuchty (Fife) – 1204/14 Vchtermukethin, 1250 Hucdirdmukedi, 1293 Utermokerdy, 1294 Utremukerty, 1350 Ochtirmokadi
uwch tir moch y tŷ = 'upper land of the pig-house'
uchder moch y dŷ = 'height of the pig-house'
uch tir moch y tyn = 'land of the pigs above the croft' (see 1204/14)
* Johnston – Probably = 'height, rising, of the swineherd'. From Gaelic *mucair* with *ty* or *dy* ending.
* Ross/Mackay – Gaelic *uachdar muc garadh* = 'upper pig enclosure'.
** The first element could be *uch* = 'above, over'; or *uchder* / *uchdwr* = 'height'; or *uwch* = 'higher, upper'. The last element meaning 'house' could be *tŷ* = 'house' in it's unlenited form, or in it's lenited form as *dŷ*. There is an outside chance that if the earliest records of 1204-1214 are the most reliable then the *thin* ending might possibly from *din* = 'fort' lenited to *ddin*, the change to *thin* being the usual result of mediaeval scribes trying to translate Welsh sounds into English or Scots using letters of the English alphabet.

Auchterneed / Achterneed (Strathpeffer) – 1499 Ouctirnede, 1619 Ochterneid
uwch tir neuadd 'upper lands of the Hall', i.e. 'big house'
achtir neuadd = 'land near-to the Hall'
* Johnston – perhaps Gaelic *uachdar neade, nid* = 'upland with the nests', Watson doubtfully connects this Gaelic *uachdar niad* – with Welsh *nant* = 'a valley'.
** I cannot find this name in Watson's book and Welsh *nant* = stream.

Auchtrievane (Kirkmabreck) –
Uwch tre faen – 'upper stone-steading' i.e. 'upper stone-built farmstead'?
* Johnston – Gaelic-locative *uachdarach* plus *bhan* = 'white upland'.

** *uwch tir ban* aspirated and metathesised to *uwchtrifan* = 'upper land on the peak', is also possible.

B

Baberton (Currie) – 1335 Kilbaberton
* Johnston – Difficult! 'Kil' in 1335 record may be Danish Kilde = 'a well' and 'Baber' may be for Badburh = 'a woman'.
** Johnston is way off-beam here. See 'Edinburgh Names'.

Bangour (W. Lothian) – 1335 Bengouer
ben gafr = 'goat hilltop'
ban gafr = 'goat peak'
* Johnston – Gaelic *beinn gobhar* = 'hill of goats'.
* Watson – Gaelic *beann ghobhar* = 'goat's peak'.
** Another possibility is *bangor* = (1) 'a (defensive) wattled fence or hedge'; (2) 'a monastery, a college'.

Bannockburn (Stirling) – 1215 Vtred Banoc, 1314 Bannockburn 1494 Bannokysborne
banog, banoc = 'little-peak', plus Scots *burn* (added later) = 'burn from the little peak'
* Johnston – Probably British *ban oc* = 'white shining stream', but a Welsh record speaks of *Mons Bannauc* = 'peaked, or horned, hill' which may have been in this region and which Watson connects with the Burn. The grounds seem slender.
* Watson – *Mons Bannauc* represents *minid bannauc,* the hilly region abounding with peaks which forms the basin of the river Carron, from the northern side of which flows the Bannock Burn.
** *banog, banoc,* = 'little-peak' Hence Bannock-burn = 'little-peak stream' i.e. a stream from a little peak in the Fintry

Hills – which is where it comes from. Alternatively *ban* = 'loud, noisy', but neither Watson's nor Johnston's researches, see above, support this interpretation. Johnston's British *ban oc* is a possibility as *ban* = 'white' is still found in Welsh dictionaries. The first element, 'Vtred', in the 1215 record could possibly hold the key to this name's earliest origins but unless this is a much misconceived form of *ystrad, 'strad,* (= broad flat valey)it must otherwise remain a complete mystery.

Barlinnie (Glasgow) –
bar llynyn = 'summit, hilltop, by the small lake'
* Johnston – Gaelic *bar linne* = 'height with the pool'.
** *bar llynyn* first aspirated to *barlynyn,* then *-yn* to *-ie* conversion gives *barlynie* and hence Barlinnie.

Barnbogle, Barnbougle (Dalmeny) – c.1177 Berenbouell, 1320 Prenbowgal 1481 Berenbougale
pren bugail = 'the herdsman's tree': first aspirated to *bren bugail* then metathesised to *bernbugail,* and so on
* Johnston – Original British *pren* = 'tree', then Gaelic *barr an buagheail* = 'height of the cowstall'.
* Watson – Earlier it is Prenbowgall, Pronbogalle, Pronbugele, for *pren bugail* = 'herdsman's tree'.
** There is a slight possibility that it derives from *bryn bugail* = 'hill of the herdsman', but this could not account for the 'Prens' and 'Prons' in the early records, as neither does Johnston's *barr an buagheail.* See 'Edinburgh Names' also.

Bathgate – 1160 Bathchet, 1200 Betchet, 1250 Bathket, 1306 Bathcet, Batchet, Batkeht, Bathcat, Bathket, 1316 Bathgetum, 1337 Bathkethe
baedd coed = (1) 'wood of the boar' or (2) place of – 'wild boar'
* Johnston – British *bath chet* or *both chet* = 'house in the wood', from Old Welsh *chet;* Welsh *coed* = 'wood'.

* Watson – It may be for *baedd goed* = 'boar's wood'.
** The records for this name give an illuminating insight into some of the numerous old forms, and variations, of *coed* which have appeared in past names, e.g. *chet, cet, ket, keht, cat,* and *kethe,* the last being the forerunner of the present-day *Keith.* In modern Welsh *baedd coed,* literally 'boar of the wood', has the meaning 'wild boar'.

Ben y Glow (Blair Atholl) –
ben-y-glaw = 'hilltop, peak, of rain'
ben-y-glaw = 'hilltop, peak, of brightness'
* Johnston – Gaelic *glo* = 'veil', therefore 'veiled, hooded, cloud-capped Ben'.
** Johnston seems to have evaded any explanation for the first two elements 'Ben' and 'y' which precede his Gaelic *glo.* My Welsh dictionaries differ significantly, three giving *glaw* = 'rain' and the other giving *glaw* the totally conflicting meaning – 'brightness'. No matter! – the one is for optimists and the other for pessimists. But which for whom?

Bervie, River (Kincardine) – 1199 Bervie, 1212 Bervyn, 1290 Haberberui
from *berwyn* = 'little boiling river', 'little seething river'
* Johnston – quotes another source as favouring *borv* = 'bubbling spring' as a possible root. He compares these with Old Gaelic *bir, bior* = 'water, a well', and with Welsh *berwi* = 'to bubble'.
* Watson – Bervie is identical with the Irish Berba, Bearbha, the Barrow. It is from the root found in Irish *berbaim* = 'I boil', Welsh *brwd* = 'hot, fervent'.
** River Bervie is *berwyn* = 'little boiling / seething' river; Thereafter *-yn* to *-ie* conversion, gives *berwie,* and an early confusion between script letters 'w' and 'v' then gives *bervie.* The town name Bervie, as is obvious from the 1290 record, derives from *aber berwie* = 'confluence of the river Bervie'.

Biggar (Lanarks) – 1170 Bigir, 1229 Bygris, 1524 Begart
Possibly *pig ardd* aspirated to *bigardd* = 'high beak', i.e. ' high beak-shaped height'.
* Johnston – Probably Norse *bygg gard'r* = 'barley field'.
** As Johnston has said before the terminal *dd* in *bigardd* drops off quite easily to give *bigar,* from which Biggar.

Birnie (Elgin) – 1190 Brenin, 1200 Brennach, 1384 Brynnay
prenyn = place of the 'little tree'
* Johnston – Probably Gaelic *braonach* = 'moist, oozy place'.
* Watson – Gaelic *braonaigh* (dative of *braonach*) = 'a moist place', which by metathesis becomes 'Birnie'.
** *prenyn* by aspiration becomes *brenyn* (see 1190 record), *-yn* to *-y* conversion gives *breny* (see 1384 record), metathesis then gives *berny* or *bernie* from which comes 'Birnie'. Additionally, *prenach* = 'little tree', in which *-ach* is an alternative diminutive.(see 1200 record). Otherwise 'Birnie' may simply be the lenited form of Pirnie, as in Pirnie (Roxburgh) which Watson attributes to Welsh *prennau / brennau*= 'trees'.

Birnam (Dunkeld) – 1508 Birnane
brenanau = place of 'little trees'
* Johnston – It is 'hero's, or warrior's, home' from Old English *biorn, beorn,* Middle English *berne, birn* and *ham.*
** Although late the 1508 record suggests *bernanau,* especially if the final 'e' in Birnane is sounded; *bernanau* would be the metathesised and lenited form of *prenanau* = place of the 'little-trees'. (see Birnie and Pirnie). 'Birnam Wood' featured importantly in Shakespeare's Macbeth. Today the place links to Dunkeld = *din caled,* an association which perhaps favours a P-Celtic root. Ross says 'this is unusually far into the Highlands to find a name with an Anglian source'.

Buchan – (Aberdeen) – 1150 Buchan, Buchain, 1249 Bochan, 1295 Bouwan, 1456 Buchane
bychan = 'little place'
* Johnston – Probably Old Celtic.
* Watson – It may be connected with Welsh *buwch* = 'cow'.
** Welsh *buwchan, buchan* = 'little-cow' is pronounced 'bewchan', 'bichan'; *bychan* is pronounced 'Buchan'.

C

Cadboll (Fearn) – 1281Kattepoll, 1478 Cadbollis, 1529 Cathabul
cad y poll = 'battle of the stream' – place-of?
* Johnston – = 'place of wild-cats' from Old Norse *kattar* / Danish *kat*
** In Scotland *pol, poll,* is said to be a British word, meaning 'small or medium-sized stream', which is believed to derive somehow from *pwll* = 'pool', possibly via it's Scots derivative *pow* = 'a sluggish stream'. Hence *cad y pwll or cad-y-poll* compares well with the record of 1281, Welsh 'd' easily confuses with Welsh 't'. It is the aspirated form of this i.e. *cad-y-poll* to *cadboll* which gives the record of 1478 and the present-day name.

Caddon Water (Selkirk) – 1175 Keledenelee, 1296 Kaledene
caled din lle = 'hard fort place'
* Johnston – Perhaps Welsh *caled din* = 'hard fort' or 'hard hill'?
* Watson – It appears to be from an early river-goddess name *Catona,* 'the warring-one'. Welsh *cad,* Gaelic *cath* = battle, the phonetics are British.
** The 1175 record accords well with *caled din lle,* especially when this is aspirated to *caledinle.* The name can be

compared to Dinas Dinlle (Caernarfon).

Cadzow (Hamilton) – 1150 Cadihou, Cadyhow, 1360 Cadyow
cad y huw = 'battle of the lullaby'. Well? – battles do have funny names. What about the Battle of the Bulge 1945?
* Johnston – Looks like Welsh *cad y*? = 'battle of the?'. Perhaps it is *cad du* = 'dark battle' with Scots *how* = 'a hollow'.

Caerketton –
caer cudyll = 'stronghold of the falcon', see Edinburgh names.

Cairnaquheen (Balmoral) –
carn y gwaun = 'cairn on the moorland pasture'
* Johnston – Gaelic *carn na chuimhne* = 'cairn of memory', 'cairn of recollection'.
** See Traquair and Quothquan for similar instances where an original '*g*' has been written down and recorded as a '*q*'.

Cairnbeddie (Perth) –
carn beddyn = 'little-grave cairn'
* Johnston – 'Cairn of Beth, or Macbeth' whose Fort was traditionally placed nearby. From Scots *cairn* plus Old Gaelic-locative *mac bead / bethad* = 'son of life'.
** First *carn beddyn,* then *-yn* to *-ie* conversion giving *carnbeddie,* hence Cairnbeddie. Pronunciation of *dd* is 'dull' as the *th* in 'breathe'.

Cairngrassie (Stonehaven)
carn grasau = 'cairn of Graces'
carn grasyn then -yn to -ie conversion to *carngrasie* = 'cairn of little-Grace'
* Johnston – Gaelic *cairn graise* = 'cairn of grace / divine blessing'.
** Another possibility is, as above, but with *gras* = 'gift'.

Cairnie / Cairney (Huntly) –
carddenyn = 'little-copse'
carnyn = 'little cairn'
* Johnston – Gaelic locative *cairneach* = 'rocky place'.

* Watson – Refers to Cardnye, Cardenys (Aberdeen), now Cairnie. He derives these from *Cardden* = 'a copse', a derivation entirely divorced from the element *carn* = 'cairn'.
** The usual *-yn* to *-ie* conversion gives *carddenie* from *carddenyn* and *carnie* from *carnyn.* Watson's derivation is more soundly based, relying as it does on established early records.

Cairn Toul (Braemar) –
carn twll = 'cairn hole' i.e. cairn, in or by, the hole
* Johnston – Gaelic *cairn t'sabhail* = 'cairn like a barn', 'cairn-shaped-hill like a barn'. The hill nearby is called 'Barn'.
** No records, so guesses only. 'Barn' may simply be *baran* = 'little summit'.

Cakemuir (Borthwick) –
ceg mawr = 'big mouth', 'big opening'
* Johnston – probably hybrid Welsh-Scots *ceg muir* = 'moor at the opening, or entrance'. Welsh *ceg* = 'opening', 'entrance'.
** No records – therefore suggestions only, local topography may provide clues.

Calder (Many, throughout Scotland) – various records, both as rivers and places. Typically 1250 Kaldor, 1293 Caldovere, 1294 Calder, and sometime Kaledour
caled dŵr, caled dwfr = 'hard water'
* Johnston – Old Gaelic *call dobhar* = 'hazel stream'.
* Watson – It is a survival of an early British *caleto dubron* = 'hard water' and is identical with river Calettwr in Wales, *caleto* is now Welsh *caled* = 'hard'.

** *caled dŵr* relates to the 1250, 1294 records and also to Watsons Kaledour; *caled dwfr* matches to the 1293 record.

Callander (Falkirk) – 1164 Calentare, 1296 Calantyre, 1350 Callanter, 1504 Kalentare
caled dŵr = 'hard water'
* Johnston – very confused! Seems to favour Gaelic *call triaith, treith* = hazel of the chieftain'. Or else Gaelic *call tir* = 'hazel land'.
* Watson – Skirts around this name but he does, unmistakably, connect it to Cawdor, Calder (which see) and to Welsh *caled dŵr.*
** Can do no better than accept Watson's dissertation.

Callander (Crieff) – 1451 Calyn et Calendrate, 1457 Calendrade, 1509 Calen et Calendrath, Calentreth, 1580 Caolrathad
Same as previous Callander (Falkirk)
Note: All records for this name are very late and therefore unreliable.

Cameron (Leven) – 1199 Cumbrun, 1200 Cambroun, 1280 Cameron, 1210 Camberoun, 1236 Camerun, 1306 Cambron
cam bron = 'bent / curved brow' – of the hill
* Johnston – Gaelic *cam brun* = 'crooked hill'.
** *cambron* accords well with the records of 1199, 1200, 1210, and 1306. The other records seem to have been subjected to some kind of metathesis whereby a spurious 'e' has somehow displaced the original 'b', or else the 'b' has simply been omitted. This is seen to have persisted through to the present-day name.

Camstraddan – (Loch lomond) – 1427 Caumstradan
cam ystraddan = 'crooked little-flat-bottomed valley'
* Johnston – Gaelic *cam sraddan* = 'crooked lanes'.
** *cam ystraddan* easily abridges to *camstraddan*.

Capplegill (Moffat) –
capel y cil = 'chapel of refuge'
* Johnston – Norse *kapilla-gil* = 'chapel glen', 'showing how far inland Norse influence went'.
** No records, only guesses. But *capel y cil* = 'chapel of refuge' or 'chapel in the nook' naturally aspirates to *capelgil.*

Carbeth (Dunkeld) –
caer bedd = 'fortlet by the grave'
* Johnston – Probably Gaelic *cathair beath* = 'fort among the birches'.
** No records – so take your pick.

Cardenden (Dunfermline) –
cardden-tyn aspirated to *cardendyn* = 'thicket, copse – by the croft'
cardden din = 'thicket by the fort'
* Johnston – See Watson.
* Watson – Welsh *cardden* = 'thicket', plus English *den* = 'den' or 'hollow', or 'dell'.
** No records, so difficult to assess the options.

Cardrosss (Helensburgh) – 1208-1233 Cardinros, Cadinros, 1275 Cardrois, 1401 Cardrose *cardden rhos* = 'thicket-moor' / 'copse moor'
* Johnston – Welsh *cerrdin ros* = 'rowan-tree promontory'.
* Watson – the meaning is perhaps 'copse-point' or more likely 'copse-moor'.
** Note that Watson gives Welsh *rhos* = 'moor' as being 'more likely'.

Cardross (Monteith) –
* Watson – the meaning here is 'copse point' see previous Cardross (Helensborough).

Carfin (Holytown) – 1489 Carnefyn
carn y ffin = 'cairn on the boundary'

* Johnston – Gaelic *carr ffion* = 'white, glistening rock'.
* Watson – 'white cairn', presumably from Gaelic *carn ffion.*
** The 1489 record definitely favours *carn-y-ffin.*

Carfraemill (Lauder) – 1458 Carffra
caer fre = 'fortification, fort, on the hill'
* Johnston – Welsh *caer* plus Gaelic *fraighe* = 'border' or 'edge', thus 'fortlet on the border'.
* Watson – Carfrae is *caer fre* = 'hill fort, from Welsh *bre* = 'a hill', 'a mount' There is a fine large 'fort' here.
** Possibly Carfraemill is *caer fre moel* = 'fortlet on the bare hill'. If however there is evidence of any sort of Mill being sited here in the past then the final element in Carfremill will simply be 'mill', if not the present name may be a throw back to much earlier times. On the other hand there is no hint of a 'mill' in the 1458 record.

Carlanrig, Caerlanrig (Hawick, Roxburgh) – 1610 Carlanerik
caer llanerch = 'fortified site, fort, in the glade'
* Johnston – Welsh *caer* = 'fort'. The latter part may be as in Lanark, from Welsh *llanerch* = 'a glade', in a wood.
* Watson – Identifies the name with Carlaverik 1511, Carlavrock 1662, and as 'Carlanryik', and 'Carlenrigg' from other sources. The name is for *caer lanerch* = 'fort in the glade'. There seems, he says, to have been a fort at this spot.
* Nicolaisen – *caer lanerch* = 'hamlet in the glade'.
** Total agreement it seems!

Carlaverock, Caerlaverock (Dumfries) – 1275 Carlauerok, 1371 Carlaverok
caer llanerch = 'fort, in or by, a glade' – in a wood
* Johnston – Perhaps a hybrid Welsh-Scots *caer laverock* = 'fort of the lark' or a hybrid Welsh-Gaelic *caer leamhreach* = 'fort, in or by, the elm-wood'.
* Watson – Sees an origin in Old Welsh *Limarch, Lifarch* later *Llywarch,* a personal name, therefore *caer Lifarch* = 'Llywarch's Fort'.

** Dorward, and Ross repeat Johnston's Gaelic *caer leamhreaich* = 'elm tree fort'. It seems that the only agreed element in this name is the acceptance that the first element is Welsh *caer*. In this case there is a high probability that the second element must at one time have been Welsh also. Reference to the early records for 'Carlanrig' are a positive invitation to treat this name as being no different, it is the same name *caer llanerch* = 'fortified site in the glade'. There is certainly a Castle on the site now and these mediaeval Castles often occupied a site previously chosen for a far more ancient fortification. The 'u' of 1275 and the 'v' of 1371 may simply be connected to an original scribal error mistaking an 'n' for a'v' or 'u'.

Carluke (Lanarks) – 1304 Carlug, 1320 Carneluke, 1567 Carlouk
caer llwch = 'fort at the wet-swampy-place'
carn llwch = 'cairn at the wet (swampy) place'
* Johnston – Gaelic *carr na luig* = 'rock by the hollow'. It's old name was Eglismalescok. = 'church of a saint called Malescok' of whom nothing is known. Watson makes a comparison with St Loesuc, Brittany.
* Watson – I can find no mention of Carluke!
* Ross – Either Brythonic Celtic *caer* = 'fort' plus Brythonic *lwch* = 'marshland', or Scottish-Gaelic *carn* = *cairn*, plus an obscure personal name.
** *caer llwch* aspirated to *caerlwch* accords well with the records of 1304 and 1567, *carn llwch* aspirated to *carnlwch* accords well with the record of 1320. Otherwise the old name Eglismalescok is Welsh *eglwys Malescok* = 'church of St Malescok'.

Carnethy – see Edinburgh place-names.

Carnoch, Carnock (Airth & Dunfermline) – 1185 Kernach, 1215 Carnock, 1250 Kernoch, 1449 Cranock, 1468 Kernock
carnach = 'little-cairn'

* Johnston – Gaelic *carnach* = 'rocky place, quarry', Gaelic *carnag* = 'pulpit'.

Carntyne (Glasgow) – 1200 Prenteineth
pren tyddyn, pren tyn = 'tree by the croft'
pren tanaidd = 'tree full of fire'
* Johnston – Seems British for 'tree among the green plots', Welsh *tyno* = 'dale', 'meadow', 'home', 'green'. The earlier Welsh *pren* has become the later Gaelic *crann* = 'tree'; then by transposing of 'r' the more familiar *carn.* But Watson says the ending is Gaelic *teineadh* = 'fire'.
* Watson – Carntyne is Gaelic *carn teineadh* = 'fire cairn'.
** Watson's interpretation does not account for the early record, Prenteineth. Alternatively there may be two names – *pren tanaidd* = 'fiery tree' being one and *carn tyn* = 'cairn croft' the other. The former having survived in the early record and the latter in the present day name?

Carnwath (Lanarks) – 1108 Carnewith, 1165 Charnewid, 1172 Karnewit, 1174 Karnewic, 1179 Karnewid, 1315 Carnewithe, 1424 Carnwith, 1451 Carnewith
caer newydd = 'new fortlet', 'newcastle'
* Johnston – Welsh *carn gwydd* = 'cairn, mound, in the shrubs or woods'.
* Watson – It is evidently *carn gwydd* lenited to *carn wydd* = 'cairn of the wood'.
** The intrusive 'e' between 'n' and 'w', in the records of 1108, 1165, 1172, 1174, 1179, 1315, and 1451, in fact in all except that of 1424, must favour *caer newydd*. The local pronunciation 'Carn-wayth' is a remarkably good retention of the original Caernewydd. David Ross has it as 'Kaerandi's ford' from an Old Scandinavian personal name! My! These Vikings get everywhere?

Carpow (Abernethy) –
caer pwll = 'fortlet by the stream'

* Johnston – Probably the 'Ceirfull' as mentioned in the Pictish Chronicles, hence Welsh *caer pwll* = 'fort at the pool'.
* Watson – 'Ceirfuill' must now be Carpow = 'fort on the sluggish stream', Welsh *pwll,* Gaelic *poll.* This specialised meaning of *pwll, poll* obtained great vogue in the south-west and occurs several times in Perthshire.
** *caer pwll* is literally 'fort, pool', but the 'Pow' in Carpow indicates that here it has it's special meaning = 'a stream', usually a 'sluggish stream' or 'pooly stream', a meaning which harks back to it's origin in Welsh *pwll* = a 'pool', 'pit', 'hole', 'pool'. Elsewhere in Scotland, the stream names *pol* and *poll* share the origins of *pow* and *pwll,* but do not necessarily describe 'sluggish' streams. Watson's passing reference to *poll* being a Gaelic word is not confirmed by my Gaelic Dictionary which gives *poll* = 'pit, 'hole', 'pond', 'mire'. The consensus nowadays is that *pol, poll,* = 'stream' are 'British' terms.

Carrick (Ayrs) – The 'Carrawg' of Taliesin? c. 7th century, 1140 Karric, 1153 Karric, 1286 Carryke
carreg = 'a rock', usually an outstanding one
* Johnston – Gaelic and Irish *carraig* = 'sea-cliff or rock'.
* Watson – Carrick is from Welsh *carreg,* 'a rock', borrowed into Gaelic as *carraig.*
** If both Watson and Johnston are right then it seems that Welsh *carreg* was 'borrowed' not into Scots-Gaelic but also into Irish-Gaelic.

Carriden (Bo'ness) – 1000 Cair Eden, 1140 Karreden, 1336 Kaaredene
caer eidyn = 'fortlet, fortress of eidyn'
* Johnston – Old Welsh *caer eiddyn* = 'fort on the slope or hillside'.
* Watson – Quotes a reference connected with the 6th century monk and historian Gildas: '*Kair Eden, a very ancient city, about two miles from the monastery of Abercurnig, now*

Abercorn'. The name is usually equated with the 'Caer Eidyn' of Old Welsh literature meaning 'fort of eidyn', but there is now neither trace nor tradition of a town or village bearing this name.
** It is probable that *'eidyn'* is either the name of a region or else a personal name it is not necessarily connected with the element 'Edin' as in Edinburgh. 'Clyddno Eiddyn' appears as a personal name in the Scottish historian W.F. Skene's genealogy of the 'Kings of the Race of Coel Hen' and Clinog Eiddyn in his genealogy of 'Kings of the Race of Macsen Guledig'.

Carrifran Gans (Moffat) –
caer y fran ganos ='fortress of the songful crow'
* Johnston – Welsh *caer y fran* = 'fort of the crow', plus Scots *gans* = 'jaws without teeth'.

Carruber, Caruber (Linlithgow) – 1296 Caribre, 1454 Caribris
caer y bre = 'fortlet on the hill'
* Johnston – British *caer aber* = 'fort by the marsh'.
** Elsewhere Johnston describes *aber* = 'marsh' as being a Gaelic word.

Carruthers (Ecclefechan) – 1334 Car-rothres, 1350 Caer Ruther
See – Johnston and Watson below.
* Johnston – *caer Rhydderch* = 'fortress of Rhydderch'.
* Watson – *caer rotri* = 'fortress of Rhodri'.
** Both Rhodri (Roderick) and Rhydderch are Welsh personal names.

Carstairs (Lanark) – 1170 Casteltarres, 1250 Castrotharis, 1301 Castrum de Tarres, 1500 Carstaris, 1540 Castalstaris, 1579 Carstaris
caer = 'fort' plus *staris, taris* = meaning unknown, but may be a personal name?

* Johnston – Old English *castel tarres* = Tarres Castle.
* Watson – The 1250 form may be Latinised, the second part may be the same as Tarras Water in Eskdale.
** This is, just possibly, an instance where the earliest record of 1170 may have already been corrupted and where the present spelling and pronunciation, backed up by the records of 1500 and 1579, may be a better guide to it's origin. The 'Castel-' of 1170 may have replaced an original *caer* and the 'Castro' of 1250 appears to be a *caer* replacement by Latin *castrum*. In this case the first element is *caer* and the second element might have been some origin of *tarres, tharis,* or *taris*. River names are mostly very old names and it would be nice to know what the name of the river Tarras means.

Carwhinelow River (Dumfries) –
caer Gwendolew see Johnston below
* Johnston – probably Welsh *caer Gwendolew* = 'fort of Gwendolew', a leader in the battle of Ardderyd 573 AD.
** *caer gwendolew* aspirates to *carwendolew*. Also, Gwenddolew appears as a personal name in Skene's genealogy of the 'Kings of the Race of Coel Hen'.

Cathcart (Glasgow) – 1158 Kerkert, 1170 Katkert, Ketkert, 1375 Catkert
caer Cart = 'fort on Cart'
coed Cart = 'wood on Cart'
cad Cart = 'battle-place on Cart'. For these and River-Cart see Johnston and Watson below
* Johnston – 1158 is Welsh *caer Cart* = 'fort on River Cart', 1170 & 1375 are *cad Cart* = 'battle-place on the River Cart'.
* Watson – Both forms, Ker- and Ket-, make good sense. Kerkert of 1158 represents *caer gert* = 'fort on River Cart', Ketkert, Katkert and Catkert of 1170, and 1375 represent *coet cert* = 'wood of Cart'. Cart (river) is perhaps connected to Irish-Gaelic *cartaim* = 'cleanse' and is probably a 'goddess' type name.

Cawdor (Nairn) – 1280 Kaledor, 1501 Caldor
caled dŵr = 'hard water'
* Johnston – see 'Calder'.
* Watson – It is named after it's burn known locally in Gaelic as *allt chaladair* but deriving from *caled dŵr* as in Calder.
** Cawdor is evidently a corruption of the common stream name 'Calder'. In my Gaelic Dictionary *caladair* = 'a calendar' and there is no word *chaladair*. This then is possibly a case, as Watson complained, of local Gaelic speakers turning a non-Gaelic name *caled* into a pseudo-Gaelic name *chaladair* by simply re-spelling it using letters from the Gaelic alphabet and then, in this case, replacing *dŵr* = 'water' with Gaelic *allt* = 'stream'.

Clunaig (Skipness) – 1511 Clynage
clynawg, clunawg = 'little meadow' or 'little moor'
* Johnston – Gaelic *cluanaig* = 'little meadow'.
** In Wales the place-name Clynnog has the meaning 'place abounding in holly trees', it is a contraction of *celynawg*. In Scots Gaelic the diminutive suffix *-ag* or *-aig* is a 'borrowing' from Welsh.

Clunas (Nairn) –
clynas, clunas = 'place-of meadows'
* Johnston – Gaelic *cluan* plus Pictish *-ais* making *cluanais* = 'little meadow place'.

Clunie (Blairgowrie) – 1164 Kluen, 1291 Clony
clynyn, clunyn = 'little meadow'
* Johnston – Gaelic *cluan* = 'meadow' plus locative *-ie* ending gives *cluanie* = 'little meadow place'
** The 1164 record Kluen could be either *clun* or *clyn* = *'meadow'*. In Welsh the pronunciation is almost identical. The 1291 record Cluny may simply be *clynyn* or *clunyn* = 'little meadow', where -yn to -ie conversion gives Clunie.

Clyne (Golspie) – 1240 Clun
clun, clyn, clyne = 'meadow' or 'moor'
* Johnston – Gaelic *claon* = 'a slope'.

Clyne (Ross) – 1231 Clon, 1264 Clyne, 1375 Clyn
clyn, clun clyne = meadow, moor, as above
* Johnston – Gaelic *claon* = 'a slope'.

Clynelish (Sutherland) –
clyn y llys aspirated to *clynylis* = 'meadow of the Court (Great House)'
* Johnston – Gaelic *claon lios* = 'slope with the garden'.

Clyntre – 1368 Duae Clintreis
clyn tre = 'meadow by the steading'
* Watson – the first part seems to be Gaelic *claon* = 'sloping', the second part is Welsh *tre, tref* = 'a stead'.
Note – Watson agrees that the second element is Welsh *tre* therefore it is reasonable to look for a Welsh interpretation for the first element as well: *clyn* or *clun* = a 'meadow' fits very nicely.

Coatbridge (Glasgow) –
* Johnston – Welsh *coet* = 'a wood'; the bridge was not built until c.1800.

Cochrane (an old Barony, Paisley) – 1384 Cochrane
coch rhen = 'red brook', see Johnston below
* Johnston – *coch rhen* = 'red brook'.

Cockpen (Dalkeith) – 1240 Kokpen, 1300 Cockpen
coch pen = 'red head' or 'red hill', see Johnston below
* Johnston – Welsh *coch pen* = 'red head' or 'red hill'.

Collin (Kircubright) –
celyn = 'holly' (place)
* Johnston Gaelic *cuileann* = 'holly' (place).

Colvend (Dalbeattie) – 1513 Culevane, 1560 Colven, 1610

Culwen
cil faen = 'refuge Stone', 'corner Stone'
* Johnston – Probably Gaelic *cul a bheinn* = 'at the back of the hill'.
** The records are late, even so they all suggest *cil faen* = 'refuge stone' / 'corner stone'.

Comrie (Crieff) – c.1268 Comry, 1271 Cumry, Comri, 1275 Cumry
cymerau = 'confluences of two, or more, rivers'
* Johnston – Gaelic-locative *comar* = 'confluence'.
* Watson – Comrie in Perthshire is at the junction of the rivers Ruchil, Lednock and Earn. In Gaelic the name is Cuimrigh, Cuimirigh. Gaelic *comar* = confluence, Welsh *cymmer* = 'a confluence of rivers'.

Comrie (Contin) – 1479 Cumre
See Comrie, Perths.

Comrie (Cairnie) – 1226 Cumery
See Comrie, Perths.

Corsewall (Stranraer) – 1430 Corswel
cors gwael aspirated to *corswael* = 'vile bog' (plenty of bogs on the Mull of Galloway!)
* Johnston – 'the cross well', here dedicated to St Columba. In Scots 'a well' is 'a wall'.

Corsock (Kirkcudbright) – 1527 Karsok
See Johnston below.
* Johnston – Welsh and Cornish *cors* = 'bog, fen', plus diminutive suffix *-oc* or *-og* gives *corsoc* = 'little bog, fen, marsh'.
** The 1527 record is late and by that time Welsh *cors* may have slipped into Scots *carse,* hence 'Karsok' of 1527.

Corstorphine – 1130 Crostorfin/Crostorphin, 1140 Crorstorfin, 1508 Corstorphyne

cors tor ffin = 'marsh or fen, rock-outcrop, boundary'
* Johnston says 'Cross of Thorfinn' an Earl of Orkney!
** Welsh *cors tor ffin*, = 'Marsh by the Rock-outcrop on the Boundary' not only fits the site exactly but also the vernacular pronunciation. See Edinburgh-names.

Coulter / Culter (Biggar) – c. 1210 Cultyr, 1229 Cultir, 1457 Cultir
cil tir = 'corner-land', 'nook-land'
cul tir = 'little-cottage land'
* Johnston – Gaelic *cul tir*, Welsh *tre* = 'back-land'.

Coupar (Angus) – 1169 Cubert, 1190 Cupre, 1296 Coupre-*in-Anegos*
cau pert = 'pretty hollow'
cau per = 'sweet hollow'
* Johnston – A puzzle! Some say Gaelic *comh-pairt* = 'partnership, common-land, common' – seems possible.
* Watson – Cupar in Fife, Coupar in Angus – also nearby Cupar-maculty, are doubtless British. The Gaelic form is *Cubar*.
** The oldest form is possibly *cau pert* = 'pretty hollow', whilst the later forms are possibly *cau per* = 'sweet hollow'; both meanings are similar. See Cupar Fife also.

Cowcaddens (Glasgow) – 1510 Kowcawdennis 1521 Kowkadens, 1531 Kowcaldenis
cau carddenas, cau carddenais = 'hollow full-of thickets'
* Johnston – Gaelic *cuil calldainn* or *cuil calltuinn* = 'nook of hazels'.
** The records are late so we rely quite heavily on the present-day name and pronunciation, nevertheless the records also support the interpretations *caucardenas, -denais*.

Craigcrook – see Edinburgh-names

Craigellachie (Aberlour) – 1680 Craig Ilachie
craig y llachau = 'crag of glistenings'
* Johnston – it is often said to be Gaelic *creag eagalach* = 'rock of warnings', but see Watson.
* Watson – Gaelic *creag eileachaidh* (from Early Irish *ailech*) = 'rock of the stony place'.
** Coupled, as it is, with a name of such obvious Welsh derivation as Aberlour it is tempting to postulate *craig y llachau* = 'crag of glistenings'; i.e. dripping with water perhaps? Scots-Gaelic *creag* is nearer to Welsh *craig* than it is to Irish-Gaelic *carraig*, possibly showing its inheritance from the Welsh rather than the Irish?

Craigie (Several) – perhaps 1266 Cragyn
craigyn = 'little crag'
* Johnston – Gaelic *creag* plus 'locative' suffix *-ie* gives *creaigie* = 'crag place'.
** *craigyn* to *craigie*, by conversion of Welsh diminutive *-yn* to Scots diminutive *-ie*. Johnston's 'Gaelic-locatives' are considered somewhat doubtful.

Craigmillar – see Edinburgh

Craigmore (Rothesay, Aberfoyle) –
craig mawr = 'big crag'
craig môr = 'sea crag'
* Johnston – *creag mor* = 'big crag'.

Craignish (Lochgilphead) – 1434 Cragginche, 1609 Creginis
craig ynys = 'crag meadow'. Or else- 'crag island'.
* Johnston – Gaelic *creag innis* = 'crag meadow'.
** Scots *inch, innis* is from Welsh *ynys.* It looks like the name suffered phonetic change i.e. Cragginche became Cragnch and then Cragnish. But the modern name retains the earlier *craig*.

Craigo – 1359 Craggow
Craigach = 'little crag', then *craigach* to *craigo* by conversion of Welsh diminutive suffix -ach to Scots *-o*. (See Balerno in Edinburgh names.)
* Johnston – Gaelic *craigach* = 'rocky place'.
** According to Watson Gaelic *ach, ag* is an adoption from Welsh *–ach*.

Cramond – see Edinburgh-names

Crawick (Sanquhar) –
See Johnston below
* Johnston – Probably Welsh *caer Rwyc* = 'fortress of Rwyc'; where Rwyc is a personal name as in the works of Taliesin the Bard.
** Johnston's interpretation is taken from Skene, the Scots Historian of Victorian Times, and is mentioned as such in Watson.

Crewe – see Edinburgh-names

Cromdale (Grantown) – 1224 Cromdol, 1237 crumbdol
crom dôl ='bent, curving meadow', *crwm dol* = 'bent, crooked meadow'
* Johnston – Pictish forms. Old Gaelic *crumb*, Gaelic *crom* = 'crooked' and Gaelic *dail*; Welsh *dôl* = meadow
* Watson – Cromdale, in Gaelic *cromdhail* = 'bent haugh', from the bend in the River Spey which sweeps round the glebe just below the parish church.
** Scots *haugh* = 'river-meadow land'.

Crossbasket (East Kilbride) – 1426 Corsbasket
cors bas cet = 'marsh at exit to the wood'
Johnston – Perhaps Old Welsh *croes pas cet* = 'cross at the exit of the wood'.
** Welsh *pas* = 'exit', but if so, more likely is *cors pas cet* aspirated to *corsbascet* = 'marsh, fen, at the exit from the wood' which accords well with the record of 1426.

Crossford (Lanark) – 1498 Corseford
cors ffordd = 'marsh by the roadway, pathway etc.'
* Johnston – is not clear.

Cruachan, Ben (Argyll) – 1375 Crechanben
ben crwcan = 'peak with small-bowl'
* Johnston – Gaelic *cruachan* = 'the haunch', 'conical stack', *cruachan* = 'a stack'.
** *crwc* = 'bucket, pail, bowl, tub', *crwcan* is the diminutive; *crwcanben* = 'small-bowl of, or by, the peak' accords well with the record of 1375. There is a bowl-shaped depression, behind Ben Cruachan, which has now been dammed to form the reservoir for the Hydro Electric power station. The Gaelic dictionary gives *cruachan* = 'hip', 'a conical hill', in which case *ben cruachan* = 'hill, conical-hill', or 'hip-shaped hill'. Neither of which seem likely.

Cruden (Aberdeen) – 1163 Invercrwdan, 1501 Croudane
crwdan = 'little round lump', possibly referring to some local landmark
* Johnston – 1163 record is probably 'confluence of the kingfisher' from Gaelic *cruidein* = kingfisher.
** The 1163 record would have started life as Abercrwdan.

Culross (Dunfermline) – 1110 Culenross, 1295 Culnross, Kyllenros
celyn rhos = 'holly moor'
Johnston – Gaelic *cuilean ros* = 'holly wood'.
Watson – It is 'holly point'.

Cummertrees (Annan) – 1223 Cumbetres, 1245 Cumbertres, 1553 Cummirtreis
cymmer drys = 'confluence among thorns or brambles'.
* Johnston – Old Gaelic *cumber*, Gaelic *comar dreas,* Welsh *cymmer drysi* = 'confluence among thorns or brambles'.
** In Irish-Gaelic *dreas* = 'a spell, a while' and the word for 'thorn' is *dealg;* neither is there any 'cumber'or 'comar', so it

would seem that both Old-Gaelic *cumber* and Gaelic *comar dreas* may have come from Welsh *cymmer* and Welsh *drys.*

Cupar (Fife) – 1183 Cupre, 1294 Coper (see Coupar, Angus also)
Possibly *cau pert* = 'pretty hollow', or *cau per* = 'sweet hollow'; both meanings are similar. But see below.
* Johnston – A puzzle! Some say Gaelic *comh-pairt* = 'partnership, common-land, common', – seems possible?
* Watson – Cupar-Fife and Coupar-Angus are doubtless British.
** Watson says nothing further about either of these except to relate them to the second element in the early records for Dalfouber. These are, 1511 Dalquhober, 1554 Dulquhowqbeir: of these he says: *the second part seems to be the same as Cupar and Drum-cooper in Fife and C(o)upar-Angus.* Elsewhere Watson interprets the *qu* in Quair as *gw* or *gu;* of these alternatives both *'quho'* and *'quhow'* in the early records would, in this instance, seem to favour *'gw'*. Taking this together with the persistent 'b' gives the second element as possibly *gwber* and invites comparison with Gwbert in Wales which is said to be *gwy pert* = 'pretty water' but could equally be *gwy per* = 'sweet water' which combines to *gwper* in the same way as *gwy pert* combines to *gwpert,* which in its aspirated form gives Gwbert. It then needs but a small leap of faith to see 'gwper' written down by mediaeval scribes as 'cwper': the confusion between 'g' pronounced and 'c' written-down has occurred in other place-names. It may be no coincidence that Cupar-Fife is on the river Eden, Coupar-Angus is on the river Isla and Dalfouber is on the river North Esk near Edzell, in which case Dolquhober may possibly be from *dol gwy ber* = *dolgwber* = 'meadow on the sweet water'.

Currie (Midloth) –
Cyrrau = 'skirts', 'skirting-edge', possibly of the pentland hills. See Edinburgh Names.

Cuthill (Prestonpans) –
See Johnston below
* Johnston – Probably Welsh *cuddigl* = 'a retreat, private-place'; from *cuddio* = 'to hide'.
** Welsh *cuddigl, cuddygl* = 'cell, small-room, bed, cubicle, retreat'.

D

Daer Water (Elvanfoot) – 1170 Deiher
dar = 'oak trees'
* Johnson – Probably Gaelic *deifir* = 'haste', 'speed' i.e. a 'rapid, frolicsome' stream; so not as Watson's Aber-dare, Wales.
* Watson – 'Daer', a tributary of the Clyde, is probably identical with the 'Dare' of Aberdare in Wales.
** There is a South Wales dialect in which 'dar' is pronounced 'dare'; as in the River Dar at Aberdare South Wales, coincidentally there is a church 'St Elvan's' in the centre of Aberdare!

Dairsie (Cupar) – 1234 Dervesyn, 1639 Dersey
derwasyn, derwaisyn = place – 'full of little oak trees', then *-yn* to *-ie* conversion, gives *derwasie, derwaisie* from which 'Dersey' and Dairsie.
* Johnston – Perhaps Old Gaelic-locative *dair bheus* = 'oak of fornication': compare with Welsh *derw* = 'oak'.
** *dar*, plural *deri* is an obsolescent word, the modern Welsh word for 'oak-tree' is *derwen*, plural *dderw*, there is also *derwin* = 'oak'. The change of ending through the sequence

-yn to *-ey* to *-ie* adds substance to O'Maolalaigh's theory on the transition of -yn endings to -y and -ie as the names became influenced by Lowland Scots, but the central 'es' in Dervesyn and the 'se' in Dersey, are elusive.

Dalbeallie (Àberlour) –
dol beili = 'meadow by the yard', e.g. a 'farmyard'
* Johnston – Gaelic *dal bile* = 'field at the rim, or margin'.

Dalgetty, Dalgaty (Aberdour) – 1178 Dalgathyn
dol gethin = 'brown meadow', *-in* conversion to *-ie* gives *dol gethie* then Dolgettie etc.
* Johnston – Gaelic *dail gaoith* (here in locative)= 'field of the wind', 'windy field'.

Dalgleish (Ettrick) – 1383 Dalglas
dol glais = 'meadow by the streamlet'
dol glas = 'green meadow' or 'grey meadow'
* Johnston – Gaelic *dal gleois* = 'field of activity', to derive from *glais* = 'green' is phonetically less likely.
* Watson – It is from Gaelic *dail g(h)lais* = 'green haugh', perhaps taken over from Welsh *dôl-las,* with the same meaning.
** Scots *haugh* = a 'piece of level ground, usually alluvial and on the banks of a river', 'river-meadow land'. Welsh *dôl-las* is the aspirated form of *dôl-y-glais.*

Dalkeith (Lothian) – 1140 Dalkied, 1145 Dalketh, Dolchet, 1336 Dalkethe
dol coed = 'meadow in the wood'
* Johnston – British for 'field in the wood'. Welsh *dol,* Gaelic *dail* = 'field': Old-Welsh *cet, chet;* Welsh *coed* = 'a wood'
* Watson – *dol coed* = 'meadow, or plateau, of the wood', *coed* = 'wood', from Early Celtic *ceto / caito*
** Modern Welsh *coed* appears in Scottish place-names in a variety of forms some of which are :- *cet, ceth, chet, kethe.*

Dallas (Forres) – 1232 Dolays, 1306 Dolays
dolas = (place) – 'full of 'meadows'
dol lais = 'meadow by the stream'.
du glais = 'dark stream' Same as Dulais and Dowlais in Wales
* Johnston – Pictish *dolais* = 'place on the plain': Welsh *dôl* = 'meadow'.
* Watson – *Dalais*, older *Dolais* is a compound of *dul, dol*, with most probably a term representing Welsh *gwas* = 'an abode, a dwelling', it means 'meadow-stance', 'holme-dwelling', or such. In Moray there is also Dalasbrachty, formerly Dolesbrachti = 'of the malthouse', from Welsh *bracty* – I have not heard or seen the corresponding Gaelic term.
** Watson's conjunction of an uncontested Welsh element *bracty* with the disputed element *doles* in Dolesbrachti would favour a Welsh origin for both and by extrapolation a Welsh origin also for Dallas. Welsh *bracty* = a 'brewery'.

Dallas (Edderton) – 1560 Doles
Same as Dallas (Forres).

Dallas (Ross) – 1574 Dollace
Same as Dallas (Forres).

Dalmahoy (Ratho) – 1272 Dalmohoy, 1295 Dalmehoy
dol ma hwy = the 'longer meadow on the piece of flat-ground'
* Johnston – Gaelic *dal mo h'Aoidh* = 'field of my dear Hugh'. Watson's derivation from St Tua is phonetically very difficult.
* Watson – *dail mo Thuae* = 'my Tua's meadow'. Tua means the' silent-one', *dol, dul* is found not uncommonly with names of Saints, indicating an old church site.
** There is an old established Church at Dalmahoy, but is it old-enough?

Dalmellington (Ayrs) – 1275 Dalmellingtoun, 1302-4 Dalmeledone
dol melin tyn = 'meadow by the mill-croft'.
* Johnston – Perhaps a hybrid Gaelic *dail meallan* = 'field among a cluster of knolls or hills', plus English *ton* = 'village' Local pronunciation is 'da-melin-ton'.
** Also possible is *dol melin* = 'meadow by the mill' plus English *ton* as a later addition? But English *ton* = a 'steading', so it is perhaps more likely that it was used to displace the earlier Welsh *tyn* = 'small cottage', 'croft' particularly as the pronunciation is so similar.

Dalmeny (Forth Estuary) – 1180 Dumanie, 1250 Dunmanyn, 1296 Dunmanyn
din meini = 'fort of stones'
din maenyn = 'fort by the small-stone'
* Johnston – Gaelic *dubh, du* = 'black' and *moine* = 'a moss', but *dun mainne* = 'hill of delay, or procrastination' is more likely.
* Watson – The first part is *dun* = 'fort', probably Gaelicized from Welsh *din*; the second part may be Welsh *meini;* plural of *maen* = 'a stone'. 'Stone-Fort' would be quite possible in an area where the forts are usually of earth – as they are in the Lothians.
** Watson's *din meini* is likely to be the more correct. See Edinburgh Names also.

Dalmuir (Dumbarton) – 1200 Dalmore, 1680 Dalmuire
dol mawr = 'big meadow'
dol mor = 'meadow by the sea'
* Johnston – Gaelic *dal mor* = 'big field'

Dalmullin (Ayrs) – 1214 Dalmulin
dol melin = 'meadow by the mill'
* Johnston – Gaelic *dail muileann* = 'field of the mill'.

Dalry – see Edinburgh Names.

Dalrymple (Ayrs) – 1300 Dalrimpill, 1467 Dalrumpill
dol crwm pwll = 'meadow in the curvature of the pool or stream'
dol crwm pol, dol crwm poll = 'meadow by the bending stream'; is more likely where *pol,* although connected to Welsh *pwll,* is Brythonic for 'stream'
* Johnston – Gaelic *dol chruim puill* = 'field on the curving stream'.
** Alternatively, *dol grym poll* aspirated to *dolrympoll* = 'meadow by the powerful stream'.

Dalton (Ecclefechan) – 1200 *Lib. Melros* Dalton
dol din = 'meadow by the fort'
dol tyn = 'meadow by the croft'
* Johnston – Either English 'dale town' or perhaps Gaelic *dall dun* = 'dark hill'.
** English *ton* often replaces an original Welsh *din,* therefore an origin in *doldin* is the more likely. But see Dalmellington.

Dewar (Heriot) –
du ar = 'black ploughed-land'. See Johnston below.
* Johnston – Probably Welsh *du ar* = 'black ploughed-land' as opposed to Gaelic *dubh ard* = 'dark height'.

Dingwall (Ross) – 1227 Dingwell, 1250 Dinkeual
aber pefryn = 'confluence of the river Pefryn'
* Johnston – Old Norse *dinga-voll-r* = 'meeting place of the 'thing', the 'council'. The local Gaelic name is 'Inver Pefferon'.
* Watson – In Ross the Peffery flows through Strathpeffer and enters the sea at *Inbhir Pheofharan,* the native name for Norse 'Dingwall'.
** The oldest name might have been *aber pefryn* = 'confluence of the Pefryn river', where the stream name *pefryn* = 'the small, bright-one'. The river is now the

'Peffery'. Conversion of *-yn* to *-y* gives *pefry* (Peffery?) from *pefryn.*

Dinnet (Aberdeen) –
dinet = 'small fort'
* Johnston – Perhaps Gaelic *dion-aite* = 'place of refuge, sanctuary'.
** *din* = 'fort' plus diminutive suffix *-et* = 'small fort'.

Dinwoodie (Lockerbie) – 1296 Dinwithie, Dunwythe, 1482 Donwethy, 1503 Dunwedy, 1578 Dumwiddie
din gwyddyn = 'hill with little trees, shrubs'
* Johnston – Welsh *din gwydd* = 'hill with shrubs' (*dd* = *th* as in 'breathe').
* Watson – British *din* can now seldom be distinguished from Gaelic *dun;* the former appears in Dinwoody, Dinwiddie (Dumfries) and in Dunwedy (Roxburgh 1504).
** *din gwyddyn* to *dinwyddyn* by lenition, then to *dinwyddie* via conversion of *yn* to *-ie,* giving the 'Dinwithie' of 1296, finally corrupted to 'Dinwoodie' today. In Scotland *din* and *dun* are interchangeable hence the 'Dunwythe' of 1296 and the records of 1503 and 1578. The present name and all the records display a remarkable consistency.

Dollar (Alloa) – *Pictish Chronicles* Dolair, 1461 Doler, 1639 Dolour
dol ar = 'ploughed meadow'. See Johnston below
* Johnston – Welsh *dol ar* = 'ploughed-land meadow'; *dol* = 'meadow'; *ar* = 'ploughed-land': or perhaps Old Gaelic, *ar* or *air* may be a mere suffix.
* Watson – Dollar is from *dol* with *ar* extension which appears to be collective.
** Watson's interpretation is, uncharacteristically, somewhat 'woolly'. Johnston's reference to Old Gaelic *ar, air* is also rather vague.

Dollar Law (Peebles) –
Same as Dollar (Alloa) with Scots *law* added.

Donibristle (Aberdour), 1169 Donibrysell, 1178 Donybrisle.
din y prysell = 'hill-fort by the copses'
* Johnston – Gaelic *dun* (here in locative) *brisg-gheal* = 'at the clear bright hill'.
* Watson – Gaelic *dunadh Breasail* = 'Breasal's fortress' from Old Irish *Breasal* = 'warrior'.
** *prysell, prysel* = 'copses' or 'groves'; *din, dun* = 'hill-fort' or 'hill', *dyn y prysel* aspirates to *dinybrysel, dunybrysel,* hence Donibristle.

Douglas (Lanarks) – 1150 Duuelglas, Duglas, 1220 Dufgles, 1298 Douglas
du glais, du glas = 'dark, black, stream'
* Johnston – Old Gaelic *dub glas* = 'black, dark, stream'.
* Watson – Gaelic *dubhghlais,* Welsh *dulas* (Old Welsh *dubleis, dugleis*) = 'black stream', becomes 'Douglas' in English.
** Johnston quotes 'Old' Gaelic, Watson quotes 'Old' Welsh. It appears then that this is a very old name, which as a river name it can be expected to be, in which case it can be expected that it's origins precede the advent of the Gaelic language into this region. There seems to be no *ghlais* = 'stream' in Irish-Gaelic; Scots-Gaelic must then have inherited the word, and therefore the name, from Welsh.

Drumclog (Strathaven) –
y-trum-y-clog = 'ridge with cliff'
* Johnston – Either Gaelic *druim clog* = 'bell ridge', or Welsh *(y) drum clog* = 'the ridge with a crag, a cliff'.
* Watson – The second part is probably Welsh *clog* = 'crag, cliff, rock'.
** *y-trum-y-clog* aspirates to *drumclog.*

Drummond (Crieff) – 1296 Droman
y-truman = 'the little-ridge'.
* Johnston – Gaelic *dromainn* = 'a ridge', from *druim* = 'the back'.
** *y-truman* aspirates to *druman.* Welsh *mynydd,* as it appears in Scottish place-names, means either 'mountain' or 'moorland hill-pasture'. It is discerned elsewhere in Scotland as 'munid', 'mount', 'monid', or suchlike forms, and in Scots-Gaelic as *monadh.* Welsh *trum* means either 'ridge' or 'summit'; *y-trum mynydd* aspirates to *drumynyd* which then anglicizes or corrupts to *drummunid* and then *drummond.*

Drumochter (Dalnaspidal) –
y-trum uwch tir = 'ridge on the the upper land'
* Johnston – It is 'upper hill-ridge summit', see Auchterarder.
* Johnston presumably means, Gaelic *dromainn uachdar tir* = 'ridge on, summit of, the top land'?
** *y-trum uwch tir* aspirates to *drumuwchtir* = 'ridge on the upper land' or 'upper-land summit'.

Drumpellier (Coatbridge) – 1174 Dumpeleter, 1203 Dunpeleder, 1232 Dunpeldre, 1545 Dunpelder, 1602 Drumpendare, 1607 Dumpelder, 1608 Dunpelder
din pelydr = 'fort of spears'
* Johnston – Originally British – Welsh *din peledyr* (plural of *paladr*) = 'fort of the spears'.
* Watson – Same as Dunpelder now Traprain Law.
** Modern Welsh *paladr,* plural *pelydr* = 'spear, shaft, stem,' the amendment of *pelydr* to 'pelyder, peleder, peleter', looks like some form of metathesis. The meaning behind the name may be 'fort of the spear-men'? See Traprain Law also.

Drymen (Stirling) – 1238 Drumyn, also Drummane
drumyn / druman = 'little ridge'
* Johnston – Gaelic *dromainn* = 'a ridge' (*dromainn* is dative/locative of *druim* = 'back').

Duddingston –
was *tref-yr-llyn* = 'steading by the lake'. See Edinburgh-Names.

Duffus (Elgin) – 1274 Duffhus, 1512 Dufous
du faes = 'dark, black; flat-field', flat-ground'
* Johnston – Gaelic *dubh uisg* = 'dark water'.
* Watson – Duffus is Gaelic *dubhais* = 'black station', from *dubh* = 'black', plus *fas* = 'station'. A *fas* is a 'stance', a nice level spot such as a drover would chose as a night's quarters for his charge.
** Welsh *faes* is the aspirated form of *maes* = 'open-field, plain, field'. Here we take 'plain, open-field' = 'flat-ground'. There is no *fas* = 'level-ground', in Irish Gaelic. In modern Scots Gaelic *fas* = 'unoccupied, uncultivated, vacant, hollow, void'.

Dumbarton (Dumbartons) 1300, 1345 Dunbretane, 1498 Dunbretane, 1600 Dumbarten, 1639 Dumbriton
This is not directly from the Welsh language, it is nevertheless associated with the history of the Welsh in Scotland. See Watson and Johnston below.
* Johnston – Gaelic *dun breatain* = 'hill-fort, hill of the Strathclyde Britons', it's older name Alcluith is also Gaelic = *ail clud* = 'rock in the river clyde'.
* Watson – Dumbarton is Gaelic *dun Breatann* = 'fortress of the Britons', once the acropolis of the Strathclyde Britons.
** The terms 'Strathclyde Britons' and 'Strathclyde Welsh' are synonymous.

Dumbuck (Old Kilpatrick) –
din buch, dun buch = 'cow-fort'
* Johnston – Gaelic *dun buic* = 'hill of the buck, he-goat'.

Dumfries (Dumfries) – 1183 Dunfres, 1189 Dunfres, 1259 Dunfres, 1395 Drumfreiss, 1465 Dumfrise, also assorted records as Dunfres, Dunfrys, Dumfres, Donfres

din prys = 'shrubwood hill-fort', 'shrubwood hill'
* Johnston – Probably from Welsh *prys*, Gaelic *phreas* so – *dun phreas* = 'copse hill'.
* Watson – In modern Scottish Gaelic the regular term for a bush is *preas*, which does not occur in Irish Gaelic. It is a survival from British, and is to be compared with Welsh *prys* = 'a covert, brushwood', and *presel* = 'a brake'.
** The second element *prys* = 'covert, brushwood, copse, grove,' is obviously Gaelicized to *phreas*, from *preas* which is itself inherited from 'British'.

Dun (Montrose) – 1250 Dun
din = 'hill-fort', *dun* = 'hill'
* Johnston – Gaelic and Irish *dun* = 'a hill' then 'a fort-on-a hill'. Welsh *din*.

Dunad (Crinan) 683 Duinn-Att
dineid = 'fortified place'
din ardd = 'high hill', 'high hill-fort'
* Johnston – Gaelic *dun fhada* = 'long hill'. Watson thinks – not!
* Watson – Skene identifies it as the Gaelic Monadhmor of early mention. Here he has gone astray; it is not Monadhmor = 'big-hill', but Mhoinn Mhor = 'big moss', 'big bog'. Dunadd was certainly an important stronghold.
** Watson's rejection of Skene is hinged on Skene's claim that Monadhmor was so called from the Moss which surrounds it. But rejection of this comparison does not invalidate Skene's identification of Dunadd as Gaelic Monadhmor = 'big hill'. We know that Gaelic *monadh* is inherited from Welsh *mynydd* so, equally, Gaelic *monadhmor* = Welsh *mynyddmawr* = 'big mountain', 'big moorland-pasture', in which case Dunadd Monadhmor is the 'high hill-fort' on the 'big moorland-pasture'.

Dunaverty (Kintyre) – 712 Aberte, 1252 Dunaverdin, 1375 Donaverdyne
aber ty = 'river-mouth by the house'
din aber ty, = 'fort at the river-mouth by the house'
din aber tyn = 'fort at the river mouth by the croft'
* Johnston – Seems to be Gaelic *dun a' bhardainn* = 'hill of the warming or summers'.
* Watson – Gaelic *dun a bhartaigh* = 'Abhartach's fort' (a personal name).
** An interesting name, easily explained in terms of Welsh *aber ty* and *din aber tyn* = 'river-mouth house', or 'fort river-mouth croft'. The earliest 712 record is simply *aber ty* = 'river-mouth by the dwelling'. The later records are embellished by the addition of *din* and the change of *ty* = house to *tyn* = 'croft'. This results in *dinabertyn* which with misplaced Gaelic lenition becomes *dinaferdyn.*

Dunbar (East Lothian) 709 Dinbaer, Dunbarre, 1072 Dunbar
din bar, dun bar = 'fort, hill-fort, on the summit'. See Watson.
* Johnston – Gaelic *dun barr* = 'fort on the height'.
* Watson – Dunbar is 'summit fort', probably taken over from British *din bar* with the same meaning.

Dunbarney (Bridge of Earn) – 1128 Drumbernin, 1214 Dunbernyn
trum prenyn = 'hill-ridge with a little tree' or 'summit with a little tree'.
* Johnston – Gaelic *dun bearna* = 'hill with the gap'.
** The 1128 record indicates *drum prenyn.* Lenition of *trum* to *drum, pren* to *bren,* and metathesis of *re* to *er* gives *drumbernyn.* The 1214 record replaces *drum* = 'ridge with *din,dun* = 'hill-fort, hill', resulting in *dunbernyn* = 'hill, hill-fort with the little tree'. Conversion of Suffix *-yn* to *-y* then gives *dunberny* and thence Dunbarney.

Dunblane (Perths) – 1200 Dumblann, Dumblein, Dunblain.

1272 Dumblin, Dubblain
din blaen = 'fort at the headwaters, the source' (of the Allan river?)
din Blaan = 'fort, hill-fort of St Blaan'
* Johnston – Gaelic *dun blann* = 'hill of St Blann', a 7th century saint, probably an Irish-trained Briton.
* Watson – *dun Blaain* = 'hill of Blann' from St Blaan, 'triumphant Blaan of the Britons', who supposedly had a monastery here.
** Blaan was a Briton so it is likely that the name of his dwelling-place would have been in the 'British' language of his day.

Dunbog, Dinbug (Cupar) – 598 Duinbolg, 1190 Dunbulc, 1250 Dunbulg, 1517 Dunbug
din bwlg = 'hill-fort, fort' on the 'bulky-round body' (a 'lumpy-hill' perhaps?)
* Johnston – Gaelic *dun bolg, dun builg* = 'massive, bellying hill'.
** The Welsh and the Irish are very close here, Welsh *bwlg* is paralleled by Irish *bolg*.

Duncow (Dumfries)
din cau = 'fort in the hollow' or 'fort in the field'. (see Glasgow).
* Johnston – Gaelic *dun gobha* = 'hill of the 'gow', a smith'.
* Watson – Duncow, older Duncoll is in Gaelic *dun-choll* = 'fort of hazels'.

Duncrub, Drumcrub (Strathearn) – 965 Dorsum Crup
drum crwb = 'hump-shaped ridge'
* Johnston – Gaelic *dun crubha* = 'hill with the haunch or shoulder' from Gaelic *crubha*, Welsh *crwb* = 'a hump'.
* Watson – It is 'hill of the hump', and may be, as Skene suggests, the 'Mons Craupius' of History. 'Craupius' would

yield *crup* in Old Welsh and *crwb* = 'a hump, haunch' in modern Welsh.
** The Latin *dorsum* of the 965 record indicates it is a *drum* = a ridge, and not a *din, dun* = a 'hill', a 'hill-fort'. It is interesting that the present name reflects the modern Welsh *crwb* and not the Old Welsh *crup*.

Dundee (Angus) – 1177 Donde, 1182 Dunde, 1200 Dundo, Dunde, Dundho
din de, dun de = 'south-fort', 'south hill-fort'
* Johnston – Probably Gaelic *dun de* = 'hill of God'.
* Watson – The Gaelic name is *dun deagh* = 'fort of daig(h)', daig being a personal name meaning 'fire'.
** The meaning of 'south fort' is evasive, perhaps a better description would be 'southern fort', or 'fort of the Southern District'?

Dundrennan (Berwicks) – 1160 Dundrainan, 1200 Dundraynane, 1461 Dundranan
din drainan, dun drainan = 'fort, hill-fort of little thorns'
* Johnston – Gaelic *draighnean* = 'hill with the thicket'.

Dunfermline (Fife) – 1109 Dumfermelyn, 1124 Dunferlin, 1134 Dunfermelitanus, 1142 Dunfermlin, 1160 Dunfermelin, Dunfermeling 1251 Dunfermline, 1375 Dunferlyne
din ber melin, dun ber melin = 'spear fort mill'
din ber melyn (dunfermelyn) = 'fort of the yellow spear'
* Johnston – Two names seem to have mingled; *ferlin etc.* is from 'Farlan' said to be one of the first colonizers of Ireland. *Fermelin etc.* may be for Gaelic *dun meallain* = 'fort on the hillock' or *dun fiar melain* = 'crooked hill of Melin', a personal name.
** *din ber melin* aspirates and evolves to *dunfermelin* (see 1160 record). Similarly *din fer melyn* goes to *dunfermelyn.* (see 1109 record).

Dunipace (Denny) – 1183 Dunipast, 1190 Dunypais, 1195 Dunipace
din-y-pas = 'fort at the pass, exit'. See Johnston below
* Johnston – Locally thought to be Gaelic *dun na bais* = 'hill of death', but as the site suggests, more probably Welsh *din y pas* = 'hill of the pass, or exit'.
** Welsh *din*, when it appears as such in Scottish place-names, usually means 'fort, hill-fort', when it means 'hill' it usually appears as *dun*, but very often an original *din* is mistakenly Gaelicized as *dun*.

Dunkeld (Perths) – 865 to 1141 Duncalden, Duincaillen, Dunicallen, 1141 Duncheldin, 1150 Dunkeld, 1420 Dunkaldyne
din caledion = 'fort of the Caledonians', – the local British 'Clan'
* Johnston – From the same root, Celtic *caled* = 'hard', as the tribe Caledonii which, it is said, derives from a personal name recorded as Caledo.
* Watson – Gaelic *dun chailleann* = 'fort of the Caledonians'.
** Interestingly the present name holds to the original Welsh *dincaledion* showing that the Gaelic records Duincaillen, Dunicallen were transitory translations into Gaelic and did not reflect common usage.

Dunmore (several) –
din mawr, dun mawr = 'big fort, hill-fort'
din mor, dun mor = 'fort, hill-fort by the sea'
* Johnston – Gaelic *dun mor* = 'big hill'.

Dunmyat, Dummyat, Demyat (Ochils) –
din maiati = 'fort, hill-fort of the Maeatae'. See Johnston below
* Johnston – *dun miati* = 'hill of the Maeatae', a subset of the Damnonii tribe; opinion has it that *miati* derives from Welsh *meiddio* = 'to dare'.

Dunnichen (Forfar) – 'early' Duin *Nechtain,* 1220 Dunnachtyn
din Nechtan = 'Nechtan's fort'
* Johnston – *din nechtan* = 'fort of Nechtan', a Pictish King.
* Watson – Dunnichen, of old Dunechtyn is 'Nechtan's fort'.
** Johnston and Watson agree that here *din* = 'fort' thereby implying Welsh *din* = 'hill-fort' and not Gaelic *dun* = 'hill'.

Dunnikier (Kirkcaldy) – 1250 Duniker
din y caer = 'fort, hill-fort; of the castle'
* Johnston – Gaelic-locative *dun ciar* – 'dark brown hill', or perhaps 'hill of the fort', as in Bankier.
** It may mean that here a later *caer* was sited on top of, or near to, an earlier *din.* Elsewhere *caer* is often found in forms like *kerr* or *keir.*

Dunning (Perth) – 1200 Dunine, later Dunyn
dinyn, dunyn = 'little fort, hill-fort'
* Johnston – Gaelic *dunan* = 'little hill', or 'little hill-fort'.
** The diminutive suffix *-yn* is Welsh, as also is *-an.*

Dunragit (Glenluce) – c.800 Dun-rechet, 1535 Dunregate
din rheged = 'hill-fort of Rheged'. See Watson below.
* Johnston – perhaps Gaelic *dun reachd* = 'hill of sorrow'.
* Watson – *din rheged* = 'fort of Rheged', the site of the old fort is on a rounded eminence called the 'Mote of Dunragit'.
** Rheged was one of the old Kingdoms of the North-Britons.

Dunrod (Kirkcudbright) – 1160 Dunrod, Dunroden
din rhod = 'wheel fort'
din rhoden = 'little-wheel fort'
* Johnston – Gaelic, either *dun roid* = 'hill, hill-fort of sweet gale, bog myrtle' or *dun rod* = 'hill, hill-fort by the road'.
** The meaning may be 'wheel-shaped fort', 'circular fort', or 'round fort'.

Duns (Berwicks) – 1296 Duns
dinas = 'fortified hill settlement'
* Johnston – Gaelic *dun* = 'a hill'. Dun with English plural becomes Duns.
** The name also appears as Dunce as in 'John Scotus Dunce', i.e. John, the Scot, from Dunce, which is probably indicative of the correct pronunciation. There is an iron-age hill fortress on what is now called Duns Law, above the town. With *din* turned to *dun*, as often occurs, the name becomes *dunas*, which again points to 'Duns' as being pronounced 'dunce'. Modern Welsh *dinas* = 'city', 'city fortress'.

Dunscore (Dumfries) – 1300 Dunescor, 1465 Dunescoir
dinas cor = 'fortified hill-settlement, of the tribe'
* Johnston – Gaelic *dun sgor* = 'hill of the sharp rock'.
** The term *cor* has more than one meaning; as *cor, cordd* = 'tribe, family'; as *cor, corrod* = 'dwarf'; 'spider', so alternatively 'city of the dwarf': or 'city of the spider'.

Dunsinane (Dunkeld) – circa 970 *Pictish Chronicles* Dunsinoen
dinasin oen = 'little hill-settlement of the lamb'
dinasin wyn = 'little hill-settlement of the lambs'
* Johnston – Probably Gaelic *dun sine, sineachan* = 'hill with the dugs, or breasts'.
** Obviously *dinas* here becomes *dunas* then *duns* as in Duns.

Dunsyre – 1180 Dunsyer, 1300 Dunsier
dinas sir = 'hill-settlement of solace'
* Johnston – Gaelic *dun siar* = 'west hill'.
** Dunsyre is at the Western end of the Pentland Hills; Johnston's interpretation is therefore the more likely, unless there is also site evidence of a hill-fortification.

Dura Den (Cupar, Fife) –
dwrau = 'waters'
dur dwr = 'hard water, or stream'
Scots 'Den' = 'narrow wooded valley'.
* Johnston – Gaelic *dobharach* = 'watery place', plus Scots 'Den' = 'wooded glen'; cognate with Old English 'Dene'.
* Watson – does not deal directly with the name Dura but an insight into what it may mean can possibly be obtained by recourse to his dissertation on the similarly sounding name Duror (early records: Durdowar, Durwoir, Durgure, Durgwyr) which Watson couples with that of Morar then states: *'Both these district names, originally names of streams. are doubtless old British names taken over into Gaelic'*. Morar, he says, is on record as Mordhowar which is in Gaelic *mordhobhar* = 'big water' (cf. Welsh *mawrdwr*) and similarly Duror is *durdhobhar* = 'hard water', 'rocky water'. Of the Scots-Gaelic *dhobhar* Watson says: *'It was doubtless borrowed from Welsh . . . '*. In modern Welsh the noun *dur* = 'steel' and the verb *durio* = 'to harden', 'to steel'.
** Since 'steel' as we know it today was invented only in fairly recent times it is possible that *durio* = 'to harden' reflects an older 'British' meaning = 'hard'. Gaelic *durdhobhar* is then paralleled by Welsh *durdwr* = 'steel water / steel stream', 'hard water / hard stream' or as Watson seems to prefer = 'rocky stream'. David Ross sees the name Duror as the name of the stream in Glen Duror and as Scottish Gaelic *dur* = 'hard', plus Scottish Gaelic *dohbar* = 'water' (*durdobhar* = 'hard water, or stream'), plus Scots 'Den' = 'narrow wooded valley'. Today Dura Den is a narrow, wooded valley through which flows the Ceres Burn, what 'Ceres' means and whether the stream always had this name is a mystery. Unfortunately we have no early records for Dura Den itself and therefore nothing to guide us.

Durie (Leven) –
dwrau = 'waters', 'streams'.
dwryn = 'little water', 'little stream'
* Johnston – Gaelic *dobharach* (as in Dura) with locative *-ie* suffix.
** It is difficult to see what Johnston is suggesting. Is it *dobharachie* or *dobharie*?. Otherwise conversion of P-Celtic *-yn* diminutive suffix to Scots *-ie,* straightforwardly changes *dwryn* to *dwrie,* from which Durie.

Duthil (Carrbridge) – 1230 Dothol, 1336 Dotheleie
dwy ddol, dau ddol = place of – 'two meadows'
* Johnston – Gaelic *tuathail* = 'north, north-side' of Creag-an-fhithich – a local derivation.
** Presumably Johnston means *dal tuathail* = 'meadow at the north-side' of the Creag? Otherwise *dauddol* – accords with 1230 record; and *dwy ddolyn, dau ddolyn* = 'two little meadows', then *dwy ddolie, dau ddolie* by change of *-yn* to *-ie.* ('dd' = 'th') – accords with 1336 record.

Dye River (Kincardine) –
dwy = the 'god', 'goddess' river. See Johnston below.
* Johnston – Perhaps Celtic for 'goddess' as in the Dwyfor and Dwybach streams, around Criccieth, northern Wales.

E

Eaglesham (Paisley) – 1158 Egilsham, 1309 Eglishame
eglwys ham = 'church village'
* Johnston – Not from Gaelic *eaglais* = 'church'; but from 'Egil 'or 'Egli' a personal name from Switzerland.
** *eglwys ham* is a hybrid; Welsh *eglwys* = 'church' plus English *ham* = 'town', 'village', 'steading', 'hamlet'. Johnston

however gets full marks for imagination!

Earn River (Perths) – 1100 Eirenn, 1190 Erne, 1195 Erin, 1300 Eran
eirin = 'plum-tree river'
* Johnston – Gaelic *eireann,* the genitive of *Eire,* now the name of the Republic of Ireland but originally a local P-Celtic Goddess.
** This is a 'river' name and is therefore likely to be pre-Gaelic and be of ancient and uncertain P-Celtic or even pre-Celtic derivation. Johnston's idea of a Goddess type river-name could well be true, but his Gaelic attribution is unlikely.

Earnock (Hamilton) –
eirynog = 'plummy' = 'place full of plum-trees' perhaps?
* Johnston – Probably Gaelic *earnach* = 'place of sloes'.

Ecclefechan (Dumfries) – 1303 Eglesfeghan, 1507 Egilfeichane, 1510 Eglisfechane, 1542 Egilphechane, 1570 Hecklefeugham
eglwys fechan = 'little church'. See Watson below.
* Johnston – Gaelic *eaglais fiachan* = 'church of St Fechan' – the 'Little Raven', Abbot of Fother, from County Meath in Ireland, in St Kentigern's time.
* Watson – can be compared to Llanfechan in Montgomeryshire; the second part, which is supposed to be the name of St Fechin of Fore, may however be the mutated form of the Welsh adjective *bechan* = 'little'. The meaning then would be 'little church'.
** As a place-name in Wales Llanfechan is said to mean 'little church'. There is no mention of a Saint Fechin in *The Book of Welsh Saints.*

Eccles (Coldstream) – 1297 Hecles
eglwys = 'the church'. See Watson below.
* Johnston – Gaelic *eaglais* = 'church'. St Mary's Nunnery

founded here in 1155.
* Watson – 'Eccles' in Berwickshire may represent Welsh *eglwys* rather than Gaelic *eaglais*, as also in Ecclesmachan.

Ecclesmachan (Uphall) – 1250 Eglismanin, Eglismauchin, 1296 Egglesmauhy, 1404 Eglismauquhy
eglwys Machan = 'church of St Machan'
* Johnston – Probably, 'church of St Machan', a disciple of the 6th century St Cadoc.
* Watson – St Machan, who is commemorated in Ecclesmachan, is said to be a disciple of St Cadoc of Llancarvan, probably a contemporary of St Kentigern (St Mungo). For the first element see Eccles.
** Cadoc / Cadog was a Welsh Saint and perhaps Machan was one also.

Eddleston (Peebles) – 1200 Edoluestone, 1296 Edalstone, 1305 Edwylstone (earlier Penteiacob)
pen ty iacob = 'headland of James' house'. See Watson below.
pen ty iacob = 'first house, (main residence) of Jacob'
* Johnston – 'Edulf's Village', in 1189 lands here were granted to Edulf, a Saxon. The Celtic name had been Pente-Jacob.
* Watson – Eddleston near Peebles, appears on record first as 'Penteiacob', a purely Welsh name, meaning 'headland of James's House'.
** *pen* has several related meanings. See earlier chapters.

Edinburgh – see separate chapter – 'Edinburgh Names'.

Eglisgirig, Eglisgreig (St Cyrus) – 1243 Ecclesgreig
eglwys graig = 'church by the crag'
* Johnston – Quotes Watson as: 'church of St Cyricus'.
** From previous names, e.g. Eccles, it is certain that Watson would hold that here Eccles = *eglwys* = 'church', in which case the likelihood of the second element also being Welsh is increased; in compound Welsh words, such as

creigfa = 'rockery', *craig* = 'rock' is sometimes seen in the form *creig* which itself aspirates to *greig*.

Eglismonichty (Monifieth) – circa 970 Eglis Monichti, 1211 Eglismenythok, 1245 Eglismeneyttock, 1260 Eglismenigcott, 1482 Eglismonichto, 1511 Eglismonitho
eglwys mynach ty = 'church by the Monk's house'
eglwys mynyddog = 'church of the mountain'
* Johnston – refers to Watson.
* Watson – It sems to be the same as Eglismenigott of 1260; the name here appears to be from 'mo-Nechtan' (i.e. 'church of Nechtan').
** The two Welsh interpretations may not be mutually exclusive, the place may well be by a 'Monk's House' *and* by a 'Mountain'. The former accords well with the records of 970 and 1482 and the latter accords well with the records of 1211, 1245 and 1511. The record of 1260 is a good example of scribal error.

Eildon Hills (Melrose) – 1120 Aeldona, Eldunum, 1143 Eldune
ail din, = 'second hill-fort', or 'secondary hill-fort'
ael din = 'brow fort' i.e. 'fort on the brow of the hill'
* Johnston – Probably a hybrid; – Gaelic *aill* = 'rock, cliff, plus Old English *dun* = 'hill', therefore = 'rock hill' or 'cliff hill'.
** The early Latin *dunum* suggests 'fort', and there is an Iron-age or Bronze-age fort atop these hills, as well as a later Roman one.

Elgin (Aberdeen) – 1140 Helgyn,
helygyn = place of – 'little-willows'
helygen = place of – 'the willow tree'
* Johnston – pronunciation by local Gaels is *'ailigin'*, a word often thought to be pre-Celtic in origin.
* Watson – Eilginn, Elgin, has been explained by Kuno

Meyer as for *eilgin* = 'little Ireland'. 'Elg' being nowadays a poetic name for Ireland. The difficulty is that the diminutive in *-in,* which is common in Irish-Gaelic, is rare with us (Scots-Gaelic).

** Johnston's 'local Gaelic pronunciation' fits almost perfectly with Welsh *helygyn.* Watson's ambivalence on Gaelic diminutives seems well founded.

Elvan Water, Elvanfoot (Beattock) – c 1170 contemporary with Brothyr-Alewyn in the same district

al-gwen = 'very white, bright', stream

* Johnston – Probably Welsh *al-gwen* = 'very white, bright', stream. Compare river Alwen, N. Wales.

* Watson – Elvan, in Strathclyde, is a British stream name.

** *al-gwen* aspirates to *alwen* but this interpretation only holds if the name is synonymous with the Brothyr 'Alewyn' mentioned in the record of 1170. Otherwise Watson's 'British' interpretation must hold and it may be no coincidence that 'Elvan' appears as a saint name in Wales. See Tala.

Erngath, Irongath Hill (Bo'ness) – 1337 Arnegayth, 1487 Ardyngity

arddyn caith = 'little-hill, little-height, of the villeins, serfs, captives'

* Johnston – Gaelic *aird an gaoith* = 'height of the wind', 'windy hill' perhaps?

* Watson – Irongath (Linlithgow) is probably Gaelic *Earrann-gaoithe* = 'marsh division'.

** *arddyn caith* aspirates to *ardyngaith,* but the records are late and must be uncertain. Otherwise slipshod enunciation could lead from *ardyngaith* to *aryngaith* and thence to Irongath and Erngath?

Errol (Carse of Gowrie) – 1190 Erolyn, 1199 Erole

yr olyn = 'the little-ravine'

ar ole = 'at the ravine'
* Johnston – Perhaps Pictish: Welsh *ar ole* = 'on the dingle'.
** Modern Welsh *ole* = 'ravine', *ar olyn* = 'at, or on the little-ravine'.

Erskine (Renfrew) – 1225 Erskin, 1227 Yrskin, 1262 Ireskin, 1300 Harskin, Irschen
ir ysgyn = 'the green ascent' See Johnston below
* Johnston – Quotes W.C. Mackenzie's suggested Welsh *ir ysgyn* = 'the green ascent'. Suits the site well. (he says).
** Modern Welsh gives *ir* = green, fresh: *esgyn, ysgyn* = 'to ascend'; *esgyniad, esgynfa* = 'ascent'. In Welsh place-names a leading *ys* is often truncated to *s* hence *irsgyn* from *ir ysgyn.*

F

Fala (Soutra) – 1250 Faulawe, 1508 Faulohill
fala = 'the outflow from lake' – place
* Johnston – Old English *fah hloew* = 'pale dun hill'.
** Below the northern edge of Soutra Hill is 'Fala Flow Loch', out of which a stream, now known as the Dean Burn, flows down through Fala village. The name echoes that of Bala, N.Wales which again has the meaning 'place at outflow from lake'; *fala* is the lenited form of *bala.*

Falkirk (Stirlings) – 1065 Egglesbreth, 1166 Ecclesia de Eiglesbrec, 1235 Varie Capele, 1298 Chapelle de Fayerie, 1298 Vayre Chapelle, 1300 Fowe Chapel, 1381 Fallkirk, 1382 Fawkirc, 1600 Fawkirk (as it is still pronounced locally today)
eglwys brith = 'spotted church'
* Johnston – Gaelic *eaglais breac* or Welsh *eglwys brith* = 'speckled church'.
* Watson – Gaelic *an eaglais bhreac,* which may represent a

British form. In these examples the English speakers knew the meaning of the Gaelic terms, as in earlier times the Gaelic speakers knew the meaning of the British terms.
** Watson infers that there was a straight progression of interpretation from 'British' through Gaelic to English, but in this area there is a distinct possibility that the language went directly from Welsh to English with the Gaelic translation coming much later. Nicolaisen deals with this name at length and in great detail; it suffices to say that the present name is Old English *faw kirk* = 'spotted church' and that this in turn derives, through several steps, from an original Welsh *eglwys brith* = 'spotted church'. It is said that 'spotted' indicates a church built of mottled stones, but there is no evidence that such a building ever existed. There is alternatively a remote possibility that it means 'church of the Spotted People' – i.e. the Picts! An intriguing thought perhaps – but probably nothing more than that.

Faslane (Gareloch) – 1351 Faslane, 1373 Fosselane
ffos y lan = 'ditch by the enclosure'
faes-y lan = 'flat-ground place', or 'flat-ground by the church'
* Johnston – Gaelic *fos*, Old Irish *foss* and Gaelic *lann, lainne* = 'on the enclosed land', an 'abode station'.

Fiddich, Glen (Mortlach) –
glyn gwyddach = 'valley of Gwyddach' where Gwyddach (earlier Pictish Guidid) is personal name = 'the little-woodsman'. See Watson below.
* Johnston – Fiddich was one of the sons of the legendary Cruithne (Picts).
* Watson – Glen Fiddich in Banffshire, given to me in Gaelic as *gleann fithich*, cannot be 'Raven's Glen' as claimed. The Welsh *guid, gwydd* are favourite elements in personal names and an early King of the Picts was named 'Guidid' = 'woodsman', which may be the British original of this same name.

** *gwydd* = 'woods', *gwyddach* = 'little woods', but the mutation *g* to *f* required to get Fwyddach, and hence 'Fiddich' as a personal name, from Gwyddach does not occur in modern Welsh. But see Fortingall for Watson's theory of Old British '*v*' developing into Pictish '*f*' on the one hand and into Welsh '*g*' on the other hand.

Findhorn (Forres) – 1153 Eren, 1595 Fyndorn, Fynderan, Fynderne. The River Findhorn is still called Findearn along part of it's course.
ffin earn = 'boundary along the river Earn'
* Johnston – Gaelic *fionn earn* = 'Earn river with white, clear banks'.
* Watson – Findhorn is the dative locative of Gaelic *Fionn-Eire* = 'white Ireland' doubtless referring to the white sands of the estuary.
** River Earn might be 'plum tree river' from *eirin* = 'plums', but is more likely pre-Celtic. All the above interpretations ignore the intrusive 'd'. A possible solution is *ffin daren, ffin deren* = 'boundary of little-oak-trees'; or alternatively 'boundary along the Oak-Trees river'. Rivers with 'Oak' names are found in Wales.

Findon (Easter Ross) – 1456 Fyndoun
ffin din, ffin dun ='boundary fort'
* Johnston – Gaelic *fionn dun* = 'clear, white hill'.
** Other Findons at Gamrie and Port Lethan, three more in England – are they Gaelic too?

Fingland (Peebles) – 1100 Findgland
ffin glyn = 'boundary valley'
* Johnston – Old Irish; Gaelic *fionn gleann* = 'white, clear glen'.
* Watson – Fingland is for *finn glend* later *fionn ghleann* = 'white glen, 'fair glen'; the term occurs four distinct times (in Lothian), once as 'Finglen', which is the same. 'Glen' appears

thirty times ; some of the instances may be Welsh.

Finnart (Loch Long) – 1350 Fynnard
ffin ardd = 'boundary height'
* Johnston – Gaelic *fionn ard* = 'clear height'.

Fintray (Kintore) – 1182 Fintreth, 1203 Fintrith, 1219 Fintrefe, 1300 Fyntre, 1316 Fyntreff
ffin tre, ffin tref = 'boundary steading'
ffin traeth = 'boundary beach'
* Johnston – Celtic for 'white, fine house', Welsh *tre, tref*; though perhaps '-treth' may mean 'shore', 'beach-of-river' or 'sea', as in Pentraeth (Menai Bridge) and Pentreth (Cornwall).
* Watson – Gaelic *finn* = 'white' plus Welsh *tre, tref* = 'stead'; the name represents Welsh *gwendref* = 'pleasant stead', which was, I consider the original.
** *traeth* = 'beach' is not necessarily along a shoreline.

Fintry (Denny, and the Cumbraes) – 1225 Fyntryf, 1238 Fyntrie
ffin tre, ffin tref = as for Fintray.

Fogo (Duns) – 1150 Fogghou, 1300 Fogov, 1352 Foggowe
* Johnston – Probably *fog how* = 'dry-grass hollow'. Welsh *ffwg* = 'dry-grass', plus Old English *holg, holh* / Scots *howe* = 'hollow'.
** My Welsh dictionaries give *ffwg* = 'volatile', 'runny'. I fear this name 'needs more work'!

Forbes (Alford) – 1300 Forbes, 1443 Forbas
ffor bas = the – 'road out', 'exit road'
* Johnston – Old Irish / Old Gaelic *forba* = 'field', 'district'; with Pictish ending of place, *-ais*.
** On today's map 'Forbes' appears as 'Forbestown' on the road out from Aberdeen to Inverness. Welsh *ffor* is an alternative spelling for *ffordd*.

Fordoun (Kincardine) – 1100 Fotherdun, Forddun, 1130 Fordouin
ffordd (y) din, dun, = the – 'road by the fort, hill-fort'
* Johnston – May be 'field with the fort', or 'wood on the hill' Gaelic *dun, duin.* plus Pictish-Gaelic *fothir* which may mean 'field'.
* Watson – Fotherdun means 'on the shank above Dunottar' rather than 'above Fordoun'. Fotherdun, being a poetic inversion of Dun-fother (now Dunottar); *fother* may be compared tentatively with Irish *fothair, fuithir,* meaning, apparently, 'a dell', 'a hollow'; and further with Welsh *godir* = 'a slope, lowland', from *go,* Old Welsh *guo,* = 'under', or 'sub-' or with Gaelic *fo* = 'under' and *'tir'* = land.
** Although Watson is not explicit on this point it seems he considers *fother* to be a Pictish term of uncertain meaning which he then attempts to derive by inference. Taking his suggested derivations a little further – Welsh *godir* is given as (1) = 'region', (2) = lowland, (3) = slope; *go, gwo* = 'under' and *tir* = land. The connection between P-Celtic Pictish *fother* and P-Celtic Welsh *godir,* including how the one could perhaps have developed from, or had common ancestry with, the other is here left open, but see Forteviot.

Forres (Morays) – 1187 Fores, 1190 Forays, 1283 Forais
fforas, fforais = place – 'full-of roadways, pathways'
* Johnston – *farais* = 'brink, edge, border', from Gaelic *foir* with common Pictish sufix *-ais* = 'place of'.
* Watson – Gaelic name 'Farais' is probably = 'little shrubbery', from *fo* = 'under' plus *ras* = 'wood'.

Forteviot (Perths) – 970 Fothertabaicht, 1165 Fortheuiet, 1175 Forteuiet, 1187 Fertheviot, 1280 Forteuyoth, 1251 Forteviot
y-godir de myat shortened and aspirated to *fordefyat* ='south lowland of the Maetae'; see Fordoun for *godir* to *For*
* Johnston – As for Fedderat (Brucklay), the first element 'For-' is from Pictish-Gaelic *foder* or *feder,* hardened form of

Old Gaelic *fother,* a word of doubtful meaning, perhaps 'field' or 'wood'. The second element *tabaicht* suggests Gaelic *t'abbachd* = 'abbey', so possibly = 'abbey slope' or 'abbey lowland'. See Fordoun. Watson prefers to derive it from *fothir* = 'lower-place'.

* Watson – Relates it to a Gaelic name, *Fothuir-tabaicht,* mentioned in the Pictish Chronicles.The first term is *fother* = 'slope' which he relates to Welsh *godir, fodir* as in Fordoun. The second element, he says, seems to be the same as the Irish place-name Tobacht, the meaning of which is obscure to him.

** There seems to be an agreement that the first element is Pictish *fother* which is somehow related to Welsh *godir* = 'under region', 'lowland', 'slope', the second element is possibly *de fyot,* where *fyot* is the lenited form of Myot, relating to the Maetae tribe, one time rulers of this area and *de* = 'southern', therefore 'southern lowland of the Maeatae'. Therefore *fordefyot* and hence Forteviot. See Dunyat, Dummyat, Demyat and Fordoun.

Fortingall (Kenmore) – 1240 Forterkil, 1300 Fothergill, 1544 Fortyrgill
y-gwerthyr cil = 'fortress church' or 'corner fortress'. See Watson below.

* Johnston – Old Gaelic *fothir* = 'field', 'wood' and, possibly, Gaelic *choill* ='wood' or *cill* = 'church' – therefore either 'field by the wood' or 'church by the wood'.

* Watson – Forter, Fortyr, Forther are all probably Gaelic forms of a term corresponding to Welsh *gwerthyr* = 'fortress', *y werthyr* = 'the fortress'; thus Forter, Fortyr, plus Gaelic *cill* = 'church', gives 'fortress church'.

** Watson's argument, given in his book, seems to be that an original British *vertur* passed into Gaelic as *fertur* then *fortyr, forter, fother,* etc.; and into Welsh as *gwerthyr,* the Gaelic form having come directly from Old British before this had passed into the stage corresponding to Old Welsh. Obviously then these Scots-Gaelic forms did not come from Irish-Gaelic and the original British *vertur* may have passed from Old British into Pictish before being *inherited* by Scots-Gaelic; in which case one could expect the meanings of *forther* etc.(Pictish?) and *gwerthyr* (Welsh) to have remained much the same. The other significant aspect of Watson's dissertation is his association of 'Pictish'/Welsh *Forter, Fother, Fortyr* with Gaelic *cill* = 'church', but on the principle that one Welsh element in a place-name indicates the presence of other Welsh elements in that same name then Watson's dissertation supports the proposition that in Scottish place-names which include a Welsh or 'Pictish' element the appearance of 'kil' as an additional element indicates the presence of Welsh *cil* having the same meaning 'church' as Gaelic *cill*.

Fortrose (Cromarty) – 1455 Forterose
godir rhos = 'lowland moor' (see Fordoun)
gwerthyr rhos = 'fortress moor' (see Fortingall)
* Johnston – Probably Gaelic *foter rois* = 'under, beneath, the promontory'.
** There is a problem here! Should 'forter' be treated as 'fortress' (see Fortingall) or as 'lowland', or 'slope', (see Fordoun)? The only record 'Forter- rose' favours the former but Johnston favours the latter. In either case '-rose' = *rhos* = 'moor'. Therefore, firstly *gwerthyr rhos* = 'fortress moor', and secondly *godir rhos* = 'lowland moor'. According to some of Watson's arguments it would seem that Gaelic *foter, fothir* is from a British root *vo tir* = 'under land' which passed into Scots-Gaelic, or Pictish, as *fo tir*, then *fothir*, and into Welsh as *go tir*, then *godir*.

Fossoway (Kinross) – 1220 Fossedmege, 1476 Fossochquhuy
ffossed mig = 'ditchy bog' (= Fossedmege)
ffossach cae = 'little-ditch field' (= Fossochquhuy)

* Johnston – Gaelic *fasadh mhaga* = 'dwelling in the plain', Old Gaelic *fasach mhaga.*
* Watson – In Gaelic Fossoway was first *fossadmag*, later *fosadmhagh* = 'level plain'.
** Watson gives the Welsh equivalent of *fossadmagh* as *gwastadfa* = 'a level place'. The 1220 record fits *ffossed mig*, the 1476 record fits *ffossach cae.*

Fowlis (Crieff) – 1147 Foulis, 1195 Fowlis, 1198 Fougles, 1208 Foglais
ffwg glais lenited to *ffwglais, ffwlais* = 'volatile, turbulent, stream'
* Johnston, refers to Watson – Gaelic *fo-ghlais, folais* = 'under-stream', 'sub-stream', 'rivulet'.

Fruid Water (Hart Fell) –
* Johnston – Welsh *ffrwd* = 'impulsive, hasty' stream
** Modern Welsh *ffrwd* = 'stream', 'torrent'.

G

Gadgirth (Coylton) – 1508 Gaitgirth, 1558 Gadgirth
y coed garth = 'the wood by the garth'
* Johnston – Probably from Northern England Dialect *gad* = 'a land measure of varying length' plus *girth, garth* = 'enclosure'.
** Old Welsh *y cait garth* aspirated to *gaitgarth.* Welsh *garth* can have various meanings – 'enclosure or fold', 'garden', 'hill-ridge', 'buttress'. Alternatively *y cad garth* lenited to *gadgarth* = 'battle ridge' or any of the other meanongs of *garth*. However the records are late and therefore uncertain.

Galashiels (Borders) – 1237 Galuschel, 1416 Gallowschel, 1442 Galowayscheelis, 1503 Galloschelis

* Johnston – a hybrid = 'huts by the Gala River', Scots *shiels* = 'huts', plus the Welsh, *gal gwy, gal wy* = 'clear, fair stream' or else *gwala* = 'the full stream', for the name of the Gala River.
** Welsh *gal* = 'spread-out', 'clear', 'fair'; *gwy, wy* = 'water', 'fluid'. Hence the name Gala Water?

Galbraith Inch (Loch Lomond) – 1342 to 1362 Galbrath, 1464 Gawbrath
ynys gal braith = 'island speckled with reed(s)'
* Johnston – Gaelic *gall-Breatnach* = 'stranger', 'Briton or Welshman,' or 'Lowlander'. A family of 'Galbraith', 1492 Galbreytht, used to live here.
** In the suggested Welsh interpretation *cal* = 'reed' aspirates to *gal*. The practice of naming a place after the name of its owners or inhabitants is extremely rare in Scotland or any of the other Celtic areas. It is more common in England. Here it is more likely the family took their name from the place.

Galbrathe (Wigtown) – 1296 Galbrathe
See Galbraith (Loch Lomond) above.

Gargunnock (Stirling) – 1470 Gargunnow
caer gynog = 'crowned fort'
caer gynach = 'little-wedge fort', 'little chisel-shaped, fort'
* Johnston – Perhaps Gaelic *gart guineach* = 'sharp-pointed enclosure'.
** Welsh *caer gynog* aspirates to *gaergynog* and *caer gynach* to *gaergynach* which may be exhibiting the not uncommon change of -ach to -o thus giving *gaergyno* from which Gargunnow. But the record is late.

Garnkirk (Glasgow) – 1116 Lengartheyn, 1515 to 1566 Gartynkirk
llan garthyn = 'church with small enclosure, garden', or 'church by the little hill-ridge'

* Johnston – Gaelic *gartan cearc, gartan circe* = 'little enclosure for hens'. But it seems 1116 Lengartheyn, where *len* = Old Celtic for 'church' (Gaelic *lann*, Welsh *llan*), is then = 'little enclosure church'. Later 'kirk' simply replaces *len, lann.*
** *llangarthyn.*aspirates to *langarthyn.* Later Scots *kirk* replaces *llan* to give *garthynkirk.* It is unsure from whence Johnston obtains his 'Old Celtic' *len,* and in any case Gaelic *lann* is simply Welsh *llan* in what Watson describes as 'Gaelic Dress'!

Garscadden (Irvine) – 1373 Gartscadane
garth sgadan = 'herrings garden, enclosure' (Fish-yard perhaps?)
* Johnston – *gart sgadan* = 'enclosure for herrings' (for curing?).

Garscube (Glasgow) – 1457, 1458 Gartskcube
garth ysgub = 'corn-sheaf enclosure'. (Corn-Yard perhaps?)
* Johnston – Scots-Gaelic *gart sguaib* = 'enclosure for corn-sheaves'.
** As in other Welsh instances the 'y' in *ysgub* discards to give *garthsgub* wherein the *ths* coalesces to give *garsgub* from which Garscube.

Gartclosh (Stirling) –
garth clais = 'enclosure ditch', or 'hill-ridge rivulet' – or combinations of either.
* Johnston – Gaelic *gart clois* = 'enclosure ditch'.

Gartclush (Lanarks) –
See Gartclosh.

Gartcosh (Glasgow) – 1520 Gartgois
garth caws = 'cheese enclosure'. (Cheese-yard, Cheese-shop?)
* Johnston – Scots-Gaelic *gart cois* = 'enclosure with the hole or cave'.

** Cartgois may be the aspirated form *garthgaws,* whereas the modern name retains the original unaspirated form *garthcaws?*

Garth (Aberfeldy) –
garth = 'enclosure', 'enclosed space', 'fold', 'garden', 'hill-ridge'
* Johnston – Old English *geard,* Old Norse *gard-r,* Middle English *garth* = 'enclosure', 'garden'.
** In this area the influence of the Old P-Celtic Welsh language must surely hold sway over alien English or Norse possibilities?

Garthdee (Aberdeen) –
garth de = 'southern enclosure', or = 'southern hill-ridge'
* Johnston – Aberdeen Scots *garth* = 'dam, weir, for catching fish', also = 'gravel, river-shingle'.
** My Scots Dictionary gives *garth* = either 'enclosure, garden, yard' or 'shallow part of river, stretch of shingle – used as ford'. Johnston makes no attempt to explain the element '*-dee*'.

Gartmore (Aberfoyle) –
garth mawr =' big enclosure, or garden', or else = 'big hill-ridge'
* Johnston – Gaelic *gart mor* = 'big enclosure'.

Gartnavel (Glasgow) –
*garthyn afa*l = 'little apple garden' (little apple orchard?)
* Johnston – Gaelic *gart n' abhal* = 'enclosure with the apples', i.e. 'Orchard' or 'Applegarth'.

Gartocharn (Balloch) – 1485 Gartcarne, 1494 Garncarn, 1605 Gartoquharne
garth carn, garth-y-carn = 'enclosure with cairn' or else 'hill-ridge of the cairn'
* Johnston – Gaelic *gart a' chairn* = 'enclosure with the cairn'.

** *garthcarn* fits the 1485 record, *garthycarn* the 1605 record. The 1494 record id obviously a scribal error.

Garturk (Coatbridge) –
garth twrch = 'boar, hog, enclosure', 'Pig-yard'
* Johnston – Gaelic *gart torc, gart tuirc* = 'enclosure of the boar(s) or hog(s)'.

Garvald (East Lothian) – 1250 Garvald
garw allt = 'rough wooded-hillside along a stream'
* Johnston – Gaelic *garbh alld, garbh allt* = 'rough stream'.
* Watson – *garbh-allt* = 'rough burn'; the primary meaning of *allt* is 'steep, precipice' and it is rather notable to find it used in the modern sense of 'burn' so early as 1210.
** Modern Scots-Gaelic *allt* is given as 'river with precipitous banks', 'a stream', 'a brook'. It is not found in Irish-Gaelic. Modern Welsh *gallt, allt* = 'the side of a hill', 'wooded hill-side', 'woody-cliff', 'tract of woodland', 'a wood', 'a hill'.

Gelder Burn (Balmoral) –
gal dwr = 'clear, fair stream' or else 'spread-out stream'
* Johnston – Gaelic *geal dobhar* = 'clear, fair stream'.
* Watson – Gaelic *gealdhobhar* = 'bright stream' (Watson also says – *dobur, dhobar,* a name for water, was *doubtless borrowed from Welsh*).
** Modern Scots-Gaelic *geal* = 'white', 'clear', 'bright', or else = 'leech', So 'leech-stream' could also be a possibility?

Giffen (Ayr) – 1233 Giffin, 1278 Gyffin
See Johnston below.
* Johnston – As the sites show, Welsh *cefn* = 'a ridge'.

Giffnock (Glasgow) –
See Johnston below.
* Johnston – It is a diminutive of Giffen = 'little-ridge' (i.e. *cefnog, cefnoc*).

Gillespie (Old Luce) – early reference is 'Pont Killespiek'
cil esgob aspirated to *gilesgyb* = 'sanctuary, church of the Bishop'.
* Johnston – Gaelic *cill easbuig* = 'cell, church of the Bishop'.
** The first word-element, *gill,* is best satisfied by the Welsh *gil* this being the soft aspiration (lenited) form of *cil,* but the second word-element, *espie,* is best satisfied by the Gaelic *easbuig*. On the principle that whereas an original Welsh name is open to partial Gaelicisation but there is no mechanism by which a later Gaelic name can suffer partial Welshification, it has to be assumed that the original name was once wholly Welsh and in this case was probably *gil esgyb* as above.

Glasgow – 1116 Glascu, 1136 Glasgu, 1158 Glascow, 1157-78 Glascu
glas cau, glasgau = 'green hollow'
glas cae, glasgae = 'green field'
* Johnston – Welsh *glas cu* = 'dear stream'. The 'stream' in question is possibly the Molendinar. As likely is Welsh *glas cau* = 'green hollows' which agrees with the vulgar pronunciation Gles-cay.
* Watson – Welsh *glas gu,* the first part is *glas* = 'green', the second part, with 'c' mutated to 'g' after the adjective, is the same as in Linlithgow, and the name most probably means 'green hollow', which was doubtless descriptive of the ancient site.
** Modern Glaswegians take a highly selective and imaginatively romantic attitude to the name of their city and prefer to describe it as the 'Dear Green Place'. Edinburgh residents have a less romantic interpretation!

Glasmont (Kirkcaldy) – 1178 Glasmonth
glas munt, glas mynydd = 'green mount, mountain', 'green moorland-pasture'

** mont, month, mount, monad, mounth etc., are commonly found corruptions indicative of an original *mynydd.* The 1178 record fits *glasmynydd* but the present name fits *glasmwnt* better. The meanings are similar.

Glass River (Beauly) – early reference – 1309 Straglass
glas = 'green', 'grey', 'blue'
* Johnston – Gaelic *glas* = 'grey, dark looking'.
** The 1309 record will probably be *ystrad glas* = Broad-valley of the Grey River, Green River'. Slovenly speech habits soon reduce *ystrad glas* to Straglass.

Glass (Huntly) –
glais = a 'ditch, or 'stream'
glas = 'green / grey' stream, as 'glass' river at Beauly
* Johnston – Old Gaelic *glas* = 'a River'.

Glas(s)ford (Hamilton) – 1210 Glasfruth, Glasfurth,1296 Glasford
See Johnston below.
* Johnston – Original Welsh *glas ffridd, glas frith* = 'green mountain pasture': or Gaelic *glas frith* = 'green forest' ('forest' = 'wild mountain place).

Glasterlaw (Forfar) –
glas tir = 'green land', with English 'Law' added at some later date
* Johnston – hybrid, Gaelic *glas tir* = 'green land' plus Old English *hloew* = hill.
** Interesting to observe that Welsh *glas tir* is exactly paralleled here by both Scots-Gaelic and Irish-Gaelic *glas tir.*

Glencairn (Thornhill) – 1179 Glencarn
glyn carn = 'valley of the cairn'
* Johnston – Gaelic *gleann carn* = 'glen of the cairn': Gaelic *carn, cairn* = 'cairn', 'heap of stones'.
** The word *carn* can be found in my Scots Gaelic

dictionary, but not *cairn* – which does however appear in my Scots dictionary. Neither appear in my Irish Gaelic dictionary. So did Welsh *carn* pass first into Scots? – or did it pass first into Scots Gaelic?

Glencaple (Dumfries) – 1240 Glencaple
glyn cau pwll = 'valley (glen) with a pool in the hollow'
glyn cae pwll = 'valley (glen)with a pool in the field'
* Johnston – Gaelic *glen capull, glen capuill* = 'valley of the mare'.
** The pronunciation invited by the spelling Glencaple would favour the *glyn cau pwll* option, particularly if *pwll* is aspirated to *pwl*. Most place-names are topographical which would favour the Welsh interpretation.

Glencorse (Penicuik) –
glyn cors = 'valley, of the marsh, from the marsh'
* Johnston – Gaelic *glen crosg* = 'valley of the crossing'.
** See Edinburgh-Names also.

Glencruitten (Oban) – 1502 Glencrutten
glyn croten = 'valley of the little-girl'
glyn crwtyn = 'valley of the little-boy'
glyn crwthen = 'valley of the little-hunchback-person'
* Johnston – Gaelic *gleann cruitein* = 'valley of the little-hump-back'.

Glendinning (Westerkirk) – 1384 Glendonwyne, 1471 Glendinwyne
glyn din gwyn – See Johnston below.
* Johnston – Welsh *glyn din gwyn* = 'glen of the fair hill'.
** Welsh *gwyn* aspirates to *wyn,* and so *glyndingwyn* becomes *glyndinwyn.* Welsh *glyn* becomes Glen in Scotland, *glyn din gwyn* can also be seen as 'valley of the white fort'.

Gleneagles (Blackford) – 1165 Gleninglese, 1508 Glennegas
glyn eglwys = 'valley of the church'

* Johnston – Gaelic *gleann n' eaglaise* = 'glen of the church'.
** Perhaps also Scots *glen inglis* = 'glen of the English'.

Glenelg (Inverness) – 1282 Glenhelk, 1292 Glenelg
glyn helyg = 'valley of willow-trees'
* Johnston – Probably from a man, Eilg = 'the noble'. The root akin to Elgin.
** See Elgin = 'little-willow-trees'.

Glenfinnan (Inverness)
glyn ffinan – 'little-boundary valley'
* Johnston – see Watson below.
* Watson – *gleann Fhionghuin* = 'Fingon's glen', a personal name.
** There is also a St Finan who is remembered in Lumphanan Aberdeens,.but the name is more likely to be topographical.

Glengarnock (Kilbirnie) –
glyn carnoc aspirated to *glyn garnoc* = 'valley of the little-cairn'
* Johnston – *gleann gearanach* = 'glen of the sighing, groaning', river.

Gleniffer (Paisley) –
See Johnston below.
* Johnston – Perhaps Welsh *glyn dyfr* = 'glen with the stream'; 'd' lost by aspiration.
** No records = no certainty.

Glenorchy, Glenurchy (Dalmally) – 1240 Glenerochy, 1292 Glenurwy, 1510 Glenvrquha
glyn erchyn = 'valley of the river Erchyn'; for *erchyn* see Note below
* Johnston – Gaelic *glen urchaid* = 'glen Orchy'. Urchaidh, as the river name is 'doubtful'. Watson's Old Celtic *ar cet* = 'on the wood' seems far fetched. Others have related it to

Welsh *erch* = 'gloomy', and the 1240 form could be Gaelic *glen earrach, erraiche* = 'the bottom of a dish'.
* Watson – the Glen takes its name from the River Orchy, Urchaidh which may be from an early *are-cet-ia* = 'on-wood-stream'. Welsh *coed* = 'wood'.
** Extrapolating from Johnston's reference to 'other-sources', modern Welsh *erch* = 'frightful', 'mottled, speckled', 'dun, dark-brown, dusky', 'dismal, dire'. A diminutive of *erch* is *erchyn,* which converts to *erchy.* Thus *glyn erchy* = 'valley of the little dark-brown stream' (or any of the other four different meanings of *erch*), possibly referring to its degree of peatiness?

Glentrool – 1375 Glentrewall
glyn tre gwal aspirated to *glyntrewal* = 'valley of the steading with a wall'
* Johnston – *gleann t-sruthail* = 'glen of the stream'.
** 'steading with a wall' reads better as the 'walled steading'.

Gogar – see Edinburgh-names.

Gogo Burn (Largs) –
y gogach then *gogo* by change of *-ach* to *-o,* = 'little cuckoo stream'
* Johnston – Perhaps Norse *gauk-a* = 'cuckoo's, or 'gowk's, stream'. Compare too, Welsh *gogof* = 'a cave'.
** Johnston is away with the Vikings – again!

Gorbals (Glasgow) – 1521 Gorbaldis
See Johnston below.
* Johnston – Difficult! Perhaps Welsh *gor buw-allt* = 'spacious cattle hillside'.

Gorgie – see Edinburgh-names.

Govan (Glasgow) – 1134 Guven, 1150 Gvuan, 1275 Govan, 1518 Gwuan

gorfaen – 'chief (i.e. most important) stone'
* Johnston – It may be Welsh *cu faen* = 'dear rock'.
** *gor faen* obviously refers to an ancient stone of some sort, such as a Standing Stone. Govan Church is the repository of several Pictish Stones.

Gullane (E Lothian) – 1200 Golin, 1250 Golyn, 1458 Goulyne, Guling
y-collen aspirated to *golen* = 'hazel-tree'
* Johnston – Perhaps originally Welsh *golyn* = 'guard of a sword', referring to the shape of the site; but now Gaelic *guallan* = a 'shoulder'.
** In Wales it is normal for the name of any farm, house or steading to be known only by it's specific description without any preliminary generic description such as *ty* or *tre* unless the other term counting towards it's make-up was also nonspecific. For example *tre cefn cwrt* = 'farmstead yard on the ridge' would be simply *'cefn-cwrt'* but *tre dŵr* = 'farmstead on the water' would remain *tredwr* because *dŵr* = 'water' is not sufficiently specific. Something of the same sort may have happened here where an original *tre-y-collen* = 'farmstead by the hazel-tree' became simply *y-collen, gollen, golen* = 'hazel-tree' it being understood as meaning 'hazel tree farm'.

I

(Inch) Devannoc (Loch Lomond) – 1776 Devannoc, 1804 Tavanach
ty mynach = 'house of the monk', (Inch Devannoc = *ynys dy mynach* = 'island of the monk's house')
* Johnston – Probably Gaelic *tigh na mhanach* = 'house of two monks'.

** The word element *ty* meaning 'house' can sometimes, when coupled to a Saint's or a 'saintly' name, have the meaning of a place of worship. In Wales the description 'Ty Dewi', literally meaning 'House of David', is affectionately applied to St David's Cathedral. There are numerous islands in Loch Lomond but it is unlikely that there will be two with such similar names as Inch Devannoc and Inchtavanach. It is likely therefore that these are just two different names for the same place, especially as the meaning of Devannoc is said to be associated with a 'house of monks' and on the island of **Inchtavannach** it is known that there was once a monastery. In which case see Inchtavanach entry for a more detailed assessment. It is of passing interest to compare these two place-names with that of **Defynnog** in Wales, recorded as 'Deuannoc' in 1202-1214 then 'Devennoc' in 1254. It's meaning is presently held to be 'obscure', but the similarity between the early records for Inch Devannoc, Inchtavanach and Defynnog suggest that this may well be one of the few cases where the interpretation of a Scottish place-name could perhaps assist in the interpretation of a Welsh place-name?

Inchkeith (Firth of Forth) – 1200 Insula-ked, 1461 Ynchkeyth, now Inchkeith
ynys coed = 'wooded island'
* Johnston – provides no interpretation, except to quote Skene's suggestion that it derives from the name of some son of a Pictish Prince.
* Watson – Relates the second element 'keith' to Old Welsh *coet,* Welsh *coed,* and to various appearances as *chet, keht, keth, ket, kethe,* in the records of the name Bathgate. The first element as 'ynys', 'inch' is confirmed in the record of 1200 as 'Insula' = 'island'
** The records very neatly demonstrate the development of Welsh *ynys* through *ynch* to Scots *inch* and the connection to

insula confirms that at least one of it's meanings is 'island'.

Inchmoan, Inchmoin (Loch Lomond) – 1350 Ynysmoin, 1454 Inchemone
ynys mwyn = 'island' of – (a) 'riches', – (b) 'mineral-ore', or else = 'dear, gentle, island'
* Johnston – Gaelic *innis moine* = 'island of moss'.
** This again is an explicit instance, clearly displaying the change of Welsh *ynys* into Scots *inch* between the 1350 'Ynys-' and the 1454 'Inch-'. The Welsh name for the island of Anglesey is Ynys Mon, pronounced Unnis Moan!

Inchtavanach (Loch Lomond) – 1395 Elanvanow : also called Devannoc
ynys ty fynach = 'monks house island'
* Johnston – *eileann mhanach* = 'island of monks'.
** It would seem that this is an absolutely classic case of an original P-Celtic name being translated directly into it's Q-Celtic Gaelic equivalent with little or no change of meaning but where it is the earlier P-Celtic form which is seen to have survived and been retained in the present-day name. Based on Johnston's 'island of monks' it is possible to surmise an earlier P-Celtic form in which the first element would be related to Welsh *ynys* = 'island' and the second element would be *tŷ mynach* = 'house of the monk'. The usurpation of Welsh *Ynys* by Scots *Inch* is commonplace and *ty mynach* aspirates to *tyfynach,* we can then see the evolution of the name from *ynys tyfynach* to *Inch Tyfynach* and so to the present day Inchtavanach. The 1395 record 'Elanvanow' has to reflect either a spurious or temporary translation into Gaelic and the recorded alias 'Devannoc' could simply be *ty mynach* in its wholly lenited form as *dyfynach*. The evidence must be that the Gaelic *eileann mhanach* was never in common usage. It is worth noting that it is Johnston's Gaelic interpretation of Elanvanow which sets in motion the

reasoning leading eventually to the ensuing Welsh interpretations for both Devannoc and Inchtavanach. See also Davanach (Inch) which Johnston lists separately but which surely relates to the same place.

Inchture (Errol) – 1183 Inchethore
ynys dŵr aspirates to *ynys y ddŵr* = 'water meadow', (compare 1183 Inchethore)
ynys twr = 'tower island'
* Johnston – Probably Gaelic *innis a thoire* = 'mead of the pursuit or search'.
** Welsh 'd' easily slips back into 't', and 'dd' into 'th', Thus *ynysdwr* slips to *ynystwr* and so to Inchture; *ynys-y-ddwr* slips to *ynysythwr* and so to Inchethore. Otherwise *ynys twr* = 'tower island' which forwards to Scots Inch Twr and so to Inchture, Welsh *ynys* can mean 'an island' or 'a meadow' particularly 'a water meadow'.

In(n)istrynich (Loch Awe) – 1662 Inchstrenick
ynys draenawc = 'thorny-island' or 'thorny-meadow'
* Johnston – Probably Gaelic *innis strianach* = 'isle of badgers'.
** *ynysdraenawc* aspirates to *ynystraenawc,* thence *ynys* to Scots *inch* and so to *inchstraenawc* and to the Inchstrenick of 1662. Alternatively *ynystraenawc* reduces as in Welsh place-names to *straenawc* (strenick) and Scots Inch is added later?

Innerleithen (Peebles) – 1160 Innerlethan, 1275 Innerlethain
aber laithan = 'mouth-of the pliant-little-stream'
* Johnston – Confluence of the river Leithan, where Leithen may be from Gaelic *liath, leithe* = 'grey', or else as River Leith from Welsh *lleithio* = 'to moisten. The *-an, -en* is a suffix.
* Watson – It is perhaps connected with Welsh *llaith* = 'damp, moist'.
** The second element is, as Watson says, more likely to be

Welsh *llaithan*, a diminutive of *llaith*, for which we have the meanings – 'soft, damp, moist', or 'pliant', – 'little-stream'. The other meaning of *llaith* is 'death! But then it's diminutive *llaithan* would mean 'slightly-dead' – which is not a happy state to be in! Since the first element is Welsh it is probable that at one time the second element would also have been Welsh. Changing *Inner* (*ie. Inver*) for it's predecessor *Aber* gives the name as possibly originating in 'Aberlaithan' = 'confluence of the little soft, damp, pliant, stream'.

Innerwick (Dunbar) – 1173 Ennyrwic, 1250 Inuerwike
aber wig = 'river-mouth cove'
* Johnston – Probably Old Norse *eng-r vik* = 'close, narrow, bay'. A rare case of Norse settlement in this region.

** If the second element is Welsh *wig* then the original name would possibly have been Aberwig, where *wig* is the aspirated form of *gwig* = either 'a wood, a forest', – or else 'a cove'. In the latter case Innerwick = Aberwig = 'river-mouth cove'. Johnston once again conjures up mythical Vikings!

Irvine River (Ayrshire) – for early records see Irvine Town below
Either *hir waen* = River from the 'long wet-moorland-pasture', or pre-Celtic and of obscure meaning.
* Johnston – Celtic for 'fresh, green river' as in River Irfon, Ceredigion. Welsh *ir, yr* = 'fresh, green' and *afon* = river.
** See Irvine Town below.

Irvine Town (Ayrshire) – 1173 reference to Strathyrewen-*in-galwegia*, 1190 Hirun, 1200 Irewin, 1205 Irving, 1295 Orewin
hir waen = 'long wet-moorland-pasture'.
** The consistent 'h', and the 'w' instead of 'v' in the early records does not support Johnston's interpretation for the river-name. The early 'Strathyrewen' suggests a possible *ystrad hir y waen* = 'long wide-valley, of wet-moorland'. This might describe the location of the town, but not the name of

the River – unless the river takes it's name from the valley it runs through. More likely, perhaps, is that the river name is pre-Celtic and obscure and is only coincidentally connected with that of the valley and the Town. See Irvine River above.

J

Jed River (Roxburgh) –
See Johnston below.
* Johnston – 'Jed' is probably from Welsh *gwd* = 'a turn, a twist'.

Jedburgh (Roxburgh) – 800 Gedwearde, 952 Iudanbyrig, 1100 Geddewrde, 1130 Gedword, 1145 Jaddeuurd, 1160 Jeddeburgh, 1251 Jedwarth, 1500 Jedward, 1586 Geddart
gwd-y-gwrda = that stretch of the river Jed (*gwd*) belonging to the Nobleman, the Chief (*y-gwrda*)
* Johnston – hybrid, Welsh *gwd* = River Jed, plus Old English *worth, word* = 'open space' or 'farm'. Therefore = 'farm on the river Jed'.
** Discounting the records of 952 and 1160, which are obviously of English construction, all other records are consistent with an earlier form based on *gwd*. One tentative suggestion is *gwd y gwrda* = 'Jed of the nobleman', i.e. that stretch of river belonging to him; *gwd y gwrda* aspirates to *gwdywrda,* providing a good match to the records of 800, 1100 and 1130 and, with the 'g' softened as in 'George', a reasonable match to those of 1145, 1251 and 1500. The records of 952 and 1160 show English influence and simply mean 'township on the river Jed'.

K

Keir (many!) –
caer = a 'small fortification' of some sort. See Johnston and Watson below.
* Johnston – Pictish/Welsh *caer* = 'fort'.
* Watson – The old spelling *ceir* is reflected elsewhere in the English form 'Keir'.

Keith (Banffs) – 1187 Geth, 1220 Ket
coed = 'a wood'
* Johnston – Celtic for 'wood', Old Welsh *cet, chet,* – Welsh *coed.*
* Watson – Early Celtic *ceto-* (for *caito*) means 'wood', Old Welsh *coet,* now *coed.*
** *coed* is seen in older forms as *cet, ket, ceth* which mutates to *geth,* and *kethe* from which Keith is developed.

Keithan (Keith) – 1130 Chethec, 1200 Kethet
coedan = a 'small wood'
* Johnston – diminutive of Keith = 'Little Keith'.
* Watson – as for Keith.
** The modern name is an invitation to consider the diminutive suffix *-an* giving Keithan = 'little-wood', but the early record suffixes are *-ec* and *-et,* the former may represent the diminutive suffixes *-oc* or *-awc* and the latter may be, as Johnston says, a 't' in error for a 'c', but this is not certain. The alternative for Kethet is *kethe* with the suffix *-et* giving *kethet* = place-of 'woodiness'. The variation in meaning is only slight.

Keithock (Brechin) –
coedoc, coedawc = 'little-wood'
Note: Suffixes *-oc* and *-awc* are older forms of the diminutive suffix *-og.* Otherwise as for Keithan.

Kelly, Kellie (Buchan, also Carnbee and Arbirlot) – 1183 Kellin, 1280 Kelly, 1140 Chellin
celyn = 'holly'
* Johnston – Probably Pictish/Welsh *celyn* = 'holly'.
** *-yn* conversion to *-y* or *-ie* gives *cely, celie* hence Kelly, Kellie.

Kelso (Roxburgh) – 1126 Calkou, 1145 Chelchehov, 1153 Calchoh, 1158 Kelcou, 1420 Kelsowe, 1447 Calcouia, 1554 Kalyhow
calch-y-mynydd, calch fynydd = 'lime mountain'
* Johnston – Old Welsh *calchvynyd* = 'chalk, limestone height' from Welsh *mynyd.* The first element is Old English *cealc* = 'chalk, lime' and the second is Scots *heugh, howe* = height.
* Watson – Quotes Skene's identification of Kelso as the Calchvynydd = 'chalk mount' of an early account, and relates this to the 'Chalkheugh' (chalk-hill) in present-day Kelso, in which Welsh *mynydd* is translated into *heugh* = 'height'.
** All the early records favour Welsh *calch* = 'lime', rather than English *cealc* of the same meaning.

Kilbirnie (Beith, Ayrs) – 1413 Kilbyrny
cil y prenau = 'sheltered-nook with trees'
cil brennau = 'church by the trees'
* Johnston – Probably from St Brendan, a friend of St Columba.
* Watson – Kilbirnie is supposedly 'Brendan's Church'.
** *cil-y-prenau,* first aspirated to *cilbrenau* then metathesised to *cilbernau* would lead to Kilbirnie, but the only record is late and it may be that the origin is *cilprenyn* = 'sheltered-nook of the little-tree' from which the same process plus change of *-yn* to *-y,* gives *cilberny.* This accords quite nicely with Kilbyrny. There seems to be no certain evidence connecting the place to St Brendan.

Kilbowie (Clydebank) – 1233 Cullbuthe, 1273 Cultbovy, 1330 Cultboy
cil bwthyn = 'corner by the little-cottage', 'back of the little-cottage'
* Johnston – Gaelic *cul buidhe* = 'yellow back' (of the hill).
** *bwthyn* to *bwthy* then *bwthie* by *yn* to *y* or *ie* conversion, the 'th' shown in the 1223 record seems to have reduced to 'v' by 1273 and has disappeared by 1330 when *bwthie* was presumably truncated to *bwie*; – from which '-bowie'.

Kildary (Invergordon) –
cil daryn = 'shelter of little-oak-trees' or 'church by little oak trees'
* Johnston – Gaelic *caol daire* = 'narrow oakwood'.
** *cil daryn* to *cildary* via conversion of *-yn* to *–y*.

Kildrummy (Rhynie) – 1238 Keldrumin, 1280 Kildrummy, 1295 Kildromy
cil drumyn = 'corner of the little-ridge', 'shelter by the little ridge'
* Johnston – Gaelic *coil droma* = 'wood on the hill-ridge' from *druim* = 'the back, the ridge'.
* Watson – Kildrummy, formerly Kindrummie, is for Gaelic *cionn droma* = 'at ridge end'.
** Watson's 'Kindrummie' is not supported by any of Johnston's early records and must be considered suspect. *cil drumyn* to *cildrumy* via conversion of *-yn* to *–y*.

Killin (Perth) – 1318 Kyllin
cilyn = 'little nook' : 'little sheltered-place', or 'little church'
cil llyn = 'sanctuary by the lake'
* Johnston – Probably gaelic *cill ffion* = 'white church'.
* Watson – *cill ffion* = 'white church' or – *cill Fionn* = 'church of St Fionn', 'though none of that name appears on record'.
** The 1318 record Kyllin tallies remarkably well with *cil llyn*.

Killintringan, Killentringan (Portpatrick) – early reference as Kilantrinzean

cilan ty Ringan = 'little sheltered nook, (sanctuary) by the house of St Ringan' or little church house of St Ringan'.

* Johnston – = 'church of St Ringan', this being a soubriquet of St Ninian, a 'British' saint. The name must be 'late Gaelic'.

** In Wales the word 'house' is often taken, in context, to mean 'church'. e.g. St David's Cathedral is 'Tyddewi' in Welsh. In which case *cilantyringan* could mean 'St Ninian's "church" in the little sheltered-nook'. Of course, what passed for a 'church' in those days is a matter of pure conjecture. It needs also to be mentioned that in Welsh place-names the word *cil* sometimes has the meaning 'cove', as in Cilborth (Llangrannog). In which case *cilan tŷ ringan* = 'small cove by Ninian's church' and it is this meaning of *cil* which best suits the site here.

Kilmadock (Doune) –

cil Madoc = 'cell, sanctuary, church, of St Madoc' – as he is known in Wales

* Johnston – *cill Modoc* = 'church of St Modoc', a Welsh Saint.

* Watson – It is 'my-Doc's church', and the Saint in question is 'Docus the Briton', where Docus may be the shortened form of 'Cadog of Llancarvan', the eminent Welsh saint of the 6th century; the commemoration of which is therefore an indication of British influence.

** It is interesting to observe Watson's implied statement that a 'Welsh Saint' is here an indication of 'British influence'.

Kilmeny (Fife) – 1250 Kylmanyn, 1518 Kilmainy

cil maenyn = 'cell, sanctuary, church, by the Stone', or else 'sheltered-nook, corner, by the Stone'

* Johnston – Relates it to Kilmeny (Isla) for which Gaelic

cille mhanaich = 'cell, church, of the monk', has been suggested.
* Watson – Kilmeny in Fife and Isla is for Gaelic *cille m'eithne* = 'my Eithne's church'. The Isla name in Gaelic is now *cill mheinidh* for *cill M'h Eithne.*
** *cil maenyn* becomes *cilmaeny* by usual change of *-yn* to *-y.* Alternatively *cil meini* = 'cell, church, shelter or sanctuary – stones'.

Kilrymont – (the old name for **St Andrews**)
pen rhi mynydd = 'far-end-of the King's rough-pasture-land'
cil rhi mynydd = 'place-of-worship on the king's rough-pasture-land'
* Johnston – Kilrymont is the old name for St Andrew's; Old Gaelic *cind righ monaigh* = 'head of the King's mount'.
* Watson – *Rigmonad* is most probably the Gaelicized form of a British name: the place was doubtless the seat, or near the seat, of the British rulers of Fife.
** Scots Gaelic *monadh* is recognised as being derived from Welsh *mynydd,* it is not found in Irish-Gaelic, and Scots gaelic *ceann* = 'head' often usurps an earlier Welsh *pen* = 'head, far-end-of'. Simon Taylor, *The Uses of Place-Names,* argues cogently that *monadh* in this instance signifies 'rough-grazing' land. This definition agrees with that referred to by Watson as being one of the meanings of *mynydd* i.e. 'common, or wild-unenclosed-land' – not necessarily hilly. Thus we have *pen rhi mynydd* becoming *ceann rhi mynydd* and then *cen righ monadh,* which can be compared with Johnston's *cind righ monaigh*. But a likelier possibility is *cil rhi mynydd* where *cil,* as has been argued before, has a meaning similar to *llan* in Wales. Thus *cil rhi mynydd* = 'place-of-worship on the king's rough-pasture-land'. One of the many forms in which Welsh *mynydd* appears in Scottish place-names is *mont* and Celtic 'c' is written down by mediaeval scribes as English 'k'. Thus *cilrhymynydd* becomes *kilrhymont;* hence 'Kilrymont'.

Kilwinning (Ayrs) – 1160 Killvinin, 1184 Ecelesia St Vinini, 1300 Kynwenyn, 1357 Kylvyynnyne
* Johnston – *cil Vinin* or *cil Wynnin* = 'Church of St' Vinin' or 'Church of St' Wynnin' These names being the Welsh form of St Finnan.
** Johnston's acceptance of the Welsh *cil* as meaning 'church'.

Kincardine (Firth of Forth) – 1195 Kincardin, 1277 Kincardyn, 1337 Kyncardyn
pen cardden, partially Gaelicized to *ceann cardden* = 'far-end of the thicket'
* Johnston – Pictish/Gaelic *cinn chardain* = 'at the end of the wood'; from Welsh *cerddyn* = 'a wood, a brake'.
* Watson – Another British term of common occurrence is *carden,* Welsh *cardden,* = 'thicket, brake'. The Gaelic combination *cinn chardain* = 'copse-end, wood-end' occurs in several places as Kincardine.
** The word *chardain* does not appear anywhere in my Scots-Gaelic Dictionary. If this is a hybrid of Gaelic *'ceann, cinn'* and Welsh *cardden,* then the original name would have been either wholly Gaelic or wholly Welsh; but whereas a wholly Welsh name could be partly Gaelicizised by later Gaelic speakers there is no mechanism whereby a later wholly Gaelic construction could be partly Cymricized by the language which preceded it. It can therefore be reasonably assumed that the original name was wholly Welsh, in which case it may have been *pen cardden* = 'at the far-end of the copse, thicket', which retains the interpretations given by Watson and Johnston. On the other hand it could very simply be wholly Welsh *cyn cardden* = 'wedge-wood' i.e. a wedge-shaped copse, wood.

Kinghorn (Fife) – 1136 Chingor, 1140 Kingorn, Kingornum, 1150 Kyngor, Kyngoren, 1280 Kinkorn
See Watson below.

* Watson – Postulates a lost Welsh word *gronn* or *gorn* = 'marsh'. In which case he gives it as a hybrid Gaelic-Welsh *ceann gorn* = bog-head'.
** Otherwise a wholly Welsh *cyn gorn* = 'wedge-shaped, chisel-shaped, marsh', is possible.

Kingledores Burn (Tweedsmuir) – 1200 Kingledores, 1359 Kylgildorys
cynghel dyrys' = 'concealed, tangled place', so Kingledores Burn = *'nant cynghael dyrys'* = 'stream from the concealed, tangled place'.
* Johnston – Probably Gaelic *cinn gheal doruis* = 'at the head of the clear opening'.
** *cyngheldyrys* is pronounced 'kingeldurris.

Kingoldrum (Kirriemuir) – 1454 Kyncaldrum
cyn caled trum = 'wedge-shaped, hard, ridge
* Johnston – Gaelic *ceann caoil druim* = 'at the head of the narrow ridge'.
* Watson – Gaelic *ceann coll (or call) druim* = 'head of hazel ridge'.
** *trum* lenits to *drum* to give *cyncaledrum* (Kyncaldrum) and further lenition of 'c' to 'g' gives *cyngaledrum* (Kingoldrum).

Kininmonth (Mintlaw) – 1165 Kininmunth
cynyn mynydd = 'small-wedge mountain'
cynyn mwnt = 'small-wedge mount'
* Johnston – Gaelic *cinn fionn monaidh* = 'at the head of the white, or clear, hill'.
* Watson – Gaelic *ceann fionn monadh* = 'head of white hill'.
** 'month', 'munth' are common Anglicised representations of Welsh *mynydd*, as also is Gaelic *monaidh*.

Kinnaird – 1281 Kinard
cyn ardd = 'wedge, chisel shaped hill', 'the high wedge'
* Johnston – Gaelic *cinn aird* = 'at the head of the height'.
** This is an interesting example of a name which could

ostensibly be either of wholly Welsh origin, *cyn ard(d)* = 'wedge-shaped height'; or a later, wholly Gaelic, *ceann aird* = 'head of the height'; or a hybrid Gaelic-Welsh, *ceann ard(d)* = 'head, or end, of the promontory'; this last deriving from an original Welsh *pen ardd* as in Penarth, Wales, but in which Gaelic *cenn* has later been substituted for Welsh *pen.*

Kinneil (Bo'ness) – 1250 Kinel, 1336/7 Kynnevel
pen gwal, pen y wal = 'far end of the wall'
* Johnston – Paraphrased version of Watson, see below.
* Watson – In the earliest reference Bede, in 720, speaks of a 'place called in the Pictish language *Peanfahel*, but in English *Penneltun'*, as marking the Eastern end of the Antonine Wall. Nennius circa 800 cites *guaul* as being the British name for the Wall. Later, in the 10th century, is a reference to *'Penguaual* which in Scots-Gaelic is called *Cenail'*. Thus, here we have four different forms of the same name; (1) *Peanfahel* which is Pictish; (2) *Penguaul* which is British, i.e. Early Welsh; (3) *Cenail* which is Gaelic and (4) *Penneltun* which is an English rendering of *Peanfahel* with *tun* added. Here then we have a clear instance of a British compound name *(Penguaul)* becoming first half-Gaelic *(Penfahel)* and finally wholly Gaelic *(Cenail).*
** Penguaul = *pen gwal, pen y wal* = 'far end of the wall', later transcripted as 'Pictish' *penfahel* and later still Gaelicized to *ceann-fhail* = *cenail* = Kinneil. This name exemplifies the complex interaction between Welsh *pen* and Gaelic *ceann*. As Watson sums it up: *'Doubtless many a British 'pen' has been displaced by Gaelic 'cenn', and what is true in this case is true of other British terms, though the nature of the case seldom admits of proof.'*

Kirkcaldy (Fife) – 1038 Kirkaladunt, 1093 Kirkaladunt, 1128 Kircalethyn, 1130 Kircaladin, 1150 Kircalathin, Kircaladin, Kirkaldin, 1451 Kirkcaldy
caer caled din = 'fortification, on the hard-fort

* Johnston – Gaelic *cathair Calatin* = 'fort of Calatin', a personal name from a family of Irish magicians. Otherwise Gaelic *cala dion, cala-dion-ait* = 'harbour of refuge'.
* Watson – *caer caled din* = 'fortress by the hard old-fort'. This supposes an early *Caleto-dunon* = 'hard fort' to which *caer* was prefixed later.
** Although not a diminutive it seems that here the ending of *din* has been subjected to the same change from Celtic suffix *'-in'* to Scots suffix *'y'* or *'ie'*. Hence the 1451 and present-day Kirkcaldy from the Kirkaldin of 1150.

Kittlegairy Hill (Peebles)
cudyll y caerau = 'strongholds of the falcon
* Johnston – May be *gaelic tigh coill giorra* = 'house in the short wood' – or suchlike.
** *cudyll y careau* aspirates to *cudylgaerau.*

L

Lanark – 1116 Pathelanerche, 1159 Lannarch, 1172 Barlanark, 1289 Lanark, 1375 Lanrik
llanerch = 'glade' – in a wood
* Johnston – Welsh *llanerch* = a 'forest glade' 'glade in the woods.
* Watson – *llanerch* = a' clear space', 'a glade', Lanark is pronounced locally as Lainrick, as it is in Lanrick (Loch Venachar), Lanrick (Callander) – both these in Gaelic nomenclature as *laraig* for *lanraig,* also Lendrick (Kirriemuir)
** The oldest record is Pathelanerche but both Watson and Johnston have chosen to ignore this. It is certainly obscure but a possible suggestion is to equate 'pathe' to Welsh *peth* meaning 'thing' or 'part' and which Watson associates with Pictish *pit* to which he gives the meaning a 'croft' perhaps

equating this to a 'part' or 'share' – of land? Thence Pathelanerche = *peth y lanerch* = 'croft in the glade' where the *'e'* in *peth* is pronounced somewhat like the 'a' in English 'gale'. As a place-name 'croft-in-the-glade' seems significantly more plausible than just 'glade'. For the 1172 record see Barlanark itself, but this record may just be a misrendition.

Landale, Landells (Berwicks) – 1188 Laundelis, 1296 Laundles, Landel
llan dol = 'church in the field', or more simply 'enclosure field'.
* Johnston – British *lann dail* = 'church in the field'. Old Welsh, Breton, Gaelic *lann*, Welsh *llan* is rare in Scotland but see Lhanbryde, Longforgan etc. It means 'a level, fertile spot', then 'an enclosure', then 'a church'.
** Johnston rightly states that Welsh *llan* = 'church' is rare in Scotland, but see elsewhere for arguments that Welsh *cil* was used instead but having, in Scotland, the same meaning = 'church'.

Landifferone, Lindifferone (Monimail) – 1315 Lediferine
lle dyffryn = a 'place in the water-course, river-valley'
* Johnston – probably British for 'enclosure by the little stream', from Welsh *dyffryn*.
** Johnston ignores the one and only record, Lediferine, and instead gives his interpretation of the present day name, Landifferone, as *lan dyffryn* = 'enclosure in the water-course, river-valley'. But equally Lindifferone may me *lyn dyffryn* = 'lake in the water-course, river-valley'.

Lanrick (Callander) – 1669 Lennerick, 1791 Lanrick
Same as Lanark, which see.

Lauder (Berwicks) – 1250 Lawedir, 1298 Loweder, 1334 Lawadyr
llaw y dir = a 'hand of land'

llawiau dir = 'hands of land'
llaw tir = 'wretched, mean, land'
* Johnston – Probably the same as Lowther = Old Irish *lothur* = 'canal', Breton *laouer* = 'trench', Otherwise 'Leuther' was a tribe of North Esk.
** *llaw* = ''wretched, sad, small, mean' or 'hand'. *tir* = 'land'. The meaning of 'hand of land' is admittedly obscure.

Lawers Ben (Perths) – 1150 Lauer
pen llafar = 'summit by the Lafar (noisy) stream'
* Johnston – some say Gaelic *lathar* = 'a hoof' so – 'cloven ben'. I did not find natives say *Labhar* as suggested by Watson.
* Watson – Lawers, in Gaelic *Labhar,* is primarily the name of a stream, then of a district. *Labhar* is for *labora,* Welsh *llafar* – 'loud, resounding', Scots Gaelic *labhar* is not found in Irish Gaelic Dictionaries.
** The Ben, according to Watson, takes it's name from the *Labhar* a stream rising alongside it, and running down it. Since Scots Gaelic *labhar* is unknown in Irish it would appear that *labhar* was actually inherited from Welsh *llafar* = the 'noisy' one, When using early scripts 'u' was often confused with 'v' and vice versa, hence 'Lauer' instead of 'Laver' for 'Lafar' in the early record.

Leith (Lothian) –
llaith = 'soft, moist, damp'
llaith = 'death'
* Johnston – It is from Welsh *lleithio* = 'to moisten'.
* Watson – It is perhaps connected with Welsh *llaith* = 'damp, moist' or *lleithio* = 'moisten'.
** Leith town takes its name from the Water of Leith, the river which flows through Edinburgh to reach the sea at Leith. The river name is either *llaith, lleith* = 'damp-moist-river', or *llaith* = 'water-of-death'. See Edinburgh Names.

Lennox (Dumbarton) – 1174 Leuenaichs, 1175 Levenax, 1210 Levenach, 1234 Lenox, 1296 Levenaux, Lumenach
llwyfenog, lwyfenog = 'place abounding in elm trees'
llwyfenach, lwyfenach = 'little elm tree'
lwyfenachas = 'place abounding in little elm-trees'
lle mynach = *lefynach* = 'place of monks'
* Johnston – Old Gaelic *lemnaigh,* Gaelic *leamhanach* = 'place abounding in elm trees'.
* Watson – Relates the name to a district around Loch Lomond and to the river Leven = 'elm-water', in Welsh *llwyfen,* in Gaelic *leamhain,* which flows from the Loch. He expands this theme by quoting instances of *leamhain* in Irish place-names. He then introduces a description *leamhnach* seemingly meaning 'a man from the district around the river *leamhain'* or simply 'Lennox-man', and identifies early records such as 1199 Leuenax, and 1259 Levenax, as being English plurals, *leamhnachs,* of singular *leamhnach.*
** It is not clear to me how the description *leamhnachs* = 'Lennox-men' can be applied to a district, but if the suffix 's' in *leamhnachs* is not English plural but English possessive then we have *leamhanach's* = 'Lennox-man's district' = Lennox. The reasoning is tortuous. The early records, with the sole exception of that of 1234, strongly support an original *le mynach / le fynach* but it is the Lenox of 1234 which has, for whatever reason, survived.

Lennoxtown (Stirling) –
It may or may not be closely connected to Lennox – which see. But either 'town in the Lennox district' or 'place of monks'.

Leslie (Garioch) – 1180 Lesslyn, 1232 (and often thereafter) Lescelyn, 1300 Lessly
llys celyn = place of 'holly-berries'
llys lle = 'big-house place'

* Johnston – Pictish-Welsh *llys celyn* = 'court, garden, of hollies'.
** Welsh *llys* = 'court, hall, great house' but also has an older meaning = 'berries', so alternatively 'place of holly-berries'. The 1300 record, 'Lessly', and present-day, 'Leslie', exhibit the classic conversion of *-yn* to *-y* and eventually to *-ie*.

Leslie (Fife) – named from Leslie, Garioch.

Leswalt (Stranraer) – 1426 Leswalt, 1607 Lesswoll
llys gwellt aspirated to *lyswelt* = 'sward by the great-house'
* Johnston – British-Welsh *llys gwelt* = 'enclosure for grass' (quoting Watson).
* Watson – It is 'enclosure for grass'.
** *llys* = 'court, big-house', *gwellt* = 'grass, sward, straw'. The records are late and so not wholly reliable, an intriguing alternative is *lle swllt* = *leswlt* = 'place of treasure'!

Leven Loch (Kinross) – 955 Lochleuine, 1145 Lochlewin, 1156 Lochuleuene
llefn, lefn = 'smooth', Loch *lefn* = 'smooth Loch'
* Johnston – Welsh *llefn* = 'smooth'-Loch, would suit'. As also would Gaelic *leamhain* = 'an elm' or Gaelic *sleamhuinn* = 'smooth'.
* Watson – Gaelic *leamhain* = 'elm-tree'.
** Welsh *llwyfen* = 'elm-tree' also suits.

Levern (Paisley) –
Same as in Loch Leven = Welsh *llefn,* (Scots-Gaelic *sleamhain),* = 'smooth' or *llwyfen, leamhain* = 'elm'; as for Loch Leven above.

Lhanbryde, Lanbryde (Elgin) – 1210, 1215 Lamnabride, Lamanbride, 1391 Lambride
llan y Bride = 'church of St Bride'

llan braith = 'spotted church'. See Falkirk for the meaning = 'church of the Picts'

* Johnston – Gaelic *lann na Brid* = 'church of St Bride'.

* Watson – it is = 'church of St Bride'.

** None of the above suggestions account for the consistent element, 'Lam-', in all the records but linguists tell us that an 'n' follwed by a 'b' to become 'nb' is as a result of slovenly speech, often mispronounced as 'mb'. See Dunbarton / Dumbarton.

Lincluden (Dumfries) – 1452 Lyncludene

See Johnston below.

* Johnston – Welsh *llyn Cluden* = 'lake, or pool, on the River Cluden'.

** Cluden = 'little Clyde' – possibly.

Lindean (Selkirk) – 1275 Lyndon, 1353 Lindene

See Johnston and Watson below.

* Johnston – Welsh *llyn din* = 'lake, or pool, by the fort, hill-fort'.

* Watson – Lyndon is simply Old British or Early-Celtic for 'pool', 'lake'; Welsh *llyn*.

Lindores (Newburgh) – 1182 Lundors, 1199 Lundoris, 1203 Londors

llyn dyrys = 'tangled lake'

* Johnston – Gaelic *linne doruis* = 'lake at the opening' or hybrid Welsh-Gaelic *llyn doruis* = 'same meaning'.

** *dyrys* = 'confused, intricate, tangled'. Alternatively *llyn dwrais* = 'lake of many waters' or *llyn dwrus* = 'lake of powerful water'.

Linlathan (Dundee) – 1359 Lumlethyen

llwm lyda = *lwmlydan* = 'broad surface', 'bare area'

* Johnston – Gaelic *lom leathan* = 'broad, bare, surface'.

Linlithgow (W. Lothian). – 1138 Linlidcu, 1144 Linlidcu, 1147 Linlitcu, 1150 Linlithcu, 1156 Lillidchu, 1264 Lenlithgow
llyn llaith cau = 'lake in the soft, damp hollow'
* Johnston – British – Welsh *llyn lled cu* = 'dear broad lake'.
* Watson – The first part is Welsh *llyn* = 'lake', hence Linlithgow = 'lake of Lithgow' where 'Lithgow' = Welsh *llaith* = 'damp', 'moist' – or possibly Welsh *llwyd* = 'grey' plus Welsh cau = 'hollow'. So, finally the name is *llyn llaith cau* = 'lake in the damp, soft, hollow' or *llyn llwyd cau* = 'grey lake in the hollow'.
** The above is a distillation of Watson's dissertations, upon which Johnston had this to say – 'Much in Watson (p.384) is quite fantastic'. I have noticed elsewhere that Watson can be equally unimpressed by some of Johnston's deliberations! Nevertheless Watson's *llyn llaith cau* = 'lake in soft, damp, hollow' fits the site exactly.

Lintrathern (Kirriemuir) – 1250 Lumtrethyn, Luntrethyn.
llwm traethyn = 'bare little beach'
llwm traethen = 'bare, barren, sand-bank'
* Johnston – hybrid; Gaelic *lom, luim* = 'bare spot' plus Welsh *traethen* = 'sand-bank'.
** In Wales a *traeth* can be a 'beach' by the sea, but also an area of sand or silt alongside a river, or on it's own anywhere – even up in the mountains. e.g. *traeth y mynydd* on Mynydd Illtud in the Brecon Beacons National Park.

Lochaber (Fort William) – 1297 Lochabor, 1309 Lochabre
llwch aber = 'swampy ground by the river-mouth'
* Johnston – Gaelic *loch abar* = 'lake by the marsh'.
* Watson – *loch abar* = as Johnston.
** Adamnan's very early record of circa 700 gives it as 'Stagnum Aporum' = 'swamp marsh'. Obviously taking *apor* = Gaelic *abar*. But if *apor* = Welsh *aber* then it is 'swamp river-

mouth'. Johnston's taking *stagnum* = *loch* = *lake* is somewhat dubious.

Lomond Ben (Dumbartons)
y-pen-llumon / benlumon = 'beacon hill', 'beacon top'
* Johnston – The root here is Pictish-Welsh *llumon* ='beacon'; referring primarily to Ben Lomond and also the Lomond Hills in Fife. Loch Lomond then takes its name from the Ben.

Lomond Loch (Dumbartons) –
See Ben Lomond.
* Watson – an early Latin reference is to 'the swamp of Lumonoy' and another is to the 'great lake of Lummonu, which the English call Lochleuen in the land of the Picts'. 'Lumonoy' and 'Lummonu' are, in modern Welsh, *Llumonwy*.
** *Llumonwy* = 'the Water of the Beacon' i.e. the Loch at the foot of what is now Ben Lomond. The Latin reference to 'stagnum Lumonoy' = the 'swamp of Llumonoy' translates directly into Welsh as *llwch llumonwy* = 'the swampy-ground by beacon-lake' i.e. what is now Loch Lomond. It is interesting that this connects Scottish *loch* to Welsh *llwch*.

Lomond Hills (Fife) –
See Ben Lomond and Loch Lomond.

Longformacus (Berwick) – 1340 Langeford Makhous, 1430 Lochyr-macus
llan ffordd Maccus = 'cell, sanctuary, on Maccus's road'
* Johnston – Gaelic *lann fothir Maccus* = 'church on the field, or slope, of Maccus', – a personal name known in this district as the root of the name Maxwell.
* Watson – Gaelic *longphort Maccus* = 'camp or residence of Maccus'.
** Scots-Gaelic *longphort,* from *long port* is literally 'ship-haven' and is matched exactly by Welsh *llongborth* from *llong*

porth having that same meaning. It can be seen that Welsh *porth* aspirates into *borth* in *llongborth* and Scots-Gaelic *port* aspirates to *phort* in *longphort*. There is no equivalent in Irish-Gaelic where *long port* = 'ship-harbour' and *longfort* = 'camp, fort'. Scots-Gaelic *longphort* appears to have incorporated all the meanings from both Irish and Welsh. There seems to be something of a linguistic conundrum in all this!
The local pronunciation today is still LANG-FFOR-MACKUS with the stress on the penultimate 'a' in Maccus.

Longmorn (Elgin) –
llan Morgan = 'area, sanctuary, of Morgan' – the holy-man
* Johnston – Gaelic *lann Morgan* = 'church of Morgan' – a 'saint'. Old name was Longmorgan.
** In the Scots-Gaelic Dictionary *lann* = 'an inclosure, land-area'. In the Irish-Gaelic Dictionary *lann* = 'blade' or 'fish-scale'. In Welsh Dictionaries *llan* = 'area, yard, church, parish'. The local pronunciation is probably Lang-Morgan or perhaps Lang-morr'n?

Longniddrie (Lothian) – 1424 Langnudre, 1595 Langnedre
llan neuadd dre, lanneuadre = 'area, sanctuary, in the hall, big-room, of the steading'.
llan newydd dre = *lanewydre* = 'yard, sanctuary by the new steading'
* Johnston – Probably hybrid, 'long' = Gaelic *lann,* and 'niddrie' = Welsh *nuadh tref* = 'new house, settlement'.
* Watson – The first element is simply English 'long'; succeeded by Welsh *newydd tre* = 'new stead'.
** Johnston seems to have confused the Welsh element *newydd* with Scots-Gaelic *nuadh.* Otherwise note Welsh *llan* is here corrupted to Scots 'long' and Welsh *newydd tre* to *niddrie / nidre.* is it possible that the double *dd* in the present day '-niddrie' is a throwback to the double dd in *newydd*?

Lossie River (Elgin) –
lloesau, loesau = 'river of sighs'
* Johnston – The root is perhaps Welsh *lloesi* = 'to pour'.
* Watson – Old Gaelic *lossa* = 'river of herbs', from *lus* = a 'herb'.
** Alternatively *llysiau* = 'herbage'. These are all pure guesses, nothing is certain, the root may equally be pre-Celtic and it's meaning therefore lost to us.

Lossiemouth –
The Town's name is taken from that of the river and is relatively modern.

Lothian – 970 Loonia, 1091 Lodene, 1095 lodoneium, 1145 Lodonesia, 11166 Laudonia, 1200 Louthion, 1600 Lawdien. See entry in Edinburgh Names

Lugar River (Auchinleck) – 1200 Lugar, 1202 Lughor
llychwr / llwchwr = 'dawn, daylight'
llychwyr = 'dusk, twilight'
* Johnston – Perhaps the same root as Leuchars = Gaelic *luachuair* = 'rushes'.
* Watson – Probably from Welsh *llug* = 'bright'.
** The 1202 record suggests comparison with the river Loughor in Wales, which is from *llwchwr, llychwr* = 'bright-river', 'daybreak river', 'dawn-river', or alternatively *llychwyr* = 'twilight-river', the exact opposite!

Luggie Water (Cumbernauld) – 1300 Luggy
llugwy = 'the bright-one', a 'goddess' name
* Johnston – Might be from Gaelic *lag, luig* = 'a hollow'. Perhaps the name of a Celtic river deity 'Lug', as in Welsh *llug* = 'bright'.
* Watson – *llugwy* = 'the bright-one'.
** See entry for Luggie in River-Names.

Lugton (Dalkeith) –
See Johnston below.
* Johnston – Very likely a corruption of Welsh *llug din* = 'bright hill'.
** Welsh *din* = 'fort, hill-fort', but it is very often mistakenly anglicized to *-ton* = 'town, village, hamlet, etc.'

Lynturk (Alford) –
llyn twrch, lyntwrch = 'wild-boar lake'
* Johnston – Gaelic *linne,* Welsh *llyn* = 'pool', and Gaelic *tuirc, torc* = 'wild boar'.
** Johnston really ought to have completed the wholly Welsh alternative i.e. *llyn twrch* = 'pool, lake, of the wild boar'.

M

Manor (Peebles) – 1186 Maineure, 1323 Mener
See Johnston and Watson below.
* Johnston – Local pronunciation is 'maener'. Welsh *maenor* = 'stone-built mansion', 'manor'.
* Watson – Welsh *maenor,* spelled 'Mainavre' in Domesday Book, and said to mean 'the stone-built residence of the chief of a district'.
** Modern Welsh *maenor* = 'manor, district'.

Manuel (Polmont) – 1190 Manuell, 1301 Manewell
maen-y-gwel, maenwel = 'stone of the sight'. See Johnston below.
* Johnston – Quite likely it is Welsh *maen gwel* = 'rock of the sight or view'.
** The lenited form of *gwel* is *wel* hence *maenwel* = 'sight-stone', i.e. 'prospect-stone'?

Mark, Markie Rivers (several) –
march = 'horse'
marchyn = 'little-horse'
* Johnston – Gaelic *marc* = 'horse'.
* Watson – *marcaidh* = 'horse-stream'. Occurs elsewhere in the names of tributaries of the Deveron, Spey, Feshie, & Fechlin and suggests a compound like Welsh *marchnant* = 'horse-brook'.
** Welsh *marchyn* = 'little horse'. then *marchy, marchie* by transformation of *-yn* to *-y* or *-ie.*
See Rosemarkie also.

Markinch (Fife) – 1055 Marchinke, 1183 Marchinge, 1200 Marcinche, 1290 Markynchs
march ynys = 'horse meadow' or 'horse island'
* Johnston – Gaelic *marc innis* = 'horse meadow'.
* Watson – A British-Gaelic name, Gaelic *marc,* Welsh *march* = 'horse'.
** The early *march* element of 1055 and the *ynchs* element of 1200 would seem to favour Welsh *march ynys* = 'horse-meadow', or 'horse-island' rather than Gaelic *marc innis* = same meaning. The elements *-inke, -inge, -inche,* and *-ynchs* partly illustrate the development of Welsh *ynys* into Scots *inch.*

Masson Glen (Kilmun) –
glyn maesan = 'valley with the little-flat-field'
* Johnston – Gaelic *gleann measain* = 'glen of the puppy-dog'.

May Island (Forth Estuary) – 1143 & 1200 Mai, 1165 Insula Mai
ynys mai = 'island of flat-ground'
* Johnston – Norse *ma-ey* = 'sea-mew's island'.
** *maes, faes, mai, fai, ma, fa* = 'flat-ground', 'flat-field', therefore May Island = *ynys mai* = 'flat-ground Island',

which it is! The 1165 record replaces Welsh *ynys* with Latin *insula* but retains the Welsh *mai*. The meaning is unchanged.

Maybole (Ayrs) – 1275 Mayboill, 1371 Mayboyl
mai boll = 'open flat-ground', 'open flat-field', 'open plain'
mai bwth gell = *maibwthel* = 'flat-ground by the dun-coloured hut'
* Johnston – Gaelic '*magh baoghail*' = 'plain, moor of danger'.
** There are other sources which have suggested a possible Old English *maege bopl* = 'lord's hall of the maidens', said to have been recorded as such in the 'late 12th century' as Maybothel. It is admitted, however, that 'this is suspiciously far West for a *bopl* name' and this attribution must be considered as no more credible than any other. Besides which the '12th century Maybothel' bears an uncanny resemblance to the suggested *maibwthel* which is the aspirated form of *mai bwth gell*.

Medwin River (Carnwath) –
med wyn = 'fair, white, middle-river' or 'holy, blessed, middle-river'
* Johnston – British *med abhuin* = 'river, extended and full'.
** Welsh *med afon* = 'river – extended, full', or else 'middle river'. The second element 'win' more likely derives from *gwyn*, *gwen* aspirated to *wyn*, *wen* = 'fair, white' or 'holy, blessed'.

Meggat Water (Peebles) – 1206 Meggete
miget = 'bogginess', Megget Water = 'river from the place of bogginess'
* Johnston – Gaelic *meigaid* = 'cry of a kid'.
* Watson – Welsh *mig* with abstract and collective ending *-et* later *-ed*, the meaning is then '(water of) bogginess'.
** *mig* is a 'bog' but the suffix '*-et*' or '*-ed*' converts a noun into an abstract noun, e.g. *mig* = 'bog' into *miget* = 'bogginess', the source of the Megget Water is decidedly

boggy, but the area is not famous for its goats!

Megginch (Errol) – circa 1200 Melginch, 1240 Melginge, 'later' Melkinche
maelog ynys = 'princely island' or 'princely meadow, water-meadow'
* Johnston – Perhaps Old Celtic *'mal(a)g'* = 'noble' plus *innis* = 'meadow'.
** Once again Johnston's 'Old Gaelic' (*malag)* looks not very different from Welsh *maelog.*

Meigle (Newtyle) – early record Mygdele, 1183 Miggil, 1296 Miggyl, 1378 Mygghil, 1379 Mygille
mig dol lle = 'bog-meadow place', 'quagmire-meadow place'
mig lle, migle = 'bog-place'
* Johnston – see Watson.
* Watson – Welsh *mig* = 'bog' plus *dol* = 'meadow'; *dol* can become *del* in certain linguistic circumstances.
** Watson seems to have restricted his explanation to 'Mygdele', which is admittedly the earliest record, but there is no 'd' in subsequent records. Positing an original *mig dol lle* = *migdele* = 'bog meadow place' where *dol* is later dropped, gives the shortened form *mig lle* = *migle* = 'bog place', and then by metathesis *migel* as, perhaps, in the records from 1183 to 1379. The modern name holds truer to the preceding *migle.*

Meldrum (Garioch) – 1291 Melgedrom, 1296 Melkidrum
maelog-y-trum, maelogdrum = 'princely hill-ridge'
* Johnston – Seems same as Megginch, if so then Gaelic *mal(a)g drum* = 'noble hill-ridge'.

Melrose (Roxburgh) – 700 Mailros, 1124 Malros, Melros
moel rhos = 'bare moor' or 'bare-hill on the moor'
* Johnston – British *maol ros, mail ros* = 'bare moor'.
** Melrose nestles in the lee of the Eildon Hills – which see.

Mendick (West Linton) – 1190 Menedicte, 1215 Mynedicht, Mynidicht
mynyddig = 'little-mountain' or 'little moorland-pasture'
* Johnston – British-Welsh *mynyddig* = 'hilly' is probably abnormal, but Cornish *menedh ithic* = 'large hill' is a suitable description.
* Watson – The first part looks like Welsh *mynydd.*
** *mynyddig* = 'little mountain', but *mynydd dig* = 'mountain of anger', *munid* is a common, corrupted form, of *mynydd.*

Menmuir (Brechin) – 1280 Menmoreth
maen mawr = the 'great Stone'
* Johnston – Probably like Irish *meen mor* = 'big mountain meadow'.
** Welsh *maen mawr, maen mor* = 'big stone', 'great stone'; a Pictish Stone perhaps? There is at least one of these now in Brechin cathedral.

Menstrie (Alloa) – 1261 Mestryn, 1263 Mestreth, 1315 Mestry, 1392 Menstry, 1505 Menstray
maestre, maestref = 'flat-field by the steading'
maen ystre, maenystref = 'stone steading'
* Johnston – see Watson.
* Watson – The 'n' (from 1392 on) seems to be intrusive, and the name is probably Welsh *maes dref, maes tref* = 'hamlet in the plain'.
** Watson's solution *maes dref* comes from *maes y tref,* which without the definite article, and therefore unlenited, is simply *maes tre.* Elsewhere Johnston notes the existence of *ystre, ystref* as another Welsh word for 'hamlet', 'steading, which suggests an alternative *maen ystre* = *maenystre* = *maenstre* = 'stone steading', or perhaps 'stone by the steading'. This would account for the present-day name and the records of 1392 and 1505, but not the others, for which *maestre* is better suited.

Menteith (Perth) – 1175-1178 Menetethe, Menetethet, 1185 Meneted, 1234 Mynynteth, Mynteth, 1724 Monteath
mynydd Teith = 'mountain, or hill pasture-land, of Teith', where Teith is a district rather than the River itself
* Johnston – Gaelic *moine teith* = 'moss, moor, of the river Teith'.
* Watson – Skirts around the subject somewhat but seems to be agreeing with Menteith = *mynydd Teith.*
** 'menet', 'mynt' & 'mont' are classic representations of a perhaps earlier-existing Welsh *mynydd* = 'mountain' or 'high, rough, moorland, pasture-land'.

Methven (Perth) – 1150 Matefen, 1172-1178 Afen, 1211 Methfen, 1304 Mehtven, 1371, 1376 Methven, 1500 Mechwynn
medd faen = 'middle stone', 'middle marker'. See Ross below.
* Johnston – It is pronounced 'Meffan'; otherwise see Watson.
* Watson – The name seems to be for Welsh *medd faen* = 'mead stone'.
* Ross – Brythonic *medd faen,* Welsh *med faen* = 'middle-stone' or 'middle-marker', as of a boundary.
** The pronunciation of med faen easily slips into 'meffan'.

Mey (Dunnet) –
mai = 'a plain' or 'flat-ground', 'piece of flat ground'
* Johnston – Gaelic-locative *magh* = 'a plain'.
** See May Island also.

Midmar (Echt, Aberdeens) – 1300 Migmarre
See Johnston and Watson below.
* Johnston – Probably Welsh *mig, mign* = 'bog' – of Mar
* Watson – Welsh *mig mar* = 'bog of mar' – it is the lowest part of Mar.

Migdale (Bonar bridge) –
mig dol = 'bog meadow'
* Johnston – Probably = 'midge-dale'.

Migvie (Tarland) – 1160 Migaveth, 1183 Miguwith
mig y fedd = 'bog of the grave, tomb'. See Watson below.
* Johnston – hybrid Welsh *mig* = 'bog' plus Gaelic *eaghmaidh* = 'hill-face', therefore = 'bog by the hill-face'.
* Watson – Welsh *mig* = 'bog' plus Gaelic *eaghaidh* (which he does not translate).

Migvie (Stratherrick), (Kirriemuir) – as for Migvie (Tarland).

Milleur (Loch Ryan) – early record as Pont Mullawyr
mul awyr = 'sad sky'
moel awyr = 'bare, featureless – sky'
maelor = 'market' place
* Johnston – Gaelic *meall odhar* = 'grey hill'.
** Of the above alternatives the 'early record' Pont Mullawyr would favour Welsh *pont maelor* = 'market bridge'.

Millig (Hellensbrugh) – 1294 Muleig, 1664 Milligs
moelig = 'little bare-hill'
* Johnston – Diminutive of Gaelic *maol* = 'little round-hill'.

Minigaff, Monigaff (Newton Stuart) – 1504 Monygof, 1573 Mynniegof
maen y gof = 'stone of the smith' or 'stone by the smith' i.e. his smithy?
* Johnston – Welsh *mynyd y gof* = 'hill of the smith' or Gaelic *moine gobha* = 'moor of the smith'.
** The records are late but Johnston's *mynydd-y-gof* is perhaps the more likely as the Welsh original subsequently translated into Scots-Gaelic as *moine gobha* which then gives rise to the modern name.

Minto (Denholm, Borders) – 1166 Munethov, 1275 Minto, 1296 Mynetowe, 1320 Minthov

mynyddof = 'gentle mountain'
* Johnston – Probably a hybrid, Old-Welsh *minit*, Welsh *mynydd* = 'a hill' plus Scots *how*, Old-English *holh* = 'a hollow', 'a hole'.
* Watson – Minto is near the Minto Hills 900ft high. A hybrid, the first part of which is Old-Welsh *minit*; the second part may be Scots *how* = 'a hollow' or *heugh* = 'hill'.
** The first element is *mynydd* = 'mountain', the second element is less certain but is possibly *dof* = 'gentle, tame, not-wild). Hence, *mynydd dof* and by assimilation *mynyddof* = 'tame, gentle, mountain'. Tallies well with the 1166 and1320 records.

Mochrum (Port William) – 1329 Mouchrome, 1342 Machrome
ma crom, ma crwm = 'bending flat-field', 'bowed flat field'
* Johnston – Old Gaelic-locative *mo chruim*, from *magh crom* = 'crooked plain' *
* The records are not that old so there is a definite possibility that the name is based on an early *ma crom, ma crwm*.

Molland (Drymen) –
moelan = 'small bare-topped hill'
* Johnston – Gaelic *moilean* = 'a little lump'.

Moncrieff Hill (Perths) – 726 Monid Croib, 728 Monad Croib, Monagh Craebi, 1400 Moynid Crewe
mynydd crwb, mynydd crwbi = 'hunchback mountain'
* Johnston – Gaelic *monadh craoibh* = 'hill with trees'.
* Watson – hybrid Welsh *mynydd* plus Gaelic *craobh* = 'hill of the tree', with reference to some conspicuous tree, possibly a tribal tree.

Monimusk (Alford) – 1170 Monimusc, 1315 Monimusk
mon y mwswg = 'isolated-place in the moss' where moss = bog?

mynydd-y-mwswg = 'mountain, hill, in the bog' or 'rough-pasture by the bog'
* Johnston – Gaelic *moine muiseig* 'bog of the scolding woman'.
** In Scottish place-names *mynydd* is often seen in the reduced form 'mon'.

Monkcroft (Perth) – 1271 Mukracht, 1609 Muckcroft
moch rhocheid = 'grunting pigs' (place of)
* Johnston – Gaelic *mucaireachd* = 'a herding of swine'.

Montrose (Angus) – 1178 Munros, 1200 Monros, 1296 Montrose, 1332 Monros, 1488 Montros
mwn rhos = 'neck of the moor', possibly where the moor narrows to form a headland
* Johnston – Gaelic *moine rois* = 'moss on the promontory', which applies to the site of Old Montrose ('moss' = 'bog'?).
* Watson – In Gaelic *mon-rois* = 'moor of the cape', *mon* being the short form of *monadh*.
** The recurrent 't' of 1296, 1488 and now, might suggest *mwnt rhos* = 'little mound on the moor' as an alternative. Elsewhere Watson gives Gaelic *monadh* as being 'borrowed' from Welsh *mynydd*.

Morar (Inverness) – circa 970 Morderer, 1343 Morhover, 1371 Moruar, 1372 Moreobyr
mor dwr = 'sea water' : 'sea stream'. See Watson below.
* Johnston – It is Gaelic *mor dhobar* = 'big water'.
* Watson – Early forms are Mordhobhar, Moreovyr, Morowore: These are doubtless old British names taken over into Gaelic.
** If Watson is right then it is possibly from *mor dwr* = 'sea stream' or *mor dwr / mawr dwr* = 'big stream'. The former meaning is the more likely as the river Morar is only some 100 yds long from it's source in Loch Morar to it's emptying into the sea.

Moray (North East) – 1100 Moreb, 1136 Muref, 1199 Morewe, 1205 Muraef, 1295 Moref
mor tref, mor tre = 'sea steading'
* Johnston – The first part is Gaelic *muir, mor* = 'sea' and the second part is probably the old locative *-aibh* so *moraibh* = place – 'by the sea'. But though there is no 't' in the old forms Watson is sure it is Celtic *mori treb* = 'sea-settlement', Welsh *'tref, tre'* = 'a house'.
** In Gaelic 'sea' is *muir,* in Welsh 'sea' is *mor* – a word I cannot find in my Gaelic dictionary, the inference therefore is that this name originates in the Welsh language rather than the Gaelic. Even so, both Watson's and Johnston's arguments are somewhat tenuous. Welsh 'b' mutates into 'f' so all the records except that of 1199 seem consistent. But the meaning remains elusive!

More, Ben –

** In Scotland there are 'many' hills with the name 'Ben More', – some of which undoubtedly originated as Welsh *Ben Mawr* = 'Big-Hill'.

Morphie (St Cyrus) – 1370 Morphy, Morfy
morfa, morfai = 'sea plain'
morfa = 'sea-brink', 'sea-marsh'
* Johnston – Probably Pictish-Welsh *morfa* = 'a moor, marsh'.
* Watson – Welsh *morfa* = 'sea-plain'. Morphie is on the coast and on an elevated plain on the North side of the Esk.
** *morfa* is from *mor* = 'sea', and *fa*-also-*fai* = 'flat-ground', 'flat-field', 'plain'. Clearly *mor fai* can account for the *'phy'* & *'fy'* endings in the early records. When combined into one compound word as *morfa* the meaning changes to = 'sea-brink', 'sea-marsh, bog, fen', but in this particular place there seems little argument against the conclusion Morphie = *mor fai* = 'flat ground by the sea'.

Mossfennan (Broughton) – 1249 Mospennoc, 1296 Mesfennon
maes ffynnon = 'flat-field by the well'
maes penoc = 'flat-field by the little-hill-top'
* Johnston – Probably original Welsh *maes pennog* = 'plain with the little-hill', influenced by English *moss* and Gaelic *bheinan* = 'little ben'.
* Watson – In some cases at least *maes* appears as *moss* as in Mossfennan where the second element may be Welsh *ffynnon* = 'a well'.
** It seems the place started life with the name *maespenoc* but later took the name *maes fynnon.*

Mossgiel (Mauchline) –
maes y cil, maesgil = 'field in the corner, nook'
* Johnston – Old Norse *gil* = 'narrow glen'.
** *maes* appearing here in the form 'moss', *y cil* lenited to *gil,* then assimilated to give *mossgil* hence Mossgiel.

Mosspaul (Ewes Water) –
maes pwll = 'flat-field by the stream'
* Johnston – The 'paul' is probably Welsh *pwll* = 'pool, stream'.
** If *maes* shows as *moss* then we have *maes pwll* = *mosspwl* = 'flat-field, open-ground, by the pool – or stream'. The likelihood here is, as Johnston suggests, that 'paul' in Mosspaul is for *pol* or *poll,* both of which derive from *pwll* but with the amended meaning 'pooly-stream', 'sluggish-stream' or simply 'stream'.

Mosspeeble (Ewes dale) – 1506 Mospeble
maes pebyll = 'flat-ground – tents'. See Watson below.
* Watson – most probably for Welsh *maes pebyll* = 'tent field'.
** The literal meaning of *maes pebyll* is 'flat-ground, tents'; a more imaginative meaning might be 'flat-ground of the tent-people' (see Peebles).

Moulin (Pitlochry) – 1207 Molin, 1323 Molyn
moelyn = 'small bare-topped hill'
* Johnston – See Watson.
* Watson – Gaelic *maolinn* = ' bare round-hillock'.

Mounthooly (Borders) (2. N. East)
mynydd haulwen = 'sunshine mountain'; 'sunshine rough-pasture'

* Johnston – Perhaps Gaelic *monadh chuile* = 'hill with the corner or nook'.
** *haulwen* to *haulwy* to *hauly* by conversion of '*en*' to '*y*' and ellipsis of '*w*'. In Scottish place names *mynydd* is commonly found in the form 'mount', 'mont', 'monadh' etc. Hence we get *mounthauly* = Mounthooly.

Mowhaugh (Morebattle) – 1150 Moille –
moel lle = 'bare-topped-hill place'
* Johnston – Gaelic *moil -le* = 'a heap'.
** *moel lle* lenits and amalgamates to *moille*. Subsequently Scots *haugh* = 'river-meadow land' replaces Welsh *lle* – probably as a more apt description. But maybe in 1150 there was no 'meadow'?

Moy (Inverness) – 1235 Muy, 1497 Moye
mai = 'flat ground', 'flat field', 'a plain'
* Johnston – Gaelic-locative of *magh* = *moigh* = 'at the plain'.

Mulben (Elgin) – 1328 Molben, 1367 / 1368 Mulbynne
moel ben = 'bare hill-top'
* Johnston – Gaelic *maol beinn* = 'bare round hill'.

Mye (Buchlyvie) – 1510 Mye.
mai = 'flat-ground', 'flat-field, 'a plain'
* Johnston – Gaelic *magh* = 'a plain'.
** The pronunciation of *mai* is as that of Mye.

N

Nant River, Glen Nant (Taynuilt)
nant = 'stream', (Glen Nant = *glyn nant* = 'valley with a stream')
* Johnston – Gaelic *neannta* = 'nettles'.
** Johnston's interpretation would give Glen Nant = 'valley of the river Nettles' – Not a very likely name for a Scottish river? There seems no reason to look further than Welsh 'Glyn Nant'. But also see Taychreggan.

Nethy River (Grantown) –
neddai, (neddau or neddyf) = 'adze'
* Johnston – early forms of Abernethy suggest Gaelic *an eitighich* = 'at the narrow opening, gulley'.
** Other rivers also have names relating to cutting tools or burrowing animals. But see also entry for 'Abernethy'.

Nevis (River and Ben) – 1552 Nevess, 1769 Nevish
nefus = 'the-heavenly-one', *ben nefus* = 'hill-top, summit, of the heavenly-one'
* Johnston – Local Gaelic name was *Nibheis* in 1532. Others have suggested Gaelic *ni-maise* = 'no beauty', – seemingly appropriate to this ungainly Ben. Another suggestion has been to connect it with the nymph *Nebestis,* from *neb* = 'cloud'.
* Watson – Macbain took the name from an early *Nebestis* or *Nebesta* of which the root *neb* or *nebh* is connected with clouds or water. The Gaelic spelling *nimheis* if connected to Old-Irish *nem, neim,* probably means 'venomous one'.
** Possibly related to *nef* = 'heaven'. Ben Nevis is the highest mountain in Scotland and its head is almost always in the clouds – in the heavens! It takes it's name from the river Nevis which flows away from it's summit down Glen Nevis and empties into Loch Linnhe at Fort William. A name for such a great topographical feature such as this will

surely have existed in pre-Gaelic times as also would the name of it's eponymous river. Thus Nevis could be *nefus* (pronounced 'neviss') where *-us* is a suffix converting *nef* = 'heaven' to *nefus* = 'heavenly' and giving the meaning of the river name as 'the heavenly one', possibly a 'goddess-type' river name. Similarly Ben Nevis = *y-pen-nefus,* aspirated to *ben nefus* = 'mountain of the heavenly one', a deserved tribute to its great height and massive bulk. In modern Welsh the word for heavenly is *nefol,* utilising the alternative suffix *-ol,* the meaning being unchanged. Neither one of the Gaelic alternatives is very attractive. Johnston, it would seem, was being understandably cautious by not venturing any opinion of his own, and Watson's response is equally non committal – except for his reference to McBain's 'early Nebestis / Nebesta', which he (Watson) says has its roots in *neb* or *nebh* – but whether these last are of Brythonic or Goidelic origin Watson does not say!

Newbattle (Dalkeith) – 1141 Niwebothla, 1145 Newbotill, 1295 Neubattail, 1500 Nowbattle
newydd bod lle = 'new dwelling place', 'new place of residence'
* Johnston – Old-English *neowe botl* = 'new dwelling'.
** *newydd bod lle* truncates to *newydbodle.*

Newburn (Largo) – 1135-1250 Nithbren
newydd pren = 'new tree' (Watson)
newydd bryn = 'new hill' (Johnston)
* Johnston – Probably Celtic *newydd bryn* = 'new-hill'.
* Watson – Here the second part may well be Welsh *pren* = 'tree'; the first part is Welsh *newydd* in which case Nithbren might mean 'new-tree'.
** *newydd pren* aspirates to *newyddbren* then by metathesis etc. to *newydbern* = 'new tree', possibly one of Watson's 'Tribal-Trees' as mentioned elsewhere?

Niddrie (Musselburgh) – 1249 Nodref. 1266 Noderyf, 1296 Nudreff, 1506 Nudry, 1572 Nidderie
newydd dre = 'new steading'. See Watson below.
* Johnston – Welsh *nuadh tref* = 'new house, or settlement'.
* Watson – The first part may be Welsh *newydd* ='new', the second part is *tre, tref, dre, dref* = 'a stead'. In total Niddrie = *newydd dre* = 'Newstead'.
** Johnston again seems to have mixed up Welsh *newydd* = 'new' with Scots-Gaelic *nuadh* = 'new'.

Niddrie (Winchburgh) – as for Niddrie Musselburgh

Nith River (Dumfries) – 1181 Nud, 1240 Nyth
See Johnston below.
* Johnston – Probably root is Welsh *newydd* = 'new', or Gaelic *nuadh* = 'new'.
** Johnston has got his *newydds* and his *nuadhs* right this time! But this is a river name and as such is almost certain to precede the Scots-Gaelic language.

Nyadd (Stirling)
neuadd = 'hall' see Nydie following.

Nydie (St Andrew's) – 1144 to 1220 – Nidin, 1471 Wester Nydy
neuaddyn = 'small Hall' where 'Hall' is as in 'large-residence' or 'big-room'
* Johnston – Probably Gaelic-locative *nead, nid* = 'a nest' with *-ie* locative. The 'n' in Nidin is a scribe's flourish.
** Conversion' of *-yn* to *-y* or *-ie* gives *neuaddyn* = *neuaddy* = Nydy, and *neuaddie* = Nydie. Earliest records Nidin tally with *neuaddyn*, the 1471 record tallies with *neuaddy*.

O

Ochiltree (Auchinleck) – 1200 Okeltre, 1317 Houchiltre, 1506 Uchiltre, 1537-1572 Vchiltre
uchel tre = 'high steading'. See Johnston below.
* Johnston – Welsh *uchel tre* = 'high house'.
* Watson – is not specific but in his dissertations on the Welsh element *tref* he refers to about 17 other Ochiltrees throughout Scotland.

Ochil Hills (Clackmanan) – 850 Nochel, 1461 Oychellis, 1580 Ocelli Montes
uchel = 'high' i.e. 'high hills'
* Johnston – from Welsh *uchel* = 'high'.
** The persistent 'o' in place of 'u' in these old forms may possibly hint at a dialectic variation, *ochil* in place of '*uchel*'. (See Ogle, Ogilface, Ogilvie, Ochiltree)

Ochtertyre, Auchtertyre (Lochalsh) – 1495 Wochterory, 1527 Ochtertere
uchder tir = 'land of height' = 'land at altitude' perhaps
* Johnston – Gaelic *uachdar tire* = 'upper part of the land'.
** The records are quite late and possibly more than a little corrupted. But Ochtertere tallies well with *uchder tir*.

Offerance (Buchlyvie) 1451 Offeris
See Johnston below.
* Johnston – Possibilities are based on Welsh *offeren*, Old Irish *oifrend*, Gaelic *aifrionn*, all of which = 'place of the Mass' – a 'religious service'.
** The old forms are no help.

Ogilface (Torphichen) – 1200 Ogelface, Okelfas, 1392 Ogleface, 1450 Ogilface
uchel faes = 'high flat-ground', 'high flat-field', 'high plain'. See Watson.
* Johnston – British *ocel fas* = 'high station'. Welsh *maes*

aspirated to *faes* = 'field'.
* Watson – Possibly for *uchelfaes* = 'high field'.

Ogilvie Glen (Glamis) – 1205 Ogilvin, 1296 Eggilvyne
uchel faen = 'high-stone'
* Johnston – British *ocel,* Old-Welsh *ugl* = 'high'. and perhaps Welsh *ma, fa* = 'plain', but as likely Gaelic *beinn.* (Presumably therefore British-Welsh 'valley of the high-plain' or hybrid Gaelic-Welsh 'valley of the high-mountain'.)
** It is the consistent 'n' in the endings of the two early records which favours *faen* as the second element rather than *faes, fa,* or *fai.* In Wales a 'Maen' tends to be a Stone of some significance i.e. a 'standing-stone', a 'marker-stone', a 'boundary-stone' or a Stone of some other significance. In this respect the name here could be connected with the presence of a Pictish Stone in nearby Glamis. This may also be a case, in the change of Ogilvin to Ogilvie, where the Scots inventive replacement of Celtic *-yn, -in, --en* diminutive endings by the Scots diminutive suffix *-ie, -y* or, *-i,* seems to have been extended to other '-in', '-yn', '-en' endings which are not in themselves diminutives – *glyn uchel faen* = 'high valley of the stone'.

Ogilvie (Perths) – 1172 Oggoueli, 1239 Ogeluin
uchel fai = 'high-plain', 'high open-field'. Old-Welsh *ugl fai.*
* Watson – Possibly for *uchel faes* = 'high-field'.
** The first record favours *ugl fai* but the second record with it's 'n' ending might favour *uchelfaen.* Both records can result in the present name Ogilvie. Compare with Ogilface and Ogilvie Glen.

Ogle Glen (Killin) –
ugil lle = 'high place'
* Johnston – See Ogilvie and Ochil.
** Possibly British *ocel,* Old-Welsh *ugl,* Welsh *uchel* = 'high', plus Welsh *lle, 'le',* = 'place'. Otherwise see previous

Ogilface, Ogilvie Glen and Ogilvie.

Ouse (a stream, Jedburgh) –
y-gwys / wys = 'deep, profound'
wys = 'having an aptitude for motion'!
* Johnston – Celtic for 'water'. Irish *os.* Otherwise same as English Ouse but see Oxenham.
** 'deep, profound' may not be a good description of a small stream but very apt when applied to the great Ouse rivers of England. The name there is said to be a Celtic or pre-Celtic river name meaning 'water', but these 'Celtic' English names will certainly not be 'Irish'. Another possibility is *y-gwys* aspirated to *wys* = 'pig-stream'. Several rivers and streams have 'pig', boar', or 'swine' type names and 'having an aptitude for motion' might simply mean a 'great-little-mover', or even more simply 'lively'. The description 'great-little-mover' could apply to almost any small stream.

Oxnam, Oxenham (Jedburgh) – 1150 Oxeneham, Oxanaham, 1177 Oxeham, 1360 Oxingham
ox nant ham = *ocs* (British for 'water) + *nant* (Welsh for 'stream') + *ham* (English for 'steading, farm'). The meaning then is – 'farm on the water by the stream'
* Johnston – Old-English *oxena ham* = 'oxen's home'. It stands on a little stream the Ousenan, now Oxnam, so possibly, as some think, it is as in 'Oxford', and *ox* is simply a variation of Celtic *oc* = 'water'. The district can never have been very good for oxen.
** Expanding on Johnston's theme it is possible to think of 'Ousenan' as coming from *wysen nant* = 'lively little-stream', or 'little-pig stream' and the place as initially taking it's name from it's stream, the Ousenan. Otherwise, the stream through the village is now known as Oxenham Water and this may support the hybrid *ox-nant-ham* suggestion, the terminal '*t*' in 'nant' drops off easily to give 'oxnanham' and

slovenly speech habits quickly dispose of the intrusive '*n*' to give 'oxanham'. The rest, as they say, is History!

Oykell River (Sutherland) – 1365 Okel, 1490 Ochell, 1515 Akkell
British *ocel*, Old-Welsh *ugl*, Welsh *uchel* = 'high'
* Johnston – British for 'high', Welsh *uchel*.
* Watson – The name is not Gaelic nor is it Norse, but may go back to Early-Celtic, Old-British *uxellos* which may have become something like *uckel* at the time of the Vikings (sometime after the 8th or 9th century?).

P

Paisley (Glasgow) – 1157 Passaleth, 1158 Paisleth, 1163 Passelet, Passelay, 1508 Paislay, 1550 Passele
pasg-y-lle, pasgyle = 'feeding, fattening – place'
pasg ar y lleddf = 'fattening place – on the slope'
* Johnston – Probably Welsh *pasgell llethr* = 'pasture slope'. Kuno Meyer the originator of the suggestion that the name is a corruption of Latin Basilica later withdrew it as being based on unsatisfactory evidence.
* Watson – Paisley may be of British origin. Otherwise from Latin *basilica* = 'church'.
** Johnston's *llethr* is not found in modern Welsh dictionaries and this may be a misprint for *lleddf* = 'smooth' or 'placid' or 'oblique, sloping'. Also modern *pasg* = 'a feeding', 'a fattening' and *pasgell* is a diminutive. There is however a noticeable absence of the letter 'g' in all the available records, which is not explained. An alternative possibility is *pas lle, pasle* = 'exit place' = the 'way-out' (from Glasgow maybe? – must have been popular!). But this does not account for the '*th*' endings in the earliest records which

lleddf does. To obtain something like Passaleth from *pasg ar y lleddf* would require elision of the intervening *-g ar* to give *pasylleddf*. Which is not impossible seeing that Welsh mutations cause an initial 'g' to disappear?

Palinkum (Kirkmaiden) – early reference as *Pont* Poolinkum
polyn cam = 'curving little-stream'
* Johnston – Gaelic *poll linne cam* = 'stream with crooked pool'.
** 'poll', 'pol' is said to be a P-Celtic, British term for 'stream' associated with Welsh *pwll* = 'pool', 'pit'. The diminutive of *pwll* is *pwlyn* so, similarly, one would expect the diminutive of P-Celtic *pol* to be *polyn*. In which case Poolinkum could be *polyn cam* = 'bent, or bowing, little-stream'.

Panbride (Carnoustie) – 1200 Pannebrid, 1261 Pannebride, 1485 Panbrid
pant Bride = 'St Brigit's hollow'. See Johnston and Watson below.
* Johnston – Headland of St Bridget. British-Pictish *pann* = 'head' plus 'Brid, Bride' = St Bridget.
* Watson – *pant Bride* = 'St Brigit's hollow'. Welsh *pant* = 'hollow'. Final 't' is very often dropped in Welsh, and it appears to have dropped here with us. The Parish of Panbride has two hollows with streams which unite about a mile from the sea.
** St Brigit could be any one of seventeen 'saints' of that same name!

Panmure (Carnoustie) – 1261 & 1268 Pannemore
pant mawr = 'big hollow'. See Watson below.
* Johnston – See Panbride. Gaelic *mor* = 'big', is often confused with Scots *muir* = 'moor'.
* Watson – Panmure House stands near the head of the larger hollow, (see Panbride), Panmure is therefore most

probably for *pant mawr* = 'big hollow'.

Pardovan (Linlithgow) – 1150 Pardufin, 1282 Purduuyn, 1296 Pardevyn, 1372 Pardovine, 1542 Perdovin
pawr dyfon = 'deep pasture'
* Johnston – Welsh *parr ddwfn* = 'deep-lying parcel-of-ground'. Local pronunciation is Parduvan.
* Watson – It seems to be for Welsh *par-ddwfn* = 'deep-field', with reference either to soil or to position.
** No trace of *par, parr* = 'field', 'parcel-of-ground' in my Welsh dictionaries. The nearest is *pawr* = 'pasture'. The words for 'deep' are *dwfn, dyfon,* and *dyfn,* the first two of these accord with Johnston's 'local pronunciation' = duvan.

Partick (Glasgow) – 1136 Perdeyc, 1158 Pertheck, 1172 Perdehic, 1174, 1179 Pertheic, 1186 Perthec, 1383 Perthic
perthawc = place-of 'little-bushes'. See Johnston below.
perthig = 'little-thicket'
* Johnston – Diminutive of Old Welsh *pert,* Welsh *perth* = 'thicket'. Alternatively *perthog* = place – 'full of bushes'.
* Watson – In Gaelic it is called *Pearraig, Pearthaig* which suggest an earlier British *Peredic,* but the meaning is obscure to me.
** *perthog, perthoc, perthig, perthawc,* are all diminutives of *perth* = 'bush, brake, hedge, thicket'.

Peebles (Borders) – 1116 Pobles, 1126 Pebles, 1136 Peples, 1141 Pebbles, Pebles
pebyllos, pebylos; pebyllais, pebylais = 'place of many-tents'. See Johnston and Watson below.
* Johnston – Welsh *pabell,* plural *pebyll* = 'tent, tents', place-of.
* Watson – *pebyll* = 'tents, pavilions', place-of. The term corresponds to common English 'shiel, shiels'.
** *pabell, pebyll* names occur throughout Eastern Scotland. It may be that they refer not simply to 'tents' but to 'tent-

people' i.e. to people who lived in tents, as they did in pre-Celtic times. Cairnpapple is such a name and the provenance of this site goes back to 2,500 BC.

Peffer Burn – See entry in Edinburgh Names. See also Strath Peffer

Pencaitland (East Lothian) – 1150 Pencatlet, 1210 Pencathlan, 1250 Penkatland
pen cait lan = 'enclosure at the far-end of the wood'. See Johnston and Watson below.
* Johnston – Old-Welsh *pen chet* = 'head of the wood' and *llan* = 'enclosure'.
* Watson – *pen cet llan* = 'clearing at the head of the wood'. Old-Welsh *coet* appears with fair certainty as *-cet* in Pencaitland. Before *lann* (*llan*) came to mean 'church' it meant an 'enclosure', a 'court', *pen* is for 'head, end'. Pencaitland is then 'end of the clearing in the wood'.
** Some older forms of Welsh *coed* are – *coet, cait, cet, ceth, chet* and 'far-end' is one meaning of *pen.*

Pencraig (East Linton) –
pen craig = 'head of the crag'. See Watson below.
* Watson – *pen craig* = 'rock-end'.
** *pen* has more than one meaning, see Welsh word-elements.

Penchrise Pen (Hawick) – 1368 Penercerys, 1380 Pencriz, Penchrist
See Johnston below.
* Johnston – Old Welsh *pen crys* = 'height with a band or girdle round it'.
* Watson – Includes it in his treatment of 'British' names but does not give a meaning other than *pen* = 'head, etc.'
** Modern Welsh *crys* = 'shirt, shift' or 'haste, speed'.

Pendrich, Pendreich (Bridge of Allan) – 1288 Petendreich, 1503 Pettyndreich
pethyn drych = 'small-share sight, view' then Pictized to *pet-tyn-drych* = 'little-croft view'
* Johnson – British or Pictish *pet an drych* = 'farm, croft of the view', Welsh *drych* = 'sight, aspect, spectacle'.
* Watson – hybrid British-Pictish-Welsh *pit, pett* = 'share-land', plus Scots-Gaelic *dreach* = 'aspect', 'face', – it has the specialized meaning 'hill-face' in Scottish place-names. Thus the name is 'hill-face croft', or 'croft of the hill-face'
** This is a *Pit, Pet* or *Pett* type name of which there are many in Eastern Scotland. It is generally described as 'Pictish'. Watson compares the element with Welsh *peth* and postulates an earlier P-Celtic root. It was, he says, 'taken over into Gaelic from British'. Welsh *peth* does not appear in the place-names of Wales but was evidently specialised in Pictland in the sense 'portion', 'share' and now seems to have the meaning of 'croft' in Scottish place-names.

Penicuik (Midlothian) – 1250 Penicok, 1296 Penycoke
See Johnston and Watson below.
* Johnston – Welsh *pen y cog* = 'hill of the cuckoo'.
* Watson – *pen-y-gog,* here unlenited as *pen-y-cog* = 'cuckoo's hill'.

Peninerin (South Uist) –
penyn eirin = 'little-hill with plum-trees'.
* Johnston – Gaelic *peighinn an aorainn* = 'pennyland of the mass'.
** It may be heresy to think of a Welsh name surviving in the Western Isles – but why not? This particular name positively *invites* an attempt to provide a Welsh interpretation! See also Pennycross.

Pennan (Fraserburgh) – 1654 Pennan.
penan = 'little-head' – 'little-headland'

* Johnston – British for Gaelic *ceanan* = 'little-head' – 'little headland'. Welsh *pen* is very rare North of Perth.
** Also possible is *pen nant* with final 't' dropped; 'easily done' says Watson. Thus *pennan* = 'hill by the stream', or 'headland by the stream', or simply 'far-end of the stream', or 'far-end of the headland'. The topography may help to determine which.

Pennygant (Liddesdale) –
pen-y-cant aspirated to *penygant* = 'dome-shaped hill', or 'far-end of the hoop' (rim of a circle).
*pen-y-gwan*t = as below.
* Johnston – Probably Welsh *pen y gwant* = 'height of the butt or mark'.
* Watson – It may stand for *pen y gwant* = 'head of the mark, or of the butt'.
** Another 'penny' name, but this time both Johnston and Watson agree it is not a 'Pennyland of this-or-that' but Welsh *pen-y*. Why look anywhere else?

Pennycross (Mull) – 1600 Peanagross
pen y croes = 'far-end crossroads'
* Johnston – Gaelic *peanagross* = 'pennyland of the cross'
** This is another Island name for which it is tempting to consider a Welsh derivation: *pen-y-croes* tallies with the present day name but when lenited to *pen-y-groes* = it tallies better with the 1600 record. See Pennygant also.

Pennytersan (Kilmalcolm) –
pen-y-tir-sant = 'end, far-end of the Saint's land' – possibly?
* Johnston – British *penn tarsuinn* = 'oblique hill'.
** No sign of *tarsuinn* = 'oblique' in my Dictionaries, nearest is *traws* = 'oblique, perverse'. Nor, interestingly, is there any attempt by Johnston to claim this as a 'Pennyland' name. The final 't' in *sant* drops off to give *penytirsan*.

Penpont (Dumfries) –
pen pont = 'far-end of the bridge' (see Watson). Or 'hill by the bridge' (see Johnston)
* Johnston – Welsh *penn pont* = 'hill of the bridge'.
* Watson – Penpont might, it is said, be 'derived from *pendens pons*, an arched bridge, there being a bridge of one semicircular arch supported by two steep rocks over the river Scar'. The meaning is, of course, 'Bridge-End'.

Pentland Hills – 1150 Pentlant, 1250 Pentland
See entry in Edinburgh Names.

Pentoot (Glencairn) –
pen twd = 'projecting hill', 'projecting headland'
* Johnston – *pen twt* = 'height of the look-out hill'.
** No sign of *twt* = 'look-out' in any of my Welsh Dictionaries – but *twdd* = 'that which pokes-out, or juts-out'. With the final 'dd' reduced to 'd' and then replaced by 't' we get *pentwt*.

Penvenna, Penveny (Stobo) –
pen faeni = 'headstones'
pen faenor = 'head district'
* Johnston – Welsh *pen faen* = 'head stone'.

Persie (Blairgowrie) – 1214 Parthesyn, 1529 Perse
perthosyn = place – 'full-of-little thickets'. i.e. something like a 'copse'.
* Johnston – Probably Pictish-locative *perthais* = 'wood place'.
* Watson – In the absence of old records this may be derived from *preas* = 'a copse'.
** The first element in Parthesyn could be *perth* = 'brake, thicket' (as JBJ says). Alternatively it could be *parth* = 'part, region, district', but the second element *esyn* is then obscure. A further suggestion is *perthos* = 'place full of thickets' plus the diminutive ending *-yn* giving *perthosyn* as above. Then

-yn to -ie giving *perthosie* finally truncated to *persie*.

Perth (Perths) – 1120 Pert, 1150 Perth, 1220 Perth
perth = 'thicket' – place. See Watson below.
* Johnston – Probably meant for Gaelic *barr Tha* = 'height over Tay', Welsh *perth* = 'a thicket'.
* Watson – Welsh *perth* is a bush, brake, copse, found with us in the name of the town and county of Perth.

Pettinain (Carstairs) – 1130 Padinnan, 1150 Pedynnane, Peduenane, 1580 Pettynane
ped dinan = at the – 'foot of the little hill-fort'
peth dinan Pictized to *pettdinan* = 'croft by the little hill-fort'
* Johnston – Old-Gaelic *pette nan en* = 'croft with the birds'. Otherwise *pette an athain* = 'at the little ford'.
** Welsh *ped* = 'foot', 'what bears onward'. But see Petty below.

Petty (Fort George) – 1250 Petin, 1400 Petyn
pethyn = 'little croft'. 'Pictish' – see Pettinain.
* Johnston – *pit*, spelt also *pedy, peth, pet, pette, pith, put*, is British-Pictish for a 'piece of land', then 'hamlet'. In Welsh, '*peth*'.
* Watson – British *pett* became Scots-Gaelic *peit*, the dative locative of which is seen in Petty, near Inverness.
** Conversion of '*yn*' to '*y*' gives *pethy* then *pety* from *pethyn* = 'small-part, small-share' – of land. In Scotland = 'little croft'?

Pinkie, Pinkey (Musselburgh) – 1260 Penke, 1548 Pynky
pen cae = 'top-end, far-end, of the field' – possibly.
* Johnston – British *pen ce* = 'height of Ce', (no certain meaning given for 'Ce').

Pinwinnie (Airdrie) –
pen gwyn – aspirated to *penwyn* = 'holy, blessed hill, hill-top', or simply 'white hill'

* Johnston – May be Welsh *penn gwynn* = 'white, fair, height', but as likely is Gaelic *peighinn mhoine* = 'penny-land on the moor'.

Pirn (Gala Water) – 1400 Pren, Pyrn
pren = 'a tree'
* Johnston – Welsh *pren* = 'a tree'.
* Watson – Welsh *pren* = a 'tree' occurs over a large part of Scotland. It is found by itself in Pirn, formerly Pren, near Innerleithen.
** Metathesis converts *pren* to *pern* and so to Pyrn, Pirn.

Pitmilly (Crail) – 1211 Pitmullin
peth melin = 'share-land mill', or 'croft mill', or simply 'mill cottage'?
* Johnston – Gaelic *muileann, muilinn* = 'croft with the mill'.
** Johnston does not acknowledge, or explain, the element *pit* except by including it in the given meaning. The 'Pictish' version of *peth* is *pitt* and the later 'Scots' conversion of *'in'* to *'y'* gives *peth melin* = *pittmely* and thence Pitmilly.

Pity Me (South of Jedburgh) –
peth-y-mai = 'part-of the flat-ground'
* Johnston – Welsh *peth y midd* = 'piece of the enclosed ground'. The pronunciation is 'peety mei'. Welsh *peth* is cognate with *pit* (see Petty) and final 'dd' in Welsh easily falls away.
** Is it possible that here, on the English side of the Scottish Border, we have a conversion of Welsh *peth* into Pictish *pit*? Yeeee – Haaaah!

Pluscarden (Elgin) – 1124 Ploschardin, 1226 Pluscardin
plas cardden = 'open-space in the copse'. Or – 'big-house by the copse, thicket'.
* Johnston – Pictish *plus cardin*, Welsh *plas cardden* = 'place with the wood, or brake'.
** *plas* has all the meanings – 'mansion', 'place', 'open-

space'. Johnston obviously had access to a Pictish Dictionary, something I have never been able to find!

Polmaise (Stirling) – 1147 Pollemaise, 1164 Polmase, 1372 Polmas – *mareschelle*
pwll maes, aspirated to *pwlmaes* = 'pool, or pit, in the flat-ground, flat-field'
* Johnston – Gaelic *maise* = 'pool of beauty'.
* Watson – *pwll maes* = 'pool (or hollow) of the plain'.
** If the first element is taken as 'British' – *pol, poll,* then this can have the meaning 'stream', therefore also, 'stream, in the, flat field'.

Polmont (Falkirk) – 1319 Polmunth, 1552 Polmond
pwll mynydd, from British-Welsh *pol* plus Welsh *mynydd* = 'pool or stream on the moorland pasture'
* Johnston – It is = 'stream or pool on the moorland hill', the second element *mont* = Gaelic *monadh.*
* Watson – It is 'pool hill', 'hollow hill' from *poll* = 'pool', also = 'hollow-place'.
** G.W.S. Barrow gives *pol* as a 'British' term which became *pwll* in Welsh, is found as *pol* in Old-English, passed into Scots as *pow* and possibly into Scots-Gaelic as *poll.* It can have the meanings – 'sluggish stream', 'non-sluggish stream', and 'pool'. Gaelic *monadh* derives from Welsh *mynydd.*

Ponfeigh (Lanarks) – 1370, 1371 Pollynfeyche
pwllyn buwchau = 'little-pool for the cows, cattle'
* Johnston – *poll an f(h)eidh* = 'pool of the deer'.
* Watson – *poll an fheidh* = 'the stag's water'.
** *pwllynbuwchau* lenited to *pwlynfuwchau* tallies well with the two early records. How this developed into Ponfeigh is somewhat obscure.

Posso (Peebles) – 1400 Possow, Possaw
See Watson.

* Johnston – May be British for 'calm water' – see Watson.
* Watson – Old-Welsh *poues* = 'rest, repose' plus *ma* = 'plain' gives Old-Welsh *pouisua,* whence probably Posso, a notably pleasant place on Manor Water, a situation which suggests it was the ancient seat of a British Chief.
** In modern Welsh we have *powys, pwys* = 'state of rest, repose', which can be compared to Watson's Old-Welsh *poues*. The second element which might go to the making of 'ow' or 'aw' is anyone's guess! Watson's *pouisua* is not altogether believable, nevertheless he seems convinced that this is a British-Welsh name of *some* sort.

Preasandye (Stirling) –
prysan du = 'dark, black, little-copse'.
* Johnston – Gaelic *preasan dubh* = 'dark little-thicket'.

Premnay (Insch) – 1198 Prameth
pren mai = 'tree on the flat-ground or flat-field'
* Johnston – Probably Pictish *pren a' mhaigh* = 'tree in the plain'.
** Johnston's explanation seems to ignore the early Prameth and assume the transposition of 'nm' to 'mn', making *pren a' maigh* = Prenmay = Premnay. The equivalent modern Welsh is *pren mai* = 'tree on the flat-ground, plain', Johnston's reasoning would transform this into *premnai* but the early record Prameth' remains unexplained.

Prendergast (Berwicks) – 1100 Prenegest, 1150 Prendergest
pren-y-gest = 'tree in the belly, paunch, receptacle'
pren tir gest = 'tree in the belly land', just possibly referring to a tree in a bowl-shaped depression within a narrow-necked valley?
* Johnston: Old Welsh *premter gest, premter cest* = 'Presbyter's (priest's) deep-glen'.
** The records are consistent in their spelling, 'p-r-e-n', there is no suggestion of an 'm', so unless Johnston had

further information which he has not disclosed his interpretation must surely fail? But the other postulations are also rather tortuous.

Prinside (Yetholm) – 1140 Praunwesete, Prenwensete, 1502 Prymsid

See Johnston and Watson below.

* Johnston – Hybrid Welsh *pren gwyn, gwen* = 'fair, white, tree' and English *sete* = 'seat'.

* Watson – Primside appears to be for Welsh *pren gwyn* = 'white tree' with English sete = 'seat', 'set'.

** *pren gwen* aspirates to *prenwen,* otherwise as Johnston and Watson above.

Pumpherston (Calders, Lothian) – 1684 Phumpherstoun

Anyones guess this!

* Johnston – The name 'Pumpher' is probably Danish dialect for 'short thickset man'.

** Possibly English 'ton' (steading) of a man named Pumphrey', this last being formed in the P-Celtic manner as *ap* Humphrey = Pumphrey = 'son of Humphrey'. Humphries is a common Welsh surname.

Q

Quair Water (Traquair) – 1116 Quyrd, 1174 Cuer, 1184 Queyr

gwyrdd = 'green'

gwyr = 'freshness, green-tinge'; or 'fresh, lively, pure'

* Johnston – Cornish *quirt,* later *gwer* = 'green'.

* Watson – Quair may perhaps be compared with *Gweir,* earlier *Gueir,* the river Weir, which is supposed to mean 'the clear one'.

** River name as *gwyrdd* = 'green', compares with 'quyrd' as in Quyrd of 1116. As Johnston has said previously 'Welsh 'dd' easily drops off' to change *gwyrdd* to *gwyr* pronounced 'goo-yerr', which compares well with the records of 1174 and 1184, as also does *gwyr* and the meanings of these two words are not all that different, both invoke a sense of 'greenness, freshness'. See Traquair also.

Quarrell (Carron) – 1298 Querle, 1510 Quarrell
cwarel, chwarel = 'a quarry'
* Johnston – Old Scots, Middle English for a 'Quarry'.

Quothquan (Thankerton) – 1210 Cuthquen, 1275 Knokquhan, 1403 Quodquen, 1662 Cothquhan
coed gwen = 'white, fair, wood', see Johnston below.
* Johnston – Old Welsh *chet, coit,* Welsh *coed* = 'a wood' and *gwen* = 'clear, white'. 1275 record is Gaelic *cnoc* = 'a hill'. It is a wooded-hill now.
** For the 1275 record, Gaelic *cnoc* is paralleled by Welsh *cnwc* = 'lump, hillock'.

R

Rannoch (Perths) – 1505 Rannach
rhanach = 'little-share, little-division' – presumably of land? But this is only a possibility – see Watson below.
* Johnston – Gaelic *raineach* = 'place of fern, bracken'.
* Watson – 'I have already suggested that Rannoch may be of British origin'. This suggestion appears to relate to identifying an old reference to Crog Reth as being 'a hill now called, in Gaelic, Cruach Raithneach which marks a Western boundary of the Rannoch area'. From this Watson hints that Rannoch, in modern Welsh would be *rhedinog* = 'place abundant in ferns'.

** The name Rannoch now relates to 'a district', 'a division'. Compares with Rhandirmwyn, Wales, *rhan tir mwyn* = 'pleasant share-land'. Watson obviously sses his Crog Reth as being related to *crug rhedyn* = 'mound of ferns'.

Rathen (Lonmay, Aberdeens.) – 1300 Rathyn
Possibly *rathyn* = 'little-mound'
* Johnston – Gaelic *rathain* = 'ferny place'.

Rattray (Blairgowrie) – 1291 Rotrefe, 1295 Retref, 1305 Rothtref
rath tre, rath tref = 'fortified-mound dwelling'. See Watson below.
* Johnston – Welsh or Pictish *rath tref* = 'fort, or mound-dwelling'. Welsh *tra, tre tref* = 'house'.
* Watson – The first part seems to be for Gaelic *rath*, a circular fort, usually of earth, or else Welsh *rath*, a circular fortified spot; a mound, a hill.
** The element *rath* occurs also in the place-names of Wales wherein the meaning is essentially that of 'a fort, fortified-place'.

Rattra (Borgue) – as for Rattray

Renfrew (Renfrews) – 1128 Reinfry, 1147-1152 Renfriu, 1158 Reinfrew, 1160 Renfrew
rhyn ffrwd = 'promontory torrent'
rhewin ffriw = 'stream headland'
* Johnston – Welsh *rhen friu* = 'flowing brook' – where *friu, frwd*, is from *frw, frou* = 'impulse'.
* Watson – This is clearly Welsh *rhyn-frwd* = 'point of current', the name then taken over unchanged into Gaelic, as 'Rinn-frui'.
** Watson's interpretation is explained as = 'point (promontory) of current (swiftly-flowing-water)'. Modern Welsh *rhyn* has the meanings (1) = 'hill, cape' and (2) = 'rough'; *ffrwd* = 'stream, torrent'. There is also *ffriw* = 'head,

nose' and *rhewyn*= 'stream, ditch' – giving *rhewin ffriw* = 'stream (by the) head, nose (i.e. headland)'.

Restalrig – 1210 Lestalrig, 1230 Lastalrich, 1526 Restalrig
See Johnston below and also entry in Edinburgh Names.
* Johnston – Welsh *llys tal rhych* = 'hall, mansion on the lofty ridge'. The liquids 'l' and 'r' easily interchange.

Restinnet (Forfar) – 1150 Rostinoth, 1200 Rostinot, 1268 Restenet, 1289 Rustinoth
rhos tanet, rhostaned = 'moor-of-fieriness', where 'fieriness' may be the name of the River flowing through it
* Johnston – Probably Pictish or Old Gaelic *ros tened* = 'moor of the fire'.
* Watson – Relates it to the name of it's stream which he connects to 'Tanat' the name of two rivers in Wales, obscurely derived from *tan* = 'fire'.

Rhynd (Bridge of Earn) – 1147 Rindalgros
rhyn dal groes = 'hill by the meadow and crossroads'
rhewin dal groes = 'stream in the meadow by the crossroads'
* Johnston – compare with Dalcross = Gaelic for 'spit of the promontory', *ros* = promontory.
* Watson – Gaelic *rind-dealgros* = 'point of thorn-point' the 'point' here being that formed by the conjuncture of Earn and Tay.
** Scots-Gaelic 'thorn' is *dealg*; Watson does not seem to have accounted for the last element *ros* in the early record – presumably it is 'moor'?

Rhynie (Gartly, Aberdeenshire) – 1230 Rhynyn, Ryny
Rhynyn = 'small-hill'; or 'small cape, small headland'
* Johnston – Possibly from Welsh *rhyn* = 'point' (of land).
** Conversion' of *-yn* ending to Scots *-y* or *-ie* gives both *rhyny* = Ryny and *rhynie* = Rhynie.

Rhynns of Galloway (Galloway)
See Johnston below.
* Johnston – Possibly from Welsh *rhyn* = 'point of land'.
** The Rhinns of Galloway are that part of the area which juts out into the Irish Sea and includes theMull of Galloway.

Rinnes, Ben (Aberlour) –
pen rhynos = 'far-end of the little point'
* Johnston – Rhynns with common ending *ais*.
** Johnston does not say if his 'Rhynns' is Welsh, Pictish or whatever.

Romanno bridge (West Linton) – 1116 Rothmaneic, 1200 Rumanach, 1266 Rumannoch, 1300 Roumanoch, 1530 – Romannose
rhath mynach = 'fortified-mound of the monk'
* Johnston – Gaelic *rath manaich* = 'fort, or circle, of the monk'.
* Watson – Gaelic *rath manach* = 'the monk's rath', with reference to the great Rath on the high-ground above Romanno.
** Watson compares the earthworks here with those seen on Arthur's Seat Edinburgh. If so, then the 'Rath' is certain to be pre-Gaelic and possibly pre-Celtic.

Rosemarkie (Fortrose, Black Isle) – 1128 Rosmarkensis, 1190 Rosmarkin, 1257 Rosmarkyn, Rosemarakyn
rhos marchyn = 'moor of the Little-Horse river'
* Johnston – Probably 'cape of the horse burn'.
* Watson – Rosemarkie is named after the stream beside it, in Gaelic *Maircnidh*.
** Watson gives a definite meaning neither for *maircnidh*, presumably it is 'horse-stream', nor the full name Rosemarkie including the element *rose*. The name can be considered from two divergent perspectives, depending on whether the 'moor' was named after the 'stream' or vice-

versa, in the first case the meaning is 'moor of the horse-stream', in the second the 'stream' could simply have taken it's name from the 'moor', in which case the meaning would be 'little-horse moor'. The usual conversion of *yn* to *ie* gives *rhosmarchie* from *rhosmarchyn* and hence Rosemarkie.

Roslin (Lothian) – 1240 Rosskelyn
rhos celyn = 'holly-tree moor'
* Johnston – Welsh *ros celyn* = 'moor of hollies'.
* Ross – Cumbric *ros celyn* = 'moor holly'.

Rosneath (Gareloch) – 1199 Neveth, 1225 Rosneth, 1447 Rosneveth
rhos nefed, rhos nefet = 'moor of heavenliness, holiness'
* Johnston – Gaelic *ros neimidh* = 'cape of the sacred meeting-place'.
* Watson – In Gaelic *ros neimidh* = 'promontory of the Nemet', 'cape of thc sanctuary'.
** This apparently is a 'Nemeton' name which, as G.F.S. Barrow has said, 'is almost by definition likely to be P-Celtic, *neued* (Gaulish *nemeton*) = 'sacred grove, sanctuary', even though the Q-Celtic *neimidh* must lie behind some of our modern reflexes'. If therefore this name derives from P-Celtic *nemeton* it is certainly not Gaelic. Interestingly, 'Sacred' here must mean 'Pagan'.

Rossdhu (Loch Lomond) – 1225 Rosduue, 1315 Rosedufe
Rhos du = 'black, dark moor'
* Johnston – Gaelic *ros dubh* = 'dark, black cape'.

Rossie (Fife) – 1187 Rossyn, 1488 Rossy
rhosyn = 'little-moor'
* Johnston – Perhaps Gaelic *ros-ach* here in locative = 'promontory place'.
** Usual conversion of *yn* to *y* gives *rhosy* hence *rossy* of 1488. The time interval between the two records is just that in which the *-yn* to *-y* transformation is expected to occur.

Ruthven (Perths) – 1198 Ruadeuien, Rotauin – see Ruthven (Meigle)

Ruthven (Huntly) – 1200 Ruthaven, 1300 Rothuan, Rothven, Ruven, – see Ruthven (Meigle)

Ruthven (Meigle) – 1200 Ruotheven, 1291 Rothievan
rhyd y faen = 'stone ford', probably = 'stepping- stone ford'
rhudd faen = 'red stone'
* Johnston – Old forms strongly point to Gaelic *ruadh aa bhuinn* = 'reddish river' or else Pictish or Welsh *rhudd faen* = 'red rock'.
* Watson – Whilst we might compare Welsh *rhuddfaen* = 'red stone', the name is almost certainly Gaelic *ruadh-mhaighin*: = 'red spot', 'red place'.
** Watson's 'certainty' has no place in the difficult study of Scottish place-names.

Ryan, Loch (Stranraer) – circa 150 (*Taliesin)* – Loch Reon, 1301 Louch Ryan, 1461 Lochrian
lwch Rhen = the 'local King's pool, lake'
* Johnston – Probably from Celtic *Rigon* which becomes in Welsh *Rhion* = 'Lord, Chief'.
** No *rhion* = 'lord, chief' in my Welsh dictionaries, but there is *rhen* = 'lord' and *rhiau* = 'lords'. Taliesin's Loch Reon would in modern welsh be *lwch rhen* = the 'Lord's pool', the 'Lord's fishpond' or the 'Lord's swampy, wet ground'. In all these cases 'Lord' is best interpreted as 'Ruler', 'Headman', 'local King'. The word *lwch* may be reflected in the 'Louch' of 1301?

S

Soutra (Fala) – 1160 Soltre, 1455 Sowtra, 1461 Soltra
sal tre = 'steading of the ill, frail, poor'
* Johnston – Perhaps British *sul tra, sul tre* = 'watch- tower' literally 'outlook-tower', from Welsh *sulw* = 'a sight,' 'a view'.
* Watson – Comments on the founding of a hospital in this area by Malcolm IV in 1164. He gives no suggestion for the first element *sou* but implies the second element *tra* = 'stead'.
* Nicolaisen – Interprets it as Welsh *sulw tref* = 'steading with a wide-view'.
** Today there is definite evidence that there was some form of pre-mediaeval medical activity on this site long before 1164, perhaps extending back as far as Roman, or even pre-Roman times. All of which leads more towards an interpretation such as *sal tre*. In Scotland *tre* is often found in a slightly corrupted form as *tra* which in this case gives *saltra* from which comes Soltra of 1461 in the same way as Soltre of 1160 comes from *saltre*. See Soutra Aisle, following.

Soutra Aisle –
sal tre ael = 'steading of the sick on the brow (of the hill)'
** This area is on the top of Soutra Hill which has now been identified as the site of the early hospice. It is on the northern brow of the hill above Fala Flow Loch (see Fala), the description *sal tre ael* = 'steading of the sick on the brow (of the hill)', fits the location exactly. The full modern meanings of *ael* are 'a brow', 'a jut-out', 'a skirt'. All of which apply to this location.

Stirling (Stirlings) – 1124 Strevelin, 1125 Struelin, 1182 Striuellin, 1250 Estriuelin, 1295 Strevelyn, 1455 Striviling, 1470 Sterling, 1682 Strivelinge
ynys tre felin = 'meadow by the mill steading'
* Johnston – British or Welsh *ystre felyn* = 'dwelling of

Velyn', Velyn being the aspirated form of Melyn which Johnston implies is a personal name deriving from Welsh *melyn* = 'yellow'.

* Watson – no mention.

** The 1250 form invites the interpretation *ystre felin* = 'mill dwelling', but there is the possibility that the 'ys' appearing as 'Ės' in Estriuelin, ('u' for 'v'), and reduced to 's' in all the other records indicates an original *ynys* = 'meadow'. In Welsh place names *ynys* has more than once, when fronting a name, been reduced to 'ys' or even further to 's', e.g. Sgeti (Sketty) = *ynys Geti* and Skenfrith = *ynys gynwraidd*. Thus there is the possibility that 'Stirling' originated as *ynys tre felin* = 'meadow by the mill steading', being shortened once to '*ystrefelin* giving the 1250 Estriuelin and further shortened to '*strefelin* as in all other early records. An *ynys* is usually near water, as very often is a mill. See Yester.

Strathaven (Lanarks) – 1552 Straithawane
ynys tre afon = 'meadow by the steading on the river'
ystrad afon = 'wide river valley'.

* Johnston – It is pronounced Stra-ven, with the accent on the 'a' and = 'valley of the afen, afon'.

** There is evidence that at least some of the Scots-Gaelic 'Straths' originate in the Welsh *ystrad* rather than the Irish *srath*. According to Watson the description *srath* in Ireland invariably describes an area of level ground along the shores of a lake; in Scotland *strath* usually describes a wide flat river valley between hills, and the *strath* is usually qualified by the name of the river. This corresponds exactly with the meaning of the Welsh *ystrad*. Ostensibly then this name is *ystrad* with *afon* = river added. But Strathaven straddles the Powmillon Burn, so *afon* in this case is used in a generic sense rather than with any particular meaning. The pronunciation Stra-ven invites comparison with that of Stirling i.e. Stre-velin. It is possible therefore that Straven is *ynys tre afon* = 'meadow by the steading on the river' in the same way that Stirling is *ynys tre felin* = 'meadow by the mill steading'.

Strathearn (Peebles) – 1185 Stradearn, 1190 Stradherin, Stratherne, 1220 Stradearn
ystrad Earn = 'wide-flat-valley of the river Earn'
* Johnston – It is the 'Strath of the river Earn', which see.
** The persistent 'd' favours *ystrad earn* = 'wide-flat-valley of the river Earn', where Earn is probably a pre-Celtic river-name. As in Wales the initial 'y' is discarded to give *ystrad earn* = *stradearn,* which is exactly the records of 1185 and 1220.

Strathpeffer (Dingwall) – 1350 Strathpefir
ystrad pefr = 'radiant, beautiful; wide-flat-valley'
** The second element is undoubtedly Welsh *pefr* so the first element must be Welsh also. Thus, *ystrad pefr* = 'radiant, beautiful, wide- flat-valley'.

Strathyre (Perthshire) – 1457 Strathyire
ystrad hir = 'long, wide-flat-valley', 'long strath'
ystrad tir = 'wide-flat-valley, land'
* Johnston – Gaelic *strath thire* = 'valley of the land'.

T

Talla (Borders) –
tal-y (llyn) = 'front-end of the lake'
* Johnston – Welsh *tal* = 'that which tops, or fronts, a brow (of a hill)', a name appropriate to the precipitous burn (falling down the height at the end of the reservoir).
** Welsh *tal* = 'forehead, front, end', and 'high, tall'. At the foot of the height rising up at the Southern, source-end of

Talla Reservoir is a place seen on the map as 'Talla Linfoots'. This can be compared with *Tal-y-Llyn* (Wales) = 'front-end of the lake' but here it is shortened to *tal-y* hence Talla. Otherwise, somehow from *tal* meanings given above as described by Johnston.

Tandlemuir (Lochwinnoch, Renfrews.) – 1460 Tandilmuir
tandde lle mawr = 'place of the great flaming fire'
* Johnston – Probably from Old Norse, *'tand-r, tandri'* = 'fire' from which comes Scots *'tandle, tannle'* = 'a large bonfire'.
** possibly from Welsh *tan* = 'fire', *tandde'* = 'a flaming-fire' or 'fiery' plus *lle* = 'place'. These when combined to give *tan lle* and *tandde lle* and then aspirated to *tandle* and *tanle* could well be the origins of Scots *tandle* and *tannle* as given by Johnston. The choice is then between an original, wholly Welsh *tandlemawr* = 'place of the great flaming-fire' or else a wholly Scots *tandlemuir* = 'moor of the large bonfire', or perhaps a hybrid of both.

Tantallon Castle (East Lothian) – 1300 Dentaloune, 1389 Teintalon, 1481 Temptallon, 1572 Tomtallon
din tal gwn = 'fort on the brow of the summit' or 'fort at the front-end of the apex'.
* Johnston – Welsh *din talgwn* = 'high fronted fort'. The 'Tomtallon' of 1572 may be for Gaelic *tom talain* = 'knoll of the feat of arms', an obvious misconstruction.
** *gwn* is the lenited form of *cwn* = 'top, summit, apex'; hinting that the full description might have been *din tal y cwn* = 'fort on the frontal-brow of the summit or apex', which suits the site well, but the records are a little late and show no vestige of a 'g' as in *gwn*. Otherwise it is possible to posit a mistaken second lenition of *gwn* which deletes the 'g' to give *dintalwn*?

Tarbrax (Carnwath) –
tor brochos = 'rock outcrop of the little badger'
tir brochos = 'land of the little badger'
* Johnston – Gaelic *torr breac* = 'speckled hill' with English 's' for a plural ending giving 'cs' = 'x'.
** *tor* = 'rock-outcrop' or 'rocky-hill', *broch* = 'badger', '*-os*' is a diminutive.

Tarf, Tarff (name of several 'violent' streams)
tarw = 'bull', therefore a 'bullish' river, or stream
* Johnston – Gaelic *tarbh* = 'bull'.
* Watson – Probably old Welsh name preserved in full, for Gaelic *tarbh* and Welsh *tarw* are identical.

Tarradale (Conon Bridge) – 1240 Taruedal, 1309, Taredelle, 1320 Tarrodall
tarw dol = 'meadow of the bull'
* Johnston – Norse *tarf -r dal* = 'bull dale'.
** If we take 'ue' in the earliest 1240 record as being 'w' then a possibility is 'Tarwdal' from Welsh *tarw dol* = 'bull meadow'. Welsh *dol* often appears as *dal* in Scottish place-names.

Tartravon (Torphicen, West Lothian) – 1508, 1509 Tortrevin
tor tre afon = 'rock-outcrop, rocky-hill, by the steading on the river Avon'
tir tre afon = 'land by the steading on the river Avon'
* Johnston – Welsh *tor tra afon* = 'hill or castle over the Avon'.
** Welsh *tra* = 'extremely', 'very', and 'over'- in the sense of excessive. It does not really fit as 'over' in the sense of 'above'. Welsh *tre* is often seen in the corrupt form *tra*.

Tarwilkie (Balmaclellan, Dumfries and Galloway) – 1604 Tragilhey
tre cilie aspirated to *tregilie* = 'steading at the sources of the streams'

* Johnston – British *tra, tre* = 'house', or Gaelic *tir* = 'land', plus Gaelic *giolcaidh* = 'of rushes, reeds'. So either Welsh-Gaelic hybrid *tre giolcaidh* = 'house of reeds' or Gaelic *tirgilcaidh* = 'land of rushes'.
** In Welsh Dictionaries *cil,* plural *ciliau* is given only as 'nook, corner, recess, retreat', also 'retreat, flight' and 'the back of'. In addition it appears in Welsh place-names as *cil,* plurals *ciliau* and *cilie,* with the meaning 'source of stream'. The topography around Tarwilkie should help decide which interpretation is most apt. Again we see *tre* in the form *tra.*

Tayantruan (Pitlochry) –
Possibly *tyn truan* = 'croft of the miserable wretch'
* Johnston – Gaelic *tigh an t'ortruthain* = 'house on the little black stream'.
** No records, so guesses only. Welsh *tyn* is a shortened form of *tyddyn* = 'cottage, croft'.

Taychreggan (Highlands) –
ty carregan, ty cerygan, ty cerrigan = 'house by the little-rock, little-stone'
* Johnston – Gaelic *tigh na chreagain* = 'house at the little crag'.
** On an early 20th. century postcard (seen in the hotel) it is 'Tycreggan'. A feature of the place is the large rock on the shoreline of Loch Awe, within a few yards of the house (now an hotel).

Tealing (Angus) – 1206 Thelin, 1497 Teling
ty llyn = 'house on the lake' (but where is the lake?)
* Johnston : Probably Pictish, compare with Welsh *teiling* = 'enveloping' or *telain* = 'beautiful'
** Modern Welsh : *teiling, teilwng* = 'worthy, deserving, of-merit'; *telaid* = 'beautiful', 'graceful'. Normally the sight of 'lin', 'ling', 'lyn' elements in a place-name would suggest that it is perhaps *llyn* = 'lake'. In which case *ty llyn* aspirated

to *tylyn* = 'house on the lake' is a possibility. Again, topography may help decide.

Terregles (Dumfries) – 1280 Tranagles, 1350 Travereglys, 1365 Travereglys
tref yr eglwys = 'steading by the church', 'church farm'
* Johnston – Gaelic *treamhar eaglais,* Welsh *eglwys,* ='farm of the church', also 1461 Torriculis, Torrekillis.
* Watson – *tref yr eglwys* = 'church stead'. It may be said without hesitation that 'Trever' is Welsh, it is either *tref yr –* = 'stead of the -', or *tref ar* = 'stead near the -'.

Thrieve (Kirkcudbright) –
tref = 'steading', 'farmstead', 'homestead'
* Johnston – Gaelic *treabh* = 'a farm'.
** It is possible that this is a shorthand form of a name containing *tref y-something* or *tref yr-something* or *tref ar-something,* plus an additional element which is now lost.

Throsk (Alloa) – 1246 Threske, 1252 Trost, 1311 Tresk
See Johnston below.
* Johnston – British *tre esc, tre usc* = 'house on the river', i.e. the Forth.
** Johnston is being brave here! If he is implying that the name is related to other river-names such as Esk and Usk then there is a problem. The River Usk in Wales derives it's meaning from Welsh *wysg,* Old-Welsh *uisc,* the meaning of which is thought to be 'river abounding-in-fish'. If this is true then *tre wysg* = 'steading by the river abounding-in-fish', – lucky old steading!

Tillicoultry (Dollar) – 1195 Tulycultri, 1199 Tullicultre, Tillicultry
tyle cil tre = 'steep hill at the back of the steading'
* Johnston – Gaelic *tulach cul tire* = 'hill at the back of the land'.

Tillimorgan (Culsalmond)
tyle morgan = 'Morgan's hill' (Pronunciation is Tillemorgan, accent on 'o')
* Johnston – A 'hill; but perhaps here Gaelic *teaglach Morgain* = 'ground of the family, of Morgan'. The hill is, in 1510, Knockmorgan (= Morgan's knoll).
* Watson – 'Morgan', a British name, appears in Tillymorgan, Aberdeen (presumably *tulach Morgan* = 'Morgan's hill'?).
** My Welsh dictionaries give different meanings for *tyle*; the most modern says = 'hill' or 'bed', the next two oldest say 'steep hill' and the oldest(1688) says a 'piece of land suitable for a house or upon which a house stood'. This last would give Tillimorgan = 'piece of ground where Morgan's house once stood'.

Tinnis (Yarrow,Borders) – 1455 Tynnes, 1541 Dynnesdale
dinas = See Note below.
* Johnston – Welsh *dinas* = 'fort, castle'.
* Watson – *dinas* = 'fort', With us it appears as Tinnis or Tennis, as in Tinnis, Yarrow and Tennis, Drummelzier.
** In modern Wales a *dinas* is taken to mean 'a city', but in an older archaeological sense it is perhaps better described as a 'fortified iron-age hill-settlement' as in Dinas Bran = 'hill fortress of the crow' (Powys, Wales).

Tinnis Hill (Liddesdale) – 1570 Dennys
See Tinnis, Yarrow.

Tinnies (Drummelzier) –
as for Tinnis (Yarrow).

Tipperty (Several) – 1501 Tippertay, 1591 Tippertey
ty perthi = 'house with hedges'
* Johnston – Old-Gaelic-locative of *tiobartach* = 'well place'.
* Watson – Tipperty is either for dative plural *tipratib*, later *tiobartaibh*, or a locative of *tiobartach* = 'well place'.

** The records are all rather late so not much to go on.

Torbanehill (Bathgate) –
tor ban = 'rock outcrop on the high land' or simply 'high tor' or 'white tor'
* Johnston – Gaelic *torr ban* = 'white, clear hill', with superfluous English 'hill' added as a 'tautology'.
** Welsh *ban* = a 'prominence or peak'; 'high land'; 'high or lofty' and also 'white' Therefore Welsh *tor ban* plus superfluous English 'hill'.

Tore (Inverness) –
twr = 'tower', 'heap'
tor = 'rock-outcrop, rocky-hill'; 'break, rupture'; 'belly-shaped mound'
* Johnston – Gaelic *torr* = 'heap, mound, tower', Welsh *twr* = 'tower'.
** No records so comparisons only.

Torphichen (Bathgate) – 1296 Thorfigyn, Torphychin, 1540 Torphichen
tor fychan = 'little tor'
* Johnston – Gaelic *torr phigheainn* = 'magpie's hill'.
** This area is not noted for it's magpies! See Tore (Inverness) above for the meanings of 'tor'.

Torfichen Hill (Moorfoots)
tor fychan, tor fechan = 'little tor'. Same as Torphicen.
** The barren, treeless, Moorfoot Hills are not typical Magpie territory which throws doubt on Johnston's Torphichen = 'magpie's hill'!

Torry (Aberdeens) – 1350 Torry
torrau = 'place of several, many tors'
toryn = 'little tor'
* Johnston – Gaelic *torr* = 'hill'.
** In Scottish place-names the dropping of the final *-n* from

a diminutive suffix is commonplace. Therefore *toryn* to *tory* and thence Torry.

Torweaving (Pentlands) –
tor gwyfn, gwyfyn = 'moth tor' (see Johnston below)
tor gwyfon, tor wyfon = 'gooseberry tor', 'berry tor'
* Johnston – Welsh *tor gwefyn* = 'hill of the moths, or insects'.
** *torgwyfyn* aspirates to *torwyfyn,* hence Anglicised Torweaving. Plenty of midges on the Pentland Hills!

Trabroun (Tranent) – 1296 Trebrun
tre bryn = 'hill steading', 'hill-farm'
* Johnston – Welsh *tra, tre* = 'house', and *bryn,* Old-Gaelic *brun,* = 'slope'.

Trabroun (Lauderdale) – 1170 Treuerbrun
tref-yr-bryn = see Watson below
* Watson – It is on a hillside and stands for *tref yr bryn* = 'hill-stead'.

Trailtrow (Cummertrees, Dumfries & Galloway) – 1116 Kevertrole ('k' for 'tr'), later Travertrold
tref yr trwyll = 'steading by the ring'
* Johnston – hybrid Gaelic *treabhar* = 'farm, house' plus Danish-Swedish *trold,* Old-Norse troll = 'a fairy'. Watson's Welsh *tref yr* = 'house of the - ', or *tref ar* = 'house on the - ', will not do.
** As always Watson's opinions must take precedence over those of Johnston and the first element, given by 'trever' and 'traver', will as Watson says be, Welsh *tref yr, tref ar.* Unfortunately Watson volunteers nothing for the second element and the addition of *trwyll* as the second element is but a suggestion. There is in Bristol a very old Tavern called the 'Llandogger Trow' – any connection? Johnston is away raiding and pillaging with the Vikings again!

Tranent – see Edinburgh Names.
tre nant or *tri neint* = 'stead by the stream' or place of 'three streams'

Traprain Law (Haddington, E. Lothian) – 1335 Trapren, 1370 Trapprene, 1451 Trapren
tre pren = 'steading by the tree', with Scots 'Law' = 'hill' added
* Johnston – Welsh *tra pren, tre pren* = 'house by the tree'
The old name for the Law was Dunpelder (1180) from Welsh *dyn peledyr* = 'fort of the spearshafts', *paladyr.*
* Watson – Traprain is for *tref bren* = 'tree-stead'.
** The old name for the hill, Dunpelder, has been displaced by the modern name which derives from the hamlet of Traprain at its foot. Modern Welsh *paladr* = 'shaft', 'spear', 'ray, gleam'.

Traquair (Innerleithen) – 1116 Treverquyrd, 1135 Traucrcoir, 1140 Trauequair, 1174 Trauercuer, 1225 Trefquer, 1265 Traquair, 1275 Trakwair
tref yr Quair = 'steading on the river Quair', see Note below.
* Johnston – It is 'farm', British or Gaelic *treabhar* 'on Quair Water'. But Welsh *tref, tra, tre* is 'house'.
* Watson – The name doubtless means 'stead on the Quair' or 'stead of the Quair'.
** Probably *tre gwyrdd* = 'steading by the River Quair'. The river name being *gwyrdd* = 'green', where *gwyrdd* compares well with the 'quyrd' of the 1116 record, then as JBJ has said previously 'Welsh 'dd' easily drops off' to give 'gwyr' found as 'coir','cuer', 'quer' and 'cuir' in the early records., but see entry for 'Quair' also.

Trearne (Beith, Ayrshire) – 1233 Triern, 1413 Trearne
tre eirin = 'steading among plum trees'
* Johnston – Perhaps British *tre airne* = 'house among the sloes'.

* Watson – The explanation of these names (i.e. those involving *tre, tref*) or most of them, would involve so much pure guesswork that I prefer not to attempt it.
** Modern Welsh *tre eirin* = 'steading among plum trees'. It is interesting to see that Johnston retains the Gaelic accent above the 'a' in airne even though he describes the word as 'British'.

Tremuda Bay (St Cyrus, Aberdeens) –
tre mydau = 'homestead by the arches'
* Johnston – Probably Pictish or British for 'house on the cove'. Welsh *mwdd* = 'an arch', 'a spring, 'a cove'.
** Older Welsh *mwd, mwdd* = an 'arch, vault', plural is *mydau* = 'arches', therefore *tremydau* = 'steading by the arches', 'y' is pronounced as 'u' in 'mud'. The 'arches' are a mystery – unless there are coastal 'cliff-arches' in the vicinity?

Trinafour (Struan, Highlands) –
traean y fawr = 'a third of a pasture'
* Johnston – Pictish or British for, 'house on the pasture-land' from Welsh *tra, tre* = 'house' and Pictish *four* which is cognate with Welsh *pawr* = 'pasture-land'.
* Watson – The element *four* is to be compared with Welsh *pawr* = 'pasture'. This term survived in Gaelic as *por,* genitive *puir* – Watson then relates Trinafour to *trian a' phuir* = 'third of a pasture'.
** The tenure of both Watson's and Johnston's dissertations seems to be that the element *four* is definitely not of Gaelic origin and is best described as 'Pictish', it not being easily seen to be of Welsh origin. Watson then couples it with Gaelic *trian* = 'a third' to give a Gaelic-Pictish interpretation *trian a' phuir* – as above. Johnston couples it with Welsh *tre* = 'house' to give a Pictish-Welsh interpretation *tre four* – as above. Neither addresses the question of how Welsh *pawr* became Pictish *four.* This can be explained on the

assumption that *pawr* instead of being aspirated, in the P-Celtic Welsh manner, to *bawr* was somehow aspirated, in the Q-Celtic manner, to *phawr* and thence to 'Pictish' *four*; in other words it became partly Gaelicized. Alternatively both Welsh and 'Pictish' elements could have descended from an earlier common Brittonic root, Welsh becoming *pawr* and 'Pictish'becoming *fawr* or *four*. Gaelic *trian* is paralleled by Welsh *traean* = 'a third'. Thus an origin in a Welsh / Pictish *traean y pawr, traean y four* = 'third of a pasture' cannot be considered as anything other than fitting.

Triochatan Loch (Glencoe) –
tre y chetan = 'steading in the little-wood'. See Note below.
* Johnston – Probably British *tre* = 'house' plus an obscure second element.
** Possibilities (and they are no more than that!) could be *tre-y-chetan* = 'steading by the little-wood', or *tre-ar-chetan* ='steading on the little-wood'; *chet* being an old form of modern Welsh *coed* = 'wood' with the diminutive suffix '*-an*. An intriguing alternative is *tre-y-Chattan* = 'steading of Clan Chattan'.

Troon (Ayrs) – 1371 *le* Trone, 1464 *le* Troon, *the* Truyn
trwyn = the 'nose', the 'cape, point'
* Johnston – Welsh *trwyn* = 'nose, point, cape' (of land).
* Watson – Troon is Welsh *trwyn* = 'nose, cape'.
** In his 'Four Ancient Histories of Wales' the Scottish historian Skene notes the existence of a place 'Bretrwn' which seems to occupy much the same space as modern Troon. In modern Welsh *bre* = 'hill, peak, mount, high-land, or high', thus 'Bretrwn' = 'hill on the promontory (nose, point-of-land), or 'high promontory', 'cape with high land on it'.

Troqueer (Dumfries) – 1380 Treqvere, Traquire
tre gwyrdd = 'green house'
* Johnston – *tra qair* = 'green house'.
** Johnston seems to have left the completion of this name as an 'exercise-for-the-reader'. It is the same as Traquair, but in this case as there is no associated river it must simply be *tre gwyrdd* = the 'green house'.

Trossachs, Trosachs (Callander) – 1791 Trossachs
trawsachos = place-of 'many small-traverses, crossings'
* Johnston – Not a Gaelic word, so British or Pictish.
* Watson – From Welsh *traws* Old Welsh *tros* which appears in Gaelic dress in *na Troiseachean,* the Trossachs, meaning 'the cross places', a name originally applied to the small hilly region between Loch Katrine and loch Achray. It is probably a Gaelic adaptation of Welsh *trawsfynydd* = 'cross-hill'.
** This is a controversial name possibly on account of the lateness of the earliest record. Nicolaisen states, with certainty, that 'The Trossachs' stand for Gaelic *na trosaichean* = 'the cross-hills', but omits mention of Watson's understanding that this is simply a modern Gaelic translation of an original Welsh *trawsfynydd.* Johnston supports Watson, '-not a Gaelic word', he says and indeed I cannot find a word like *tros* or *trois* in either my Scots-Gaelic or Irish-Gaelic dictionaries. In modern Welsh, *traws* = 'a traverse', 'a cross', and so possibly *trawsachos* = place-of 'many small-traverses, crossings', where *-ach* is a diminutive suffix and *-os* implies 'many-of', 'an abundance of'. In an older form of Welsh this may possibly have been represented by *trosawcos.* The descriptions 'cross-hill', 'cross-hills' are somewhat obscure but the name Trawsfynydd in Wales displays *fynydd* as the aspirated form of *mynydd* implying the presence of the definite article 'y' preceding it. The name in it's entirety would then have been *traws-y-*

mynydd = *trawsfynydd* = the 'traverse of the mountain', which makes more sense.

Trostrie (Twynolm, Dumfries & Galloway) – 1456 Trostaree, *pont* Trostari
traws tre, older *tros tre* = 'traverse (the way across) steading'
* Johnston – British *tros tire* = 'across the land'. Welsh *tir,* Gaelic *tir.* Watson's Welsh *tref* = 'house', will not suit the old forms.
* Watson – Welsh *traws,* Old Welsh *tros* = 'cross' plus *tref* = 'stead', thus *trostref* = 'cross stead'.
** I am inclined to favour Watson, there is another Trostrie (Forfar) and a Troustrie (Crail) which are very probably related and which show no sign of an intrusive 'a'; but *tref* is possibly better replaced by it's synonym *tre.* Therefore Trostrie = *trawstre* = 'cross steading' or in other words the 'traverse' of the steading'. i.e. the way across it. It is interesting to speculate on the derivation of the two records, Trostaree, -ari. Is this a case of partial metathesis where *trostre* entered some intermediate stage *trostere* before being completely metathesised to *troster* – but where neither of these metathesised forms survived? The name now retaining the original form *trostre, trawstre.*

Tundergarth (Lockerbie. Dumfries & Galloway) – 1215, 1245 Thonergayth
tyn-y-tir garth, tyndirgarth = 'croft land, hill-ridge'
* Johnston – The recorded Thonergayth, is doubtful. Perhaps from Welsh *tyndir* = 'lea land, fallow'. Old Norse and Danish *tundr,* Old English *tynder, tunder* is 'tinder'. Garth is 'enclosure'.
** Welsh *tyddyn tir* in short form as *tyn tir* aspirated to *tyndir* = 'croft land', *garth* = 'enclosure' or else 'hill-ridge', therefore *tyndirgarth* = 'croft land, enclosure' or 'croft land, hill-ridge'.

Turk, Glen (Wigtowns) – 1462 Glen Turk
glyn twrch = 'valley of the wild-boar'
* Johnston – Gaelic *torc, tuirc* = 'wild boar', so *glen tuirc* = 'valley of the wild-boar'.

Turc, Ben (Glenshee) also (Kintyre) –
y-pen-twrch aspirated to *ben twrch* = 'hill-top of the wild-boar'
* Johnston – Gaelic *bein tuirc* = 'hill of the wild boar'.

Tyndrum (Perths) –
tyn-y-trum aspirated to *tyndrum* = 'croft of the ridge', 'ridge-croft'
* Johnston – Gaelic *tigh an druim* = 'the house on the ridge'.

U

Uphall (Bathgate) –
ystrad broch = 'wide-valley of the badger'
* Johnston – It's old name was Strathbroke.
** Although there are no early records it is a fair guess that in this area it's old name 'Strathbroke' is from Welsh *ystrad broch* = 'valley of the badger'.

Urquhart (several, all with the same meaning) – Assorted records: – *Adamnan* Aircharden, 1150 Urchard, 1165 Urecard, 1200 Hurcard, 1340 Urquhart, Owrchard, 1340 Urchard
ar cardden = place 'upon, or over, the copse'
* Johnston – hybrid, Pictish *air* = 'on, upon', plus Welsh *cardden* = 'wood'. So 'wood-side'.
* Watson – Very early record as Airchartdan, here the *air* is the preposition meaning 'on, near'; in Welsh *ar*, now very often *ur* with us. The second part cannot be explained from Gaelic, and has rightly been equated with Welsh *cardden* = a

copse, the whole thus meaning 'on-wood', 'wood-side'.
** In modern Welsh *cardden* = 'thicket, brake, copse', but also = 'fort': *ar* = 'on, upon, over'; also = 'tilth, ploughed-land', and as a prefix *ar* adds intensity to what follows, thus *arcardden* = 'thick-thicket': *ar cardden* = on, upon, over the thicket, copse', or else 'on, upon, over the fort', and lastly *ar cardden* = 'ploughed-land by the copse' or 'ploughed-land by the fort'.

Usan – (Montrose)
wysan = 'small, quite-lively, stream'
* Johnston – Probably a Pictish diminutive.
** If Johnston is correct then a possibility is the adjective *wys* = 'aptitude-for-motion' i.e. 'quite-lively' coupled with a diminutive suffix *-en* or*-an* but *wys* by itself can only really apply to a river, stream or water, – name; in which case the meaning of the name in it's entirety as *wysen* or *wysan,* would have to be – 'small, quite-lively stream'. See entry for Oxenham. No records so only guesswork!

Ussie, Loch (Fodderty) – 1463 Usuy, 1476 Ouse, 1527 Housy, 1594 Ussay
wysen then *wysie* (see Note below) = 'small, quite-lively', Loch.
* Johnston – In Gaelic it is *Usaidh,* a word of unknown meaning, probably Pictish.
** Perhaps similar to Usan, coming from *wysan, wysen, or wysyn* where the final Celtic diminutive has suffered conversion to Scots 'ie' giving first *wysie* and thence Ussie. Loch Ussie then = 'small, quite-lively loch'. Alternatively was Ussie once the name of a stream feeding the Loch?

Uthrogle (Cupar) –
haidd ar uchel = 'barley on the high' place
or *uchder uchel* = 'lofty, towering, upper land
or *uwch tir uchel* = ditto

* Johnston – Gaelic *uachdar* = 'upper part', see Auchterarder and Ogle.
** Johnston does not make clear how *uachdar* can change into *Uthr-* nor does he interpret the whole name as the hybrid *uachdar uchel* the meaning of which would be 'high upper part'. The Welsh cognates *uchder* and *uwch tir* are similarly difficult and a more credible metamorphosis may be from *haidd ar uchel;* where *uchel* becomes *ogle, haiddar* is phonetically 'either' and so 'eitherogle' credibly becomes Uthrogle. This is an intriguing name but Johnston has no early records so apart from the interpretation 'ogle' = *uchel* the rest is outright conjecture anyway.

W

Wallacetown (Ayrs) –
Wallacetown = 'town of the Welsh' or 'town of Wallace-the-Welshman'
* Johnston – An old form was Walenston = 'village of the strangers', the 'Welsh', 'Britons from Strathclyde'. Old English *woel-, welisc* = 'a foreigner'. In 1160 we find mention of 'Ricardo Walas' ('Richard of Wales') who came to Riccarton, Ayrshire from the borderlands of northern Wales. It is perhaps the earliest mention of the name Wallace in Scotland.
* Watson – The people of Strathclyde continued to be described as Walenses (Welshmen) until about the end of the 12th century, and we can assume that Welsh was still spoken in Strathclyde in the reign of David 1st (1124-1153). In 1305 Edward 1st of England ordained that henceforth the customs of the Scots and Brits be discontinued (presumably this applied particularly to the Welsh and Gaelic languages?).

** It is just possible that both Riccarton and Wallacetown were named after Ricardo Walas, Richard of Wales, Richard Wallace as above, who is also said to have been the progenitor of William Wallace the 'Scottish' hero.

Walston (Biggar, Borders) – 1275 Wailston, 1293 Walyston, Walliston, 1375 Welchetoun
See Johnston below.
* Johnston – same as Wallacetown.
** It is 'town of the Welsh' as is obvious from the early records, particularly that of 1375.

Wanlockhead – (Leadhills, Borders) – 1563 Wen lec
gwen llech aspirated to *wenlech* = 'flat, white, stone', or else 'holy flat-stone'.
* Johnston – Probably Welsh *gwen llech* = 'white, clear flagstone'.
** *gwen* = 'white, fair', *gwyn* = 'white' and also 'holy, blessed', *llech* = 'flat-stone', 'slate'. The name perhaps compares with Holystone, Northumberland, and is a place of worship maybe?

Y

Yarrow, River (Selkirk, Borders) – 1120 Gierua, 1150 Gierwa, Gyrwa, 1508 Yarou
y geirw, yeirw = 'the torrent'; see Note below.
* Johnston – May be from the tribe Gyruii (Bede), but more probably Gaelic *gearr, giorra* = 'short', or *garbh* = 'rough' plus *abh* = 'stream'.
** Dorward derives this from a 'continental-Celtic' *garu* = 'rough, turbulent', which passed into Gaelic as *garbh* = 'rough, rugged, harsh'. He sees *garu* as also being the basis of the English Yar and Yare. But these are river names and

as such will, in both England and Scotland, almost certainly pre-date the arrival of either the English or the Scots and are therefore far more likely to have their roots related to Welsh *garw* = 'rough, rugged, coarse, harsh' or *garw, geirw* = 'a torrent'. The aspirated forms of *y-garw* = 'the rough' (stream); and *y-geirw* 'the torrent', are *yarw* and *yeirw*. These then have to be considered as possibilities, although the persistent terminal 'a' in the early records is still a puzzle. Johnston's *garbhabh* = 'rough stream' is pronounced 'garrav-av', which makes it somewhat unlikely?

Yester (Haddington, East Lothian) – 1295 Yestre, 1407-1410 Yhestir
llan ynys tre = 'church' in the 'farmhouse meadow' – or
llan istre = 'church' – 'below the steading'
* Johnston – Welsh *ystre* = 'a dwelling'.
** *Ystre* is possibly *ynys tre* = 'meadow by the steading' truncated, as sometimes in Welsh place-names, to *ystre*. (see Stirling). The vowel 'y' in Welsh is pronounced differently depending on it's position within a word, if it is the last syllable then it is as 'i' in 'lit'; anywhere else in the word the pronunciation is as 'u' in 'hut'. Thus *ynys* is pronounced unn-iss and the truncated *-ys*, as the last syllable, will be -iss. The pronunciation of *ystre* (= a dwelling), where 'y' is not the last syllable, would be 'uss-treh' whilst that of truncated *-ystre* = 'meadow by the steading' would be iss-treh which corresponds better to the pronunciation of todays 'Yester' where the vernacular 'ye' is more like the 'ye' in the Dickensian 'ye olde shoppe'. The only trace of the name now to be found in the Parish of Yester is Longyester Farmstead, and this is probably where the name originated. The local pronunciation of this is 'Lang Yeaster' which suggests it has it's roots in the form *llan ynys tre* truncated, aspirated and metathesised to *lanyster* = 'church in the meadow by the farmstead', rather than in the form *llan ystre* = 'church

dwelling'. A *llan* or *lan* is not necessarily a 'church' as we know it today, it can mean anything from; a simple 'enclosure' – belonging to some 'holy-man'; – an early Christian burial ground; – a rudimentary house of worship; or something a little more grand – like a 'Church'. Alternatively, and perhaps most likely, it may simply be *is tre* = 'below'(or 'under') – 'steading'. This is pronounced 'eess tray' which metathesises naturally to 'eess-ter' and so '*Yester*'.

Ythan, River (Ellon, North East) – 1373 *aqua de* Ethoyn, 1477 Ithane

See Watson below.

* Johnston – see Watson.

* Watson – The river name Ythan is the same as the Welsh 'Ieithon' of mid-Wales which is for an early *Iectona,* the 'talking one', from which comes the root of Welsh *iaith* = 'language'. It cannot be explained from Gaelic and survives from a period when Old British had passed into Early Welsh; as also did the river name Nethy.

** The early form 'Ethoyn' suggests *eithin* = 'gorse' as a possible alternative; but Watson's reasoning reads very, very sound!

Chapter 9

Edinburgh names

'Now and then the simplest explanation
turns out to be the true one'

Cadfael Chronicles, 'The Devil's Novice'

It is the purpose of this chapter to take advantage of Stuart Harris's most admirable work on Edinburgh place-names to look in detail at a relatively small area, in this case that contained within and in the immediate vicinity of the city of Edinburgh, and by abstracting all the relevant Welsh names from Harris's book gain an insight into what could result if we applied the same sort of microscopic study to Scotland as a whole. The exact area of Harris's research is not specified but it seems to be that inside a half circle of radius 9 miles centred on the middle of Princes Street and extending from South Queensferry in the west to Musselburgh in the east; a total coverage of about 125 sq. miles compared with 30,000 sq. miles for Scotland as a whole. For most entries the earliest recorded names, as found in Johnston, Watson and Harris, are given first followed by the various interpretations found in these three works of reference and finally, taking into account all previous suggestions an attempt is made to make sense of these in terms of Modern Welsh word-elements.

Allermuir Hill – 1773 Allermore (later Alamore, JBJ), 1812 Allermuir
ael-y-mor = 'seaward brow of the hill'
* Harris – Scots *aller muir*, Anglian or Old Norse *alra mor* = 'moor where alders grow'.
* Johnston – Probably Gaelic *al mor* = 'big rock'.
** Both of the above interpretations are unfitting and unlikely. The northeastern promontory of the Pentland Hills ends in three hilltops facing north across Edinburgh to the Firth of Forth. Allermuir, a smooth bare-topped eminence flanked by Caerketton to the east and Cape Law to the west, is the centre one and the highest of the three. Welsh *ael y mor* = 'brow of the sea' i.e. 'seaward brow-of-the-hill' (which it demonstrably is) is much more appropriate.

Almond (River) – 1128 Avin, 1178 Amonth, 1420 Aumond
aman = 'river', as in Cwmaman, Aberaman, southern Wales
* Harris – It may well be pre-Celtic, from the root *ombh* = 'water'.
* Johnston – Gaelic *amhainn, amhuinn* = 'river'.
* Watson – Reconstructs a hypothetical Gaulish-Brythonic word *ambona* meaning 'river', from which would come Celtic *aman* and from thence Almond. It is also, he says, the probable root of the river Aman at Aberaman S. Wales. 'The popular derivation from Gaelic *abhainn* (misspelled *amhainn*) is, of course, impossible.'
** There are other Almonds in Perthshire and West Lothian, all of whose early records display a tendency to vacillate between *amon(d)* forms and *afon* forms, both of which mean 'river'.

Arthur's Seat (Holyrood) – 1508 Arthuerissete
** The lateness of this earliest record has usually been cited

as a reason to suppose that the name originated only in late mediaeval times as a fanciful evocation of the Arthurian Romances of Welsh, French, Breton, and English writers. These fictional embellishments were however all based on Arthurian Tales now contained in 'The Mabinogion', a collection of Welsh Folk Myths written down in the 13th. and 14th. centuries but referring to events taking place some 7 centuries earlier. Naturally, since the only surviving account of these ancient folk tales is a wholly Welsh one the events in it are related as taking place in Wales itself, but there are now arguments to the effect that the exploits of the 'real Arthur' ranged farther afield and were particularly concentrated in Northern Britain in what is now the English-Scottish Borders area including the region around Edinburgh. This being so it is not altogether surprising to find almost a dozen Arthurian place names distributed along a line running from South Argyll, through Dumbartons, Lothian, Angus, Aberdeenshire and up to Glenlivet in the north east. It is unlikely that all of these can have resulted from the the mediaeval fictional Romances and there has to be the possibility that at least some of them are of more ancient origin and commemorate attributes of the 'real Arthur' rather than the 'fictional Arthur'. Thus 'Arthurissete' could be an Anglicised translation of an original '*Set Arthur*' = 'seat of Arthur' or more remotely from '*cader Arth*' = 'Arthur's 'Chair' (seat of power). Interestingly '*Cader Arth*' easily corrupts into 'Catraeth' – the legendary site of the last despairing battle fought by the Gododdin against Anglican invading forces. Although this battle is generally said to have taken place at Catterick in the north of England the historian W.F. Skene places it somewhere in southeast Stirlingshire. A site even nearer to the Gododdin stronghold of Din Eidyn (Edinburgh) would make even more sense when it is remembered that the Gododdin warriors, after nights of carousing and feasting in the 'Hall of Eidyn', sallied forth to do battle whilst suffering from the effects of severe hangovers! Even the most nightmarish of hangovers could hardly have survived the long trek from Din Eidyn to Catterick! This leaves Arthur's Seat = *Cader Arth* = Catraeth as a better bet, which may mean that this last battle was fought somewhere in the heartlands of present day Edinburgh. But see 'Craggenmarf' also.

Baads (Dreghorn) – 1540 Baddis, 1753 Bauds
baeddas = place 'full-of-boars'
* Harris – The spellings show the vowel as long; and the name, which occurs elsewhere in Lothian, with or without the added *'s'* is British *bod* = 'residence' or 'place'.
** Welsh *bod* = residence or dwelling place, but *baedd* = boar, is a better fit. (compare with *baedd coed* 'boar wood' = Bathgate). The added *'s'* or *'is'* is problematic but may be the suffix *-as* = '- full-of', '-plenty of'.

Baberton (Currie) – 1306-1329 Kilbabertone, Kilbabertoun, Kilbebirtoun, 1596 Balberton, 1599 Babertoun, 1642 Kilbabertoun (again!)
* Harris – The name can be compared with Balberton near Kinghorn Fife originally recorded as Balbretane and meaning 'farmstead of the Britons'. The 'kil' appearing in the Currie name may be from Gaelic *cul* 'back, corner-of' or Gaelic *coill* 'a wood'. The name would then mean 'back corner, or wood by the farmstead of the Britons'.
** The relative lateness of the earliest records could possibly be indicative of the presence of a Welsh speaking enclave (Britons) still existing in this area even into the 14th century.

Balerno (Currie) – 1280 Balhernoch, 1289 Balernauch, 1296 Balernaghe, 1375 Ballernache
beili eirinawc = 'enclosed-place of little-plum-trees'
* Harris – Gaelic *baile airneach* = 'sloe tree stead' or 'farm with sloe bushes'.

* Watson – same as Harris.
* Johnston – Gaelic *baile eornach* = 'barley farm'.
** The village is however in an area with mostly P-Celtic names and it is worth considering a Welsh root, especially as Watson states that the Scots-Gaelic suffix *-ach* was adopted from the Welsh suffix *-og* (earlier *awc* or *awg*). In modern Welsh we have *beili eirinog* meaning 'enclosure with little-plum-trees' which in an earlier form could have been *beili eirinawc* or *beili eirinawg*. Any of these are just as good a match to modern Balerno as are the Gaelic alternatives. Another possibility is *beili eirinach* where *-ach* is a Welsh diminutive as in the place-name Mawddach = 'the little-Mawdd river'; this with the *-ach* to *-o* conversion noted by Nicolaisen and O'Maolalaigh leads directly to *beili eirino* and then by assimilation to *beileirno*. There is also the suggestion, from Stuart Harris, that the name Balerno 'shared the same space' as the name 'Byrnie' which 'is still used locally to describe the village'. Byrnie, as Watson (p.351) hints in his treatment of the name 'Pirnie', could have derived from Welsh *brennau* – the aspirated form of *prennau* = 'the trees': Byrnie would then mean 'place of trees', echoing the fuller description 'enclosure of little-plum-trees'.

Balleny (Balerno) – 1627 Baleny, 1682 Balenie, 1753 Baleny
beili leiniau = 'farmyard on the strips-of-land'
* Harris – It is probably Gaelic *baile leanaidhe* = 'farm-place at the swampy meadows'.
** There is however every reason to associate this name with that of 'Malleny', another local name accepted to be of 'British' origin. Making this comparison and on the grounds of consistency we can equate Balleny either with a Welsh *beili lleiniau* 'enclosed-place on the strips-of-land' or else with an earlier Brythonic *beili leyna* 'enclosure by meadows' (see Malleny). The word element *Beili*, as defined in Welsh Dictionaries, has the following meanings – 'enclosure' – 'yard', 'farmyard', *lleiniau* = 'patches, strips, fillets'.

Barnbougle (Dalmeny) – 1177 Berenbouell, 1320 Prenbougal, 1481 Berenbougale (JBJ), also Pronbogalle / Pronbugele (WJW), and 1362 Barnugele, 1365 Parnbogalle earlier Pronbugele ( )
bren bugail = 'herdsman's tree' (metathesised to *bern bugail* and hence to Barnbougle)
* Harris – The forms beginning with Pren, Pron and Parn clearly indicate that the first element is from Welsh *pren* = 'a tree' and not *bryn* = 'a hill'. The second element is undoubtedly *bugail* = 'a herdsman'.
* Johnston – Originally British *pren* = 'tree', then Gaelic *barr an* = 'height-of' the *buaigheail* = 'cowstall'.
* Watson – *pren bugail* = 'herdsman's tree'. 'The cattle of the *tref*,' says Prof. J.E. Lloyd, 'grazed together in the wide pasture which surrounded the tree, under the eye of the village herdsman or *bugail*'.
** Thus Barn bougle = *bren bugail* = 'the herdsman's tree' where *bren* is the aspirated form of *pren;* seen as Pren, Pron and Parn in the earlier records.

Baws Inch (Duddingston) –
bawus ynys = 'mucky meadow'
* Harris – The second element is Scots 'inch' adopted from Welsh *ynys* = 'water meadow', but the first element could derive either from early Scots *bawser* = 'badge' or from *bausen* = 'piebald' (white-striped), or from British *bau* = 'muddy'. The Scots interpretations would give Baws Inch = 'badger water meadow' or 'white-striped water meadow', both of which seem unlikely. These compare with the British alternative 'muddy water meadow'.
** Welsh *baw* = 'muck', and *bawus* = 'mucky, dirty, dungy, filthy, miry'. Hence Baws Inch = *bawus ynys* = 'mucky meadow', 'mucky water-meadow'.

Bonaly (Colinton) – early records from 1280 onwards show Bounalyn, Benhathelyn, and Bonalyn

banolyn = 'little broom-bushes'
* Harris – The early records show the name to be British *banathel lan* = 'place of broom-bushes'.
** Welsh equivalents are *banol, banad, banadl, banadlen* = 'broom-bushes' (plural), and *banhadlen* = 'broom-bush' (singular). Taking the first option *banol* and adding the diminutive suffix *-yn* gives *banolyn* = 'little broom-bushes'. Then with the usual dropping of the final *'n'* we get *banoly,* now for some reason misspelled and mispronounced as Bonaly.

Caerketton Hill (Swanston) – 1317 Karynketil, 1539 Carkettil (surname), 1682 Kairnketten, 1763 Kiirkyetton, 1773 Kirketton, 1817 Kirkyetton, 1852 Caerketton
caer cudyll = 'fortress of the falcon'
* Harris – Based on the records of 1317 and 1682 Harris sees the first element as British *carn* = 'rocky summit' and the second element as *caid* = 'burial-cairn', with a third element *an* = 'place of'. Therefore *carn caid an* = 'rocky-summit at the place-of the burial-cairn'.
* Johnson – Cites the records of 1317 and 1539 which he interprets as Welsh *caer yn cuddial* = 'fort of refuge'.
* Watson – Probably a corruption of *caer Catel* = 'Catel's fort', Catel being a personal name.
** The significant differences in the two interpretations of Harris and Johnston are firstly the endings '-etten', '-etton' in the later records as against the endings '-etil', 'ettil' in the earliest records and secondly the interpretation of the first element as *carn* (Harris), versus – *caer yn* (Johnston). That the name is British-Welsh seems not to be doubted. Harris puts forward strong arguments to support his choice of *carn* as the first element, but his case for interpreting the second and third elements as *caid an* must fail if we accept that the early ending 'etil' of 1317 takes precedence over the later 'etten', 'etton' endings of 1682 – 1852. On the other hand Johnson's

preference for *cuddial* (modern Welsh *cuddle*) 'retreat, refuge, hiding place' is hardly a befitting description of an exposed position atop some of the most fearsome crags in the Pentland Hills. Watson, not to be outdone, quotes the records of 1543 and later as 'Carketyll' and 'Karkettil' which both reinforce the 'l' endings as opposed to the later 'n' endings, but which also reinforce the choice of *caer* as the first element, as opposed to *carn*. At the risk of adding uncertainty to uncertainty I would suggest consideration be given to *caer cudyll* = 'stronghold of the hawk (or falcon)'. The crags and cliff-faces of Caerketton would at one time have provided perfect nesting places for Peregrine falcons, and maybe still do so.

Calton Hill – 1591 through to 1700 as Caldtoun or Coldtoun
caled din = 'hard fort'
* Harris – The name appears to be Celtic, probably British. (He gives no further explanation.)
** A possibility is *caled din* = 'the hard fort', which when part Anglicized metamorphises naturally to *caled ton,* hence Calton. The hill is a natural site for a small iron-age settlement but is now so built upon that any trace of such a fort is almost certainly lost, but see Craigingallt.

Cameron – 1150 *the marsh called* Cameri, 1211-1226 Camerun, Camberun, 1264-1290 Cambrun, Kambrun, 1337 Cambroun, later Cameroun, Camron, Camroun
cam bron = 'curved hill-brow'
* Harris – It is probably British *cam rynn* = 'point-of-land at the crook'. There are eight other places named 'Cameron' in Scotland each of which features a point of high land with a stream curving around it's base.
** The name may also be related to Camborne in Cornwall, near to which is a 'Cameron Farm', in which case the meaning is Welsh *cam bron* = 'curved brow-of-the-hill'. Camborne is a metathesised version of 'Cambron'.

Alternatively *cam* here may somehow be a foreshortened form of *camas* = 'river-bend'; in which case *camas bron* = 'river-bend by the brow-of-the-hill'. (See Cammo below). Harris's interpretation however seems very valid.

Cammo – 1296 Cambo, Cambok, 1654 Kammock
camach = at the 'little-bend' in the river
* Harris – The name is British *cambaco* – 'place in the bend of the river'.
* Watson – Gaelic *cam* = 'bent' and *camach* = 'bent place'.
** There seems to be no sensible modern Welsh equivalent to *baco* unless it is *parcau* = 'fields', undergoing lenition to *barcau*. In which case *cam-y-barcau* = 'curved fields'. Otherwise *camach* = 'little-bend', probably referring to that in the nearby river Gogar, then Cammo by 'standard' *-ach* to *-o* conversion.

Carlowrie (Kirkliston) – 1337 Carlouryn, Carlouri, 1654 Kaerloury
caer llewyrn = 'fortlet of the fox'
* Harris – The name is probably British *caer lowern* = 'fort, or stockaded-place, of the fox'.
* Johnston – Probably Gaelic *carr labharaidh* = 'rock of the echo'.
* Watson – There is no proof that 'Car' = *caer* and the second part may be a man's name e.g. 'Lowrie'. (He gives no further explanation for the first element 'car'.)
** Welsh *caer llewyrn* – 'fort of the fox'. It may be that here *llewyrn* suffered aspiration of *'ll'* and some form of metathesis to give *lewryn*, and then with the usual *-yn* conversion to *-ie* we get *lewrie* and so Lowrie.

Carmel Hill (Kirkliston) –
caer moel = 'fort on the bare-hill-top'
Harris – Perhaps British *caer mail* – 'fort on the bare hill'
** Welsh *caer moel* = 'fort on the bare-topped-hill'. There is

also a Carmel in Cumbria which would tend to reinforce the identification of a P-Celtic, Welsh / British, origin.

Carnethy (Pentland Hills) –
carneddau = the 'cairns'
* Harris, Johnston and Watson all agree; it is Welsh *carneddau* = 'hill of the cairns'.
** A rare unanimity of agreement!

Carnodding (Kirkliston) –
carneddyn = 'little-cairn'
* Harris – It seems possible that it is an older British form of Welsh *carneddog* = 'rocky-place', or 'place with cairns'.
** Maybe, but Welsh *carneddyn* – 'little-cairn' is equally likely or unlikely.

Cockle Burn (Dalmeny) – 1567 onwards as Cokilburne, Cokkil Burn or similar
cagl = 'sheep-dung' stream
* Harris – The stream follows a marshy course, as also does another Cockle stream at Gogar. On this evidence Harris relates it as a possibility to British *cagal* or Gaelic *cacail* both meaning 'mire, bog' ie: 'stream from the mire' perhaps?
** Welsh *cagl* = 'mire', 'sheep-dung', 'dirt'.

Corslet (Currie) –
cors llaid = 'clay wetlands'
* Harris – Suggests a derivation from British *cors laid* = 'miry bog'. The name occurs elsewhere in Duddingston (Edinburgh) and Temple (Midlothian) and in all three cases it is associated with a waterside environment.
** Welsh *cors* = 'marsh or wetlands', *llaid* = 'mud or clay' and *llaidd* = 'soft or mild'. Of these *cors llaid* = 'clay wetlands' seems to make the most sense. Certainly this area is noted for it's heavy clay soils and the Corslet area lies in a shallow dip in the ground through which flows the Murray ('miry') Burn and which at one time may well have been marshy.

Corstorphine – 1130 Crostorfin, Crostorphin, 1140 Crorstorfin, 1296 Corstorfyn, Corstorphyn, 1508 Corstorphyne
cors tor ffin = 'marsh, fen, by the rocky-hill on the boundary'
* Johnston – Ever the romantic! – He interprets it as = 'Cross of Thorfinn'; Thorfinn being the name of a somewhat obscurely known Viking.
* Harris – despite adding the recorded names 1296 Corstorfyn, Corstorphyn, he still asserts that the name is British or Gaelic *crois Torfin* = 'Torfin's crossing'.
* Watson – The meaning is 'Torfin's crossing', rather than 'Torfin's Cross', with reference to a crossing over the hill. 'Torfin' is a personal name, reportedly connected with MacBeth.
** If however one identifies the first element as Welsh *cors* = 'a bog, marsh, fen', instead of *croes, crois* = 'a cross', and identifies the final elements as *tor* and *ffin* then the result is *cors tor ffin* = the 'marshy area (fen)' and the 'rocky-hill' (hill with rock outcrops) marking the 'boundary'. This describes the site exactly; the 'fen' which includes today's Gyle area is described at length by Harris, the 'rocky-hill' is where Edinburgh Zoo now is on Corstorphine Hill and the other end of the 'boundary' is defined by Torphin Hill which is almost due south of, and eminently visible from, Corstorphine Hill. Boundaries were seemingly important to the Tribes and Factions of Dark Age and Early Mediaeval times and were marked in various ways, a favourite being a convenient stream as at Nant-y-Ffin in Wales and Glen Finglais, (Glyn-Ffin-Glais) in Scotland.

Craggenemarf (Holyrood Park) – the name dates from 1128 onwards
carregan marth = 'little-rock of sadness'
craigan marth = 'little-crag of sadness'
* Harris – It describes the area of Holyrood Park and

Arthur's seat itself and is British for 'dead men's rock'. It may have prompted the fanciful name *Mount Dolorous* as used once for Arthur's Seat in a 12th century chronicle.
** Harris's interpretation seems to be by analogy to Welsh *carregan marw* = 'small-rock of the dead', but a closer approximation to 'Craggenmarf' is Welsh *carregan marth* = 'small-rock of sadness' and it is this latter which better relates to the description *Mount Dolorous* applied to this area by King David in the twelfth century.

Craigbrae (Dalmeny) – 1488 Cragbrey, 1506 Cragbray, 1552 Cragbrie
craig bre = the 'crag on the peak'
* Harris – The name may be wholly Celtic, e.g. British *crag bre* = 'crag or rocky-summit of the hill'.
** Welsh *craig* = 'crag'. *bre* = 'hill', 'highland', 'peak', 'mount'; and also 'high'.

Craigcrook (Costorphine Hill) – 1335 onwards Cragcrok, Cragruk, Cragcroke, Craigcruke, Craigcruke
craig crug = 'crag of the burial-mound, barrow'
Harris – Originated as a 'hill' name, British *creg crug* = 'rocky hill with hillocks or cairns on it'.
* Johnston – Probably British translated into Gaelic as *creag cruaich* = 'stack-like crag'.
** Welsh *crug* = 'hillock', 'heap', 'cairn'; 'barrow', 'tump', 'stack'; *craig* = 'crag'.

Caigenterrie (Currie) – 1720 – 1753 Craigintary
craigan tarren = 'little-crag on the knoll'
* Harris – Evidently Celtic, the name may be British *crag an taru* = 'bull's rock', but *crag an tarren* = 'rock of the knowe' would be an apt description of the prominent rocky scaur above the burn south of the house.
** Welsh *craigan* = 'little-crag'; *tarren* = 'knoll, rock, tump'. As is common in Scottish names the *-en* ending of Tarren

converts to *-ie* to give Craigantarrie and thence Craigenterrie.

Craigentinny (Restalrig) –
craigan tannau = 'little-crag of fires'
* Harris – The name is Celtic . . . more likely to be British, possibly *craggen tanan* 'little rock at a narrow place' or 'little rock of a narrow sort'.
* Watson – Craigentinnie is most probably for *creag an t-sionnaigh* = 'the fox's rock'.
** Neither of the two above suggestions ring true, Watson relates the name to Ardentinny which he interprets as ' height of the fox' but Johnston, based on quite substantial evidence says Ardentinny = 'height of fire' from Gaelic *teine* = 'fire'. Modern Welsh equivalent is *arddyn tannau* = 'little-height of fires'. Thus Craigentinny, by comparison, could equally be *craigan tannau* = 'little-crag of fires', in other words a 'beacon site'.

Craigie (Dalmeny) – 1178 Craigin, 1296 Cragyn, Cragg, 1654 Kragy
craigyn = 'little-crag'
* Harris – Celtic, probably British *cregan* = 'place of, or at, the crags'.
* Johnston – Gaelic *creag*, in locative = 'crag'.
** Welsh *craigan* / *craigyn* = 'little-crag'. The final '-yn' in *craigyn* converts to '-ie' to give Craigie.

Craigingalt (Calton)
craigyn gallt = 'little-crag on the hill, wooded-hillside'
Harris – Craigingallt is the earliest known name of the Calton Hill, appearing thus in 1456 and continuing in use until 1743. The name is British *crag an gallt* = 'crag on the hill or wooded hillside'.
** Welsh *craigan* (or *craigyn*) = 'little-crag' and *gallt* (often aspirated to *allt*) = 'hill, ascent, cliff or wood', also in South

Wales dialect = 'wooded-hillside' usually alongside a stream.

Craigmillar – 1130 Craigmilor / Craigmoilard, 1212 Craigmillar, 1374 Craigmelor
craig moel ardd = 'crag on the bare high-land', or 'crag on the high bare-hill'
* Harris – The early spellings suggest that the name is British *creg* = 'rock', at or on the *meol ard* = 'the brow of the hill', or 'the bare-summit'.
* Johnston – Gaelic *creag maol ard* = 'rock of the bare height'.
** Welsh *craig* = 'crag'; *moel* = 'bald, bare'; bare-hill, bare-hill-top'; *ardd* = 'hill', 'high-place', 'high-land'; and also 'high'.

Cramond – 1178 Caramonth, Caramonde, 1200 Karramunt, 1250 Cramond, 1292 Cramunde, 1293 Karamunde
caer aman = 'fort-place on the river'
* Harris – It is British *caer Amond* = 'fortified place on the Almond' and was evidently the native Votadinic name for the fort the Romans built there.
* Watson – The meaning is 'fort of the Almond'.
* Johnston – It is 'Fort', Welsh *caer* on the River Almond.
** Welsh *caer* = 'fort', 'fort-place'; *aman* = 'river'. The name of the river itself is on record as going through the sequence Avin, Amonth, Aumond and this is taken as evidence that the early Cramond place-name records ending in '-month, '-munt', '-monde' are simple corruptions of an earlier *aman* leading eventually to 'Almond'. (see entry for Almond River). Alternatively the endings in '-month, '-munt', '-monde' can be taken at face-value as representing either *mwnt* = 'mound, mount' or *mynydd* = 'rough-pasture-land, Common', giving the meaning as 'fort on the mound', or 'fort on the Common'.

Currie – 1210 Curey, 1230 Cory, 1246 Curri, 1392 Curry, 1402 Currie, 1434 Corry
cyrrau = 'skirting-edges' of the Pentland Hills
* Watson – These are dative of Gaelic *curragh* = 'a wet plain'.
* Johnston – Locative of Gaelic *curragh* = 'wet plain, marsh'.
* Harris – Derivation from Gaelic *curragh* = 'boggy plain' is possible but unconvincing, insofar as any 'haughs' (marshes) here are small and unremarkable – suggest that the name is British *curi* = 'a hollow', akin to Welsh *cur*.
** Welsh *cwr* = 'limit', 'border', 'edge', 'skirt'; the plural is *cyrrau*, pronounced 'kurr-eye'. The old village of Currie lies on the northern 'skirts, borders, limits, edges' of the Pentland Hills.

Dalmahoy (Ratho) – 1272 Dalmohoy, 1295 Dalmehoy, later Dalmahoye, Dalmihoi
dol ma hwy = 'meadow on the longer flat-field'
* Watson – The form indicates that it contains a Saint's name and that saint must be St Tua. *Dail mo Thuae* = 'my Tua's meadow'.
* Johnston – Gaelic *dail moh'Aoidh* = 'field of my dear Hugh'. 'Watson's derivation from St Tua is phonetically very difficult'.
* Harris – Nevertheless prefers Watson's interpretation, as 'the early spellings show the name to be British or Gaelic *da(i)l mo Thuae* = meadow of Saint Tua'.
** A more mundane, perhaps more down-to-earth, Welsh interpretation might be *dol ma hwy* = 'meadow on the longer (piece of) flat-ground'.

Dalmeny (Queensferry) – 1180 Dumanie, 1250 Dunmanyn
din maini = 'fort of stones'
din mainyn = 'fort of little-stones'
* Johnston – It is probably Gaelic *dun mainne* = 'hill of

delay or procrastination'. Ross / Mckay – Gaelic *dail mo Eithne* = 'meadow of my Eithne' (a personal name).
* Watson – First part is Welsh *din* = 'fort', the second part may be *meini* = 'stones', therefore 'fort of stones'.
* Harris – British *din meyni* = 'stone fort' or *din meyn an* = 'place of the stone fort'.
** Welsh *din meini* = 'fort of stones', or alternatively *din mainyn* = 'fort of little-stones'. Often *din* becomes *dun* and the final '-yn' in *mainyn* converts to either '-ie' or '-y' to give Dunmainie and then by assimilation Dumainie, which compares well with the record of 1180. The record of 1250 which Harris says 'was typical in the 13th century', seems truer to the original *dinmainyn*. Harris cites – *'The presence within Dalmeny of the powerful fort and settlement on Craigie Hill, with it's triple ramparts partially built in stone'.*

Dalry (City) – 1336 Dalry, early spellings also Dalry, Dalrye, Dailry
dol rhug = 'heather meadow'
* Watson – It may be Gaelic *dail an righ* = 'king's meadow' or alternatively *dail fhraoigh* = 'heathery dale'.
* Johnston – Gaelic *dail righe* = 'meadow of the king'.
* Ross / Mackay – 'May be Gaelic *dail fhraoich* = 'heather field', or *dail righ* = 'field on the slope' or *dail righ* = 'king's meadow'.
* Harris is not so sure – Early spellings Dalry, Dalrye, and Dailry show, he says, the name to be Celtic, British *dol rug,* or Gaelic *dail fhraoigh,* = 'heathery dale'. Neither history nor pronunciation supports derivation from *dail righ.*
** Welsh *dol* = 'meadow', *rhug* = 'heather', *rhi* = 'Lord', 'Chief', *rhych* = 'furrow' and *rhyn* = 'hill'; 'cape'. As there are several Dalrys elsewhere in Scotland it is very unlikely they can all be 'meadows of a king or a lord' and also unlikely that they are all 'meadows in furrows or on slopes'. Also, more often than not *dol* is found as *dal;*.the odds therefore

favour *dal rhug* = 'heather meadow'. Alternatively there is an outside possibility that it is *dol rhyn* = 'meadow on the hill'.

The Drum (Gilmerton) – 1406
y-trum = 'the ridge'
* Harris – The name is British *drum* = a 'ridge'.
** *drum* is the lenited form of *trum* = 'ridge, spine'.

The Drum (Restalrig) – 1557
See above.
** 'British' / Welsh *y-trum* = *drum* = a 'ridge'.

Drumbrae (Corstorphine)
(y) drum bre = the 'high ridge'
* Harris – 'British *drum* or Gaelic *druim* with Scots *brae* = 'steep road (*brae*) over the ridge (*drum /druim*)'.

** Welsh *drum* = 'ridge'; *bre* = 'mount' or 'hill' or 'peak' : 'highland' : 'high'. Therefore *drum bre* = 'hill ridge'; or ' high ridge'. The presence of a 'British' first element suggests that the name preceded the establishment of the Scots tongue in this area and therefore throws doubt on the second element originating as Scots *brae;* which was in any case probably inherited from Welsh *bre.*

Drumdryan (Tollcross) – 1458 Drumdriain
(y) drum drain = 'ridge of thorns, prickles'
* Harris – The name is British *drum (ar) drein* or Gaelic *druim drioghionn* = 'ridge of sloe or blackthorn'.
** Welsh *drain* = 'thorns, prickles'.

Duddingston (Arthur's Seat) – 1136- 1147 Treverlen, 1150 *Dodinus de Dodinestun,* 1295 Dodingstone, 1147 *Dodinus de Berwic*
tref yr llyn = 'steading by the lake', 'lake-steading'
tref ar llyn = 'steading on the lake'
* Harris – The name is taken from an Anglo-Norman person Dodon de Berwic. Hence 'dodin's ton' =

Duddingston. But prior to 1130 the area was called 'Treverlen' from Welsh *tre war lyn* = 'farm at or on the loch' It is tempting, says Harris, to think that it might have originated as the name of the crannog or lake-dwelling thought to have existed in the south corner of the loch.
** Welsh *tref* = 'homestead', 'hamlet', 'town'; *llyn* = 'lake' i.e. that which is now called Duddingston Loch. Interestingly 'Trevelin' is the name of a Welsh colonists' village in Patagonia, but this may alternatively be from *tre-felin* = 'mill steading'.

Dundas (Dalmeny) – from 1180 onwards
din das = 'stack-shaped fort'
* Harris – The name appears to be Gaelic *dun deas* = 'south fort' but could be British *din des.*
** Welsh *de, deau* = 'south', *deus* = 'southerly': *das* = 'stack, rick, heap'. No modern Welsh equivalent for *des.*

Dunsappie (Arthur's Seat) –
din sopyn = 'hill-fort hay-bundle'
* Watson – The second part is genitive of Gaelic *sopach* hence *dun sopach* = 'fort at place of wisps or tufts of grass'.
* Johnston – Probably the Celt's name of Arthur's Seat, *dun seapach,* here in locative = 'hill with the long tail', as it exactly looks from the south. Watson's evidence for connecting it with Torsappie is weak, Gaelic *sop* means properly 'a wisp, a loose bundle of straw' very unlikely here. The name probably goes back to the British form of the Gaelic *dun sopaich* = fort of clusters'.
** None of the two Gaelic interpretations seem particularly convincing, but Welsh *din sopyn (sypyn)* = 'hill-fort of hay-bundle' equates with Watson's Gaelic *dun sopach,* with the added advantage that the *-yn* suffix converts to *-ie* thus giving *dinsopie* or *dunsopie* from which Dunsappie; but perhaps even this explanation is not greatly credible either.

Edinburgh – circa 700 Eydden, Eidden, *Taliesin* – Dineiddyn, 1100 *Tighernac* – 'Dunedene, which the English call Edineburg', 1126 Edenburge, 1130 Dinas Etwin
din Eidyn = 'fort of Eidyn'
* Watson – Considering that it is Scotland's historic capital Watson's dissertation is disappointingly ambivalent and fails to come to any committed conclusions. He first considers the Welsh *din Eidyn* = 'hill fort of Eidyn' 'dating from the 7th. century', he then considers the Gaelic – 'modern Dun Eideann, Dunedin or Edinburgh' and finally, as everyone else has done since, dismisses any suggestion that the name derives from English 'Edwin's Burgh'; but he fails to define the meaning of either *din Eidyn* or *dun eideann.*
* Johnston – Is a little more forthcoming and besides listing all the earliest records states that 'the name is Celtic, Welsh *din* (Gaelic *dun*) = 'fort' and Old Welsh *eiddyn* (Gaelic *eadann)* = 'hill slope'. i.e. that from the Castle down to Holyrood'. (It is perhaps significant of Johnston's opinion that he gives precedence to the Welsh interpretation!)
* Ross – is more modern in his thinking. It is he says 'fort of the Rock-Face'. *Eiddyn* (Cumbric) = 'rock-face', cognate with Gaelic *aodann,* plus Old English *burh* = 'stronghold'. The latter element being a replacement for the original Cumbric prefix *din* = 'stronghold or fort'. Presumably then, according to Ross, it originated as *din eiddyn* = 'stronghold on the rock-face'.
* Harris – It is left to Harris to make some sense of these previous offerings, he interprets the meaning of *din Eidyn* as = 'hill-fort of Eidyn', where *Eidyn* is the personal name of some individual; it is not, he says, to be confused with Anglican *eoten,* Scots *etin* = 'a giant', nor with Gaelic *eadainn* or *aodainn* = 'a slope'.
** Nowadays no reputable authority disputes that the name Dunedin and it's Anglicized form Edinburgh have their origin in any source other than Welsh *din Eidyn,* the only

point of contention being the interpretation of Eidyn as either a personal name or the name of a specific area. W.F. Skene includes a 'Clinog Eiddyn' as a personal name in his genealogy of the *Kings of the Race of Macsen Guledig* and a 'Clyddno Eiddyn' in his genealogy of the *Kings of the Race of Coel Hen* – but in both cases *Eiddyn* is merely a qualifier to *Clinog* and to *Clyddno* so *Eiddyn* may still have derived either from an area or from a region. A throw-away remark by Watson discounts the Irish chronicler Tigernach's idea, circa AD638, that *eidyn* derived from Old Irish *etain* now Modern Irish *eadann, eadainn* = 'a face' which compares with modern Scots-Gaelic *aodann* = 'face, visage, countenance'.

Gorgie – 1200 Gorgin, 1250 Gorgyn, 1320 Gorgy
gorcyn, gor-y-gyn = 'upper-wedge'
* Johnston – Perhaps Welsh *gor gin* 'spacious wedge' or 'wedge-like field'.
* Harris – The early forms show it to be British *gor gyn* = 'upper wedge', probably referring to the tapering shape of this land between the river and the Craiglockhart Hills, themselves known in the 13th, century as 'Craggies de Gorgin'.
** The second element is Welsh *gyn* the aspirated form of *cyn* = 'wedge, chisel-shape', the first element can be either *gor* the aspirated form of the diminutive prefix *cor* = 'lesser, dwarf'; or the intensive prefix *gor* = 'above-, over-, high-, super-, extreme-, sur-'. In either case the whole name will be *gorgyn*, with the final '-yn' converting to '-y' and then to '-ie' to give Gorgy and Gorgie.

Inchgarvie (Queensferry) – 1491 onwards as Inchgarde, Inchgarvy and the like
ynys garw = 'rugged island'
* Harris – The name is British, akin to Gaelic *innis garbh* = 'rough island'.

* Johnston – It is 'rough, rocky, island' from Gaelic *garbh* = 'rough'.

** Welsh *ynys* = 'island', *garw* = 'rough', 'rugged', 'harsh', 'coarse', 'extreme'.

Inchkeith (Firth of Forth) – *pre* 1200 Insula Keth, 1461 Ynch Keyth
ynys coed = 'island with a wood'
* Harris – The name is British *innis cett* = 'island with a wood on it'.
** Welsh *ynys coed* / Old Welsh *ynys coet* = 'wooded island'. (See Keith, Dalkeith)

Inchmickery (Cramond) – 1654 Inchmickry, 1682 Inchmickrie, 1693 Inchmuckrie
* Johnston – Gaelic *innis an bhicaire* 'isle of the Vicar', i.e. from Inchcolm Monastery.
* Harris – The name is Celtic, probably British, akin to Gaelic *innis mucraidh* = 'isle of seals'.
** Welsh *ynys micariaid* = 'isle of vicars'. All of the records are very late and none of the above suggestions seem very convincing! Harris's seems the most reasonable.

Water of Leith (River) – 1145 Let (as in Inverlet), 1439 Leicht, 1570 Leth
llaidd = 'mild' stream
* Johnston – Welsh *lleithio* 'to moisten, overflow'.
* Watson – It can be compared with Welsh *llaith* = 'damp. moist', or *lleithio* = 'to moisten'.
* Harris – It is British akin to Welsh *llaith* = 'the water'
** Welsh *llaith* = 'damp, soft, humid', *llaidd* = 'soft, mild', *lleithio* = 'to moisten', 'to wet'. Older Welsh *llaith* = 'death'!

Leith (Town) – circa 1130 Inverlet, 1315 Inverlethe, 1439 Leight, 1570 Leth
** The Town takes it's name from the river.

Lennie – early forms are Lanin, Lanyne
llainyn = 'small-strip' of land
* Harris – The early forms 'Lanin' and 'Lanyne' from 1169 onwards show the name to be British *lein an* or Gaelic *leanain* = place 'at the long or swampy meadow'.
** No presently identifiable modern Welsh equivalent for *lein an* but *llain* = 'patch, strip, fillet', plus diminutive suffix '-yn' converted to '-ie' gives *lainie* = 'small-strip, patch or fillet'.

Lothian – Recorded from 1091 onwards in various Latin, French, or Scots forms such as: Laudonia, Leudonia (Latin); Lodoneo, de Lodoneio, Loeneis, Loenes (Norman French); Lowthian (Scots)
lleuddinion = 'land-of Lleu's fort'
* Harris – GWS Barrow points out that Lothian can be shown to be a stream name of British origin. The Lothian Burn which flows through Edinburgh may possibly be from British *lutna* = 'dark, muddy'. (See Lothian Burn)
* Watson – The oldest tradition of the name (Lothian) refers to a man called Leudonos from whom the province he ruled was called Leudonica, the Welsh form of which is Lleuddiniawn = 'the district of Lleuddin'. It is unfortunate that we have no real tradition of the name Lothian in Gaelic.
* www.cyberscotia.com – *'It seems likely that the Welsh form Lleudinyawn (12th century), derives from an earlier Brythonic form meaning the same thing = 'land of Lleu's fort', comprising the element lleu (a personal name), din (fort) and iawn (a possessive suffix, having in this case the meaning 'land-of'). On a purely linguistic level, it seems likely that the transformation of the Celtic personal name Lleu into the modern Scots Loth derives from an incorrect segmentation of the original Brythonic placename Lleuddiniawn, with the initial soft consonant of ddin being attached to the end of the lleu element yielding a spurious lleudd eventually becoming pronounced in the mouths of Scots speakers as Loth'.*

** In modern Welsh Lleuddiniawn would be *Lleuddinion.*

Lothian Burn –
llwytuan = 'litle-dark-grey' stream
* Harris – Early forms of the stream name such as Lodone, Louenyn and Louthyan suggest that the name is British *lutna* = 'dark or muddy stream'. The burn's name seems to have generated the regional name of Lothian.
** Welsh *lloedd* = 'comfort', *lloeddian* = 'small-comfort'; *llwytu* = 'dark-grey', *llwytuan* = 'litle-dark-grey'. That the Burn and the Region now have the same name may only be coincidence.

Lymphoy (Currie) – 1512 Lumphoy, 1551 Limphoy, 1552 Lymphoy
llwm fai = 'bare flat-ground'
* Harris – It is Celtic, probably from British *lom* = 'bare' and *fa,* the aspirated form of *ma,* = 'a place'.
** Welsh *llwm fa* = 'bare flat-ground', or 'bare flat-field'. The element *ma / fa* is derived as a shortened form of *maes / faes* and is also available in the form *mai / fai.* In Scotland the double *'ll'* invariably reduces to a single *'l'*, hence we can have Lymphoy = *lwmfa* or *lwmfai* = 'bare flat-ground', of which two alternatives the latter is the better phonetic match.

Malleny – 1280 on: Maleny, Malemmy, Malluny, Mallany
ma llainyn = 'flat-ground: small-strip'
ma lleiniau = 'flat ground : narrow strips-of-land'
* Harris – Early forms are Maleny, Malemmy, Mallumy, Mallany. These show the name to be Celtic, probably British, *ma leyna* = 'plain of the meadows'.
** There is no identifiable modern Welsh equivalent to Harris' 'British' *leyna* but possible substitutes are *llain* = 'patch', 'strip' 'fillet' or *llinaid* = 'flaxen'. Whence *ma llainyn* = 'small-patch-strip-fillet' of 'flat-ground' or alternatively *ma llinaidd* (pronounced ma-leen-eye-the) = 'flat-field of flax'. –

literally 'flaxen flat-ground'. Conversion of '-yn' to '-y' gives *ma llainyn* = Mallainy, hence Mallany and Malleny. Most likely is *lleiniau* = 'narrow strips of land', *ma llainiau* = 'strips of land on flat-ground'.

Meggetland –
miget llan = 'enclosed-yard of bogginess'
* Harris – The name is British *lann* = 'ground or farm-enclosure', with *miget* = 'at the boggy' burn.
** Welsh *llan / lan* = 'yard, enclosure'; *mig* = 'bog' and the suffix *-et* is equivalent to the English suffix – *ness*, hence *miget* = 'bogginess' and *miget lan* = 'bogginess yard, or enclosure'. The term 'yard' here has it's old meaning of 'yard-of-ground surrounding a house or steading'; a meaning it still has in modern day America. See Meggat Water also.

Niddrie (Musselburgh) – 1249 Nodref, 1266 Noderyf, 1296 Nudreff, 1506 Nudry
* Harris – Welsh *nuadh tref* = 'new farm'.
* Watson – The first part may be *newydd* = 'new', the second part *tref, dref;* = 'steading', the meaning would be thus Newstead.
* Johnston – Welsh *nuadh tref* = 'new house, or settlement'.
** Welsh *newydd tref* = 'new steading (ie: homestead or farmstead)'; *nuadh* is not Welsh, it is Scots-Gaelic from Irish-Gaelic *nua* = 'new, fresh'. Harris was perhaps led astray by Johnston who seems to have been responsible for the initial misconception.

Peffermill –
pefr moel = 'the bright-shining stream by the bare-hill'
* Watson, Johnston and Harris all agree that 'Peffer' is from Welsh *pefr* = 'clean, bright, shining', and that this was once the name of today's Braid Burn as it flows through the district of Peffermill. A 1630 spelling 'Peppermylne'

suggests to them that the second element is either Welsh *melin* or Gaelic *moulin*, both = 'a mill'.
** Alternatively, since the whole name Peffermill is that of a district, the second element could be Welsh *moel* = 'bare-topped-hill', describing that area wherein the Pefr Burn flows between the 'bare-hill', of Arthur's Seat, on one side and Craigmillar (*Craig Moel Ardd*) on the other. Peffermill is then the place by 'the clean, bright-shining stream and the bare-topped hill'.

Pirniehaa (Balerno) – 1812 & later Pirniehill
* Harris – Topographical evidence and that of the local pronunciation indicates that 'hill' in Pirniehill is a map error for 'hall', which itself stands for Scots *haw/ haugh* = 'a marsh'. The evidence of other 'Pirnie' names suggests that the first element *pirn* may derive from British *pren* = 'a tree', or else *peuran* = 'pasture'.
** The first element *pirn* could derive from British *prenau* = 'trees' metathesised to 'pirnie' as described by Watson for the place-names 'Pirn' (*pren*) and 'Pairney' (*prennau*). Similarly it is possibly *prenyn* = 'little-tree', metathesised to *pernyn* which with -yn converted to Scots -ie yields *pernie*, hence Pirnie.

Ratho – 1258 Ratheu, 1292 Ratho, 1315 Rathow, Rethow
rhathau = 'fortified mounds on an area-of-cleared-land'
* Watson – Gives the following meanings:- 'Gaelic *rath* = 'a circular fort', usually of earth; Welsh *rath* = 'a circular fortified spot', a 'mound' or a 'hill'.
* Johnston – Cites the plural *rathau* = 'mounds, hills'.
* Harris – Cites, 'Celtic' *ratha* = 'a place of the *rath* or *raths*', as having three meanings, (a) = forts, (b) = a 'monastic enclosure' – of the Columban Kirk, and (c) = 'a 26 acre holding'.
** This is a name of much interest and differing opinion. The spellings of all the early records are in close accord with

Welsh *rhathau* the plural of *rhath* which in Welsh dictionaries is given as meaning = 'a mound' or 'an area-of-cleared-land'. In Welsh place-names *rhath* has the meaning 'defended site, fort'. Since, in Scotland, there are quite a number of *rath* type names few, if any, of which have connections with monastic establishments Harris's second suggestion can, it seems, be disregarded. Furthermore none of these other *rath* names are to be found in the Gaelic heartlands of the West and Northwest; the inference therefore is that in Scotland the word *rath* has its origins in Welsh *rhath,* possibly incorporating all of the remaining meanings with the exception of Harris's '26 acre holding' – although this could in some cases be a specialized meaning of 'cleared land'. Taking the remaining three meanings together we have *rath* = 'fortified-circular-settlement or settlements, on a mound, sited on an area-of-cleared-land'. According to Harris there is, or was, just such a construction atop South Platt Hill, immediately west of Ratho Park.

Restalrig – Originally – Lestalric from c 1100 – 1752, the variant Restalrig introduced in the 15th century is now the name, but Lestalric is still used colloquially.
llys tal rhych = 'great-court at the front-end of the furrow'
* Harris – Early spellings Lastalric, Lastalrik, Lastalrich, Lestalric, Lestalrich, Lestalryk, suggest that it is Anglian *lastal, lestal* = 'a mire' with *ric* = narrow-strip, ditch or drainage channel'. Thus *lestal ric* = 'mire in the narrow-strip, ditch or drainage channel'.
* Johnston – Prefers Welsh *llys tal rhych* = 'hall, mansion, on the lofty-ridge'.
** Welsh *llys* = 'great-court, hall'; *tal* = 'tall, high ' or 'front-end, forehead'; *rhych* – 'furrow, groove, trench'. Hence *llys tal rych* = 'great court at the front-end of the furrow'.

Tarbrax Hill (Dreghorn) –
tor brychas = 'speckledy rock-outcropped-hill'

* Harris – It is British *tor brych* or Gaelic *torr breac* = 'speckled or brindled, hill'.
* Johnston – Gaelic *torr breac* = 'speckled hill' with English plural 's' added i.e.: *torr breac(s).*
** Welsh *tor brychas* = 'speckledy hill-with-rock-outcrops'. Alternatively *tor broch* = 'rock-outcropped-hill of the badger'.

Tormain Hill (Ratho) –
* Harris – The hill is remarkable for the cup-and-ring markings on the rocks at it's summit. The name is British *torr maen* = 'hill of the stone(s)'.
* cyberscotia.com – 'Cornish / Welsh *tor maen* = 'stone hill'.
** Welsh *tor* = 'heap, mound, belly, bulge'; *maen* = 'stone'. In Welsh place-names the element *maen* denotes a very special kind of stone, such as a 'Standing Stone'. In Welsh and Cornish place-names the P-Celtic element *tor* in it's sense of 'a heap' seems to take on the specialised, perhaps older, meaning of a 'rocky-hill' or 'hill-with-rock-outcrops' or simply 'rock-outcrops', these meanings being somewhat reflective of the Welsh verb *tori, torri* = to 'break, cut, rupture, fracture'.

Torphin –
tor ffin = 'hill-with-rock-outcrops on the boundary'
* Harris – It is British and/or Gaelic *torr fionn* = 'white steep-sided hill'.
* Watson – It is Gaelic *torr fionn* = 'white rounded-hill'.
* Johnston – Gaelic *torr fionn* = 'clear, white hill'.
** Welsh *tor* = 'rock-outcrops'; *ffin* = 'boundary, limit'. See Corstorphine also.

Chapter 10

Welsh-names for Scotch Whiskies

'Brother Cadfael saw all things in cautious balance'

Cadfael Chronicles, 'St Peters Fair'

Whisky place-names

Whisky distilleries are by their very nature sited close to water supplies which can not only be utilised to manufacture the whisky spirit itself but also to provide the necessary cooling water for the Condensers required to cool the distilled vapour from the Stills. In some distilleries a single water source, such as a local stream, suffices for both requirements; in other distilleries different water sources are used for the two requirements; e.g. spring water perhaps for the Wash tuns and river water for the Condensers. This attachment to water sources is very often reflected in the name of the distillery and hence in the name of the whisky itself and since water names are generally amongst the oldest of place-names there is a strong likelihood that at least some of them originated in the old P-Celtic Welsh languages of Scotland. The following list contains names which have already been discussed in other chapters, for these the interpretation of the name will not be repeated in detail, only the conclusion will be given here; for all other cases any justification is kept to a minimum.

Aberlour – *Aber Llawr* = 'confluence of the lowly stream' or alternatively *aber llafar* = 'confluence of the high-voiced (loud) stream'.

Ardmore – Older Welsh – *ardd mor,* Modern Welsh – *ardd mawr* = 'the great height', presumably referring to nearby Knockandy Hill *(cnwcan du* = 'little black knoll').

Balmenach – this is an interesting name inasmuch as the element *bal* is invariably construed as a Gaelic word *baile* meaning 'farm' or 'farmstead'. Here however we have as the second word element what is very possibly the Welsh word *mynach* 'monk'. To couple with this there is another Welsh word *beili* which has the various meanings 'yard, court'; 'mound'; 'outlet'; thus we have as an alternative interpretation *beili mynach* 'yard of the monk'. In other words the enclosed area around the dwelling place of the monk. Monks were amongst the pioneers of distillation processes!

Ben Nevis – *ben nefus* = 'mountain of the heavenly one', named after the river Nevis. See entries for 'Nevis' in River Names chapter and 'Ben Nevis' in Place-names chapter.

Cardhu – *caer du* ='castle-dark' (literally 'black fortlet').

Clynelish – *clyn-y-llys* = 'meadow of the Court (Great House)'.

Cragganmore – *carregan mawr* = 'big little-rock', or *craigan mawr* = 'big little-crag'.

Craigellachie – *craig-y llachau* = 'crag of gleams, glistenings'.

Dallas dhu – *dol lais du* = 'meadow by the black stream'.

Dalmore – *dol mor* = 'meadow by the sea'. Alternatively *dol mawr* 'big meadow' – The distillery itself is set in a big meadow by the sea.

Edradour – Fancifully attributed locally to Gaelic *Edred dhobar* = 'King Edred's stream' – but given in Watson as *Eadar da Dhobar* = 'between two waters' becoming by assimilation *Eadarra Dhobar;* hence 'Edradour'. This explanation, derived as it was, from a 'local Gaelic speaker' is inherently unreliable (in the immortal words of Mandy Rice Davies – 'he would say that would'nt he') and does not properly fit the present geographical situation of Edradour itself; *'dhobar'* is in any case a Scots-Gaelic word adopted from Welsh *dwr*. It has to be accepted, in principle, that if even one Welsh, or adopted from Welsh, word element is found in any placename then the likelihood is that at one time that name was wholly Welsh. Reference to a Welsh Dictionary gives the word *adroddwr* 'reciter', 'narrator'. Thus Edradour could be *addroddwr dŵr* 'storyteller stream' which by assimilation becomes *addrodwr* and hence 'Edradour'. Alternatively it could simply be *adrodwr* where the 'dd' is reduced to 'd', the meaning is unchanged. The stream flowing through the farmstead of Edradour, now a distillery, is called the Edradour Burn and the probabilities are in favour of the steading taking it's name from the stream rather than vice-versa.

Glenesk – *glyn wysg* = 'valley of the water (i.e. river)'. The distillery is situated at the mouth of the South Esk river near Montrose. See entry for river Esk in River-names chapter.

Glen Fiddich – *glyn Fiddich* = 'glen of Guidid' where Guidid is the personal name of an early Pictish King; the meaning 'woodsman' derives from Welsh *guid, gwydd* = 'woods', 'trees' or alternatively 'goose'. See place-name entry for Glen Fiddich.

Glen Keith – a modern brand name dating only from 1957 taking it's title from the town of Keith (Banffs) situated on the river Isla. Keith is from one of the old Welsh forms *coet, chet, cet,* meaning 'a wood', the modern Welsh for which is *coed;* see entry for 'Keith' in Place-names chapter. The additional 'Glen' is probably a 'promotional aid' for the Whisky.

Glenlivet – Watson says – *'it takes it's name from the river Livet which supplies the distillery with it's water. Local folklore interprets 'Livet' as meaning 'the smooth one', presumably from it's supposed association with the river Lyon of Glen Lyon'.* Watson however is somewhat ambivalent in this assessment, relating *Lyon* to Latin *lima,* Irish *liomhainn* and also to Welsh *llifo,* (from *llefn* 'smooth, placid'). In any case none of these descriptions sit well as the title of what is undoubtedly a typical rushing Highland stream and the association with the river Lyon appears as tenuous now as it did to a hesitant Watson almost 100 years ago. As the Livet feeds into the Avon (Welsh *afon*) which is itself a tributary of the Spey(name probably pre-Celtic) it is far more likely that Livet originated as a Welsh description than as an Irish or Scots Gaelic one. One suggestion would be *llifet,* (pronounced 'leevet') meaning 'flood-river' – literally 'river of floodiness' i.e. liable to flood.

Glen Lossie – The Glen takes it's name from the river Lossie = *llysiau* = 'herbage' – river'.

Glenmohr – *glyn mawr* = 'Great Glen'.

Inchgower – *ynys-y-cwr* = *ynysgwr* = 'corner, edge, meadow'. Scots Inch is inherited from Welsh *Ynys,* so Inchgwr = Inchgower.

Loch Lomond – The Loch takes it's name from Ben Lomond = *y-pen-llumon* = *ben lumon* = 'beacon mountain'.

Knockan (Highland) – *cnwcan* = ‘small knoll, hillock’.

Knockando (Moray) – *cnwcan du* = ‘small black knoll’.

Knockdhu – *cnwc du* = ‘black knoll’.

Longmorn – *llan morgan* aspirated to *lan morgan* = ‘sanctuary-enclosure of Morgan, the holy man’. The local pronunciation is ‘Langmorr’n’.

Tamdhu – *tom du* = ‘black, dark, rounded-hill, mound’.

Tomatin – Watson says *‘tom is a Welsh element which has been adopted into Scots Gaelic, – in the east ‘**tom**’ has it’s British sense of rounded-hill’.* Tomatin therefore is very possibly *tom-y-tyn* meaning ‘rounded-hill by the croft’ or *tom-ar-tyn* meaning ‘rounded hill above the croft’ where ‘croft’ = ‘small farm’; pronunciation is as ‘Tomatin’ with the stress on the penultimate ‘a’. Modern Welsh dictionaries give *tom* as a ‘mound’, a ‘heap’. An alternative interpretation given in other references is the hybrid Welsh-Gaelic *tom-aitonn* = ‘rounded hill of juniper bushes’, which is said to be an apt description of the situation. Neverthetheless the presence of the pre-Gaelic *tom* presumes an original Brythonic, Early Welsh or Middle Welsh original.

Tormore – *tor mawr (mor)* ‘big hill, with rock-outcrops’.

Inverleven – *aber llefn* = ‘confluence of the river Leven’ : Welsh *aber* is the precursor of Scots *inver* and Leven = *llefn* = ‘smooth, even, placid’.

Kinclaith – There is just a possibility, no more, that this name started life as *pen cladd* = ‘far-end-of the trench, pit, burial-place,’. Welsh *pen* = ‘head’ was often usurped by Scots-Gaelic *ceann* = ‘head’, which in place-names is seen as ‘Kin’ or ‘Ken’. Scots-Gaelic *cladh* = ‘trench, churchyard’ : Welsh *cladd* = ‘trench, pit, burying-place’.

Chapter 11

Clan & Family names

'You can fairly claim the day has not been wasted,
if something has been learned'

Cadfael Chronicles, 'A Morbid Taste for Bones'

It is an interesting fact that over 90% of British surnames can be separated into just four main categories, foremost amongst which are the 'Locality-type' names derived from a person's place of origin. The other categories are 'Occupational-type' names derived from a person's trade or occupation e.g. *'Smith' 'Archer'* etc.; 'Patronymic-type' names – derived from the first name of a person's father e.g. *'Roberts'*-(Wales), *'Robertson'*-(Lowland Scotland and Northern England), *'MacRobert'*-(Scottish Highlands and Northern Ireland), 'O'Reilly'-(Ireland) etc.; and 'Soubriquet-type' names derived from a person's nickname e.g. *'Vaughan'*-(from Welsh *Fychan* = 'little'), *Buchan*-(Scots = 'little'), and *Little*-(English = 'little').

In this chapter we are concerned only with Scottish 'Locality-type' surnames which can be related to those place-names in Scotland which can be said to have a Welsh origin. Nor will the list given here be in any way comprehensive, only a sample listing of a few of the more distinctive ones will be considered and only the outline meaning will be given as fuller assessments and derivations of these and other 'locality-type' names can be found in the main chapters on Place-names, Edinburgh-names etc. Other place-names which give rise to Scottish surnames are too numerous to mention. Recourse to any Scottish Telephone Directory will reveal such as Abernethy, Cairnie (Kearney), Calder, Callender, Currie, Dairsie (D'Arcy?), Dagleish, Dalkeith, Dalrymple, Dewar, Dalton, Dinwoodie, Dollar, Drummond, Dumfries, Dunbar, Dundee, Durie, Edinburgh, Erskine, Galbraith, Gillespie, Glendinning, Irvine, Kelly, Kilwinning, Kinnaird, Lothian, Melrose, Moncrieff, Moray (Murray?), Paisley, Prendergast, Rattray, Renfrew, Rhynd, Stirling, Trearne – all of which I have personal knowledge. There will of course be many more examples than these and in fact almost any Scottish place-name will, somewhere in the world, have a corresponding surname.

Abercrombie – *aber crwm bych* = 'mouth of the little curving stream'.

Arbuckle – *ardd bugail* = 'height of the herdsman'.

Arbuthnot – *aber byddinoedd* = 'mouth of the Byddinoedd stream' : where *byddinoedd* = 'armies, hosts' (*dd* pronounced as *th* in 'the').

Buchan – *bychan* = 'little' place. Pronunciation is as 'buchan'.

Cameron – *cam bron* = 'curved hill-brow'.

Carmichael – *caer michael* = 'Michael's fort'.

Carruthers – *caer rhydderch* = 'fortress of King Rhydderch' – a Welsh name, but a Strathclyde 'British' King.

Cochrane – *coch rhen* = 'red rivulet'.

Douglas – *du glais* = 'dark stream'.

Gordon – *gor-din* = 'grand-fortress'.

Keith – *coed* = 'wood' : *coed* is a widespread element in Scottish place-names and appears in several corrupted forms, one of which is *kethe,* from which we get Keith.

Leslie – *llys celyn* = 'court, courtyard of holly-trees'.

Ogilvie – *uchel fai* = 'high plain, level-field'.

Urquhart – *ar cardden* = place 'by the thicket'.

References & Bibliography

It is typical of the world of today that website addresses should find themselves included in this list of references, although more perhaps in the way of an acknowledgement than as a source of permanent information. I am indebted to *www.cyberscotia.com* for supporting data on the name 'Lothian' and to *www.undiscoveredscotland* for supporting information on the name 'Aberdeen.'

The History of the Celtic Place-names of Scotland, W.J. Watson 1926, Birlinn 1993.

Scottish Place-Name Papers, W.J. Watson 1889-1937, Steve Savage Publishers 2002.

Place-Names of Scotland, James B. Johnston, 3rd edition 1934, SR Publishers 1970.

Scottish Place-names, W.F.H. Nicolaisen, Batsford 1976, new edition, John Donald (Birlinn) 2001.

Scotland's Place-names, David Dorward, Mercat Press 1995.

The Place Names of Edinburgh, Stuart Harris, Gordon Wright Publishers 1996.

Scottish Place Names, George Mackay 2000, Lomond Books (reprinted 2002).

Scottish Place-names, David Ross, Birlinn 2001.

The uses of Place-names, editor Simon Taylor, Scottish Cultural Press 1998.

Place names on maps of Scotland & Wales, Ordnance Survey 1981 edition, reprinted 1995.

The Concise Scots Dictionary, Chambers 1985.

Y Geiriadur Mawr, Gomer Press – 1996 edition.

English/Welsh – Welsh/English Dictionary, Collins-Spurrell 1960.

English/Welsh – Welsh/English Dictionary, Spurrell – 4th edition 1903.

The British Language in it's Lustre, Thomas Jones, London 1688, reprint Black Pig Press 1977.

Gaelic Dictionary, Malcolm MacLennan, Mercat Press 1979.

Oxford Irish Minidictionary, Oxford University Press 1999.

Teach yourself Welsh, John T Bowen & T J Rhys Jones, English Universities Press 1960.

Languages in Britain and Ireland, editor Glanville Price, Blackwell 2000.

A Guide to Welsh Place-Names (Welsh Heritage Series), Anthony Lias, Gwasg Carreg Gwalch 1994.

The Place-Names of Wales, Hywel Wyn Owen, University of Wales Press 1998.

Welsh place names, John Jones 1979, John Jones Publishing (1996 edition).

Welsh Place-names and Their Meanings, Dewi Davies, Cambrian News 2001.

Welsh Place-Names Unzipped, Brian Davies, Y Lolfa 2001.

A Study of Breconshire Place-Names, Richard Morgan & R.F. Peter Powell, Gwasg Carreg Gwalch 1999.

1000 Cornish Place Names Explained, Julyan Holmes, Tor Mark Press Redruth 1983.

A Gazetteer of Welsh Place-Names, edited Elwyn Davies, University of Wales Press 1967.

Celtic Myths, Miranda Green, British Museum Press 1993.

Celtic Goddesses, Miranda J. Green, British Museum Press 1995.

The Triumph Tree, edited by Thomas Owain Clancy, Canongate 1998.

Scotland's Story – Part 3
Scottish Universities – Depts of Celtic Studies, First Press Publishing 1999.

King Arthur and the Lost Kingdoms, Alistair Moffat, Wiedenfeld & Nicolson 1999.

Arthur and the Britons (in Wales and Scotland), W.F. Skene (edited by Derek Bryce), Llanerch Enterprises 1988.

Brother Cadfael's Book of Days – (based on *The Cadfael Chronicles* by Ellis Peters), Robin Whiteman (2000), Headline Book Publishing 2000.

The Book of Welsh Saints, T.D. Breverton, Glyndwr Publishing. 2000.

www.cyberscotia.com

www.undiscoveredscotland.co.uk

Epilogue

What is done matters,
but what is yet to do matters far more

Cadfael Chronicles, 'Dead Man's Ransom'

It is inevitable that contained within this book there will be found at least a few assertions, attributions or opinions which will in some quarters be considered 'controversial' or even 'heretical'; nevertheless there is much that will not be disputed by those in more academic circles whose professional compass includes the study of the ancient P-Celtic place-names of Scotland variously described as Brythonic, Brittonic, Cumbric, British, Pictish, Primitive-Welsh, Old-Welsh, Middle-Welsh or Modern-Welsh. This book was written with the purpose of making this very specialist subject more accessible to the general reader by listing, describing, and adding to the various possible interpretations of these names in as simple a manner as possible. It can never be more than an introduction to a subject which is addressed in greater detail and with greater erudition in our Universities and elsewhere. Place-names can in a very real sense be considered as valid archaeological remains, subject to theories and assessments in much the same way as those other archaeological artefacts which are dug out from the ground and it is perhaps significant that all previous authoritative works on Scottish place-names have relied on modern Welsh dictionaries for the word elements used to interpret these P-Celtic place-names of Scotland. This book has adopted the same procedure and extended it, sometimes to its extreme limits, but the end result still makes surprisingly good sense. Why this should be so is beyond my capabilities to explain but the known journeyings of the Chieftain Cunedda and the Poet Aneurin from Southern Scotland to northern Wales might provide small clues to contribute to the unravelling of the mystery. In addition there is a school of thought which suggests that the collection of ancient Welsh tales known today as the Mabinogion contains stories and folk lore which relate to events and landscapes which are set, not in Wales, but in Southern Scotland; in particular these suggestions would place several of the early Arthurian episodes featured in the Mabinogion 'somewhere in Southern Scotland'. There are therefore some intriguing questions to be asked the answers to which may prove to be either fanciful, or fascinating or both!

For example:

(a) Why can the P-Celtic place-names of Scotland be so successfully explained by relating them to the modern Welsh language?

(b) Is it possible that the North British Chieftain Cunedda, his many sons, the poet Aneurin and others bring the P-Celtic language of Central Scotland to North Wales, and did this language take hold to such an extent that the language of the whole of Modern Wales is in fact directly descended from the P-Celtic Welsh of that part of North Britain?

(c) Are the tales and the folklore gathered together into the Mabinogion indigenous of Wales as it is today, or were they those of the Britons and Picto-Britons of Southern Scotland, Eastern Scotland and Northern England transposed to northern Wales by North British refugees?

Appendix A

Hilton of Cadboll

The 'Stone Bridge' between Picts and Welsh

Synopsis

This Hypothesis seeks to connect the Pictish stone **Hilton of Cadboll** to the Folk Tale **Pwyll and Rhiannon** in that collection of ancient Welsh tales known as the **Mabinogion** and thereby define a bond between the Pictish Culture and the Welsh Culture of the peoples of the so-called Dark Ages. It endeavours to do this firstly by relating the **Lady Rider** on the Stone to the Celtic goddess '**Epona**', secondly by associating the **Mirror and Comb** on the Stone to ancient **Mother Goddess** figures of whom Epona was one and Rhiannon (Rigantona) another, thirdly by demonstrating connections between **Epona**, together with other Mother Goddess figures, to the central Character of '**Rhiannon**' as she appears in the Folk Tale and fourthly by relating each and every one of the other sculptures on The Stone to events and characters in The Folk Tale. The lynch-pin of the argument is the identification of an irrefutable correspondence between the characteristic features exhibited by the **Sculpture of the Lady Rider on the Stone** and the characteristic features exhibited by several of the **Sculptures of Epona** as found in various Museums. This correlation is strong enough to be considered self-evident and is possibly the only piece of *real* evidence so far found on any Pictish Stone which could relate that particular Stone to another external entity.

Hilton of Cadboll – Pwyll and Rhiannon

1 Introduction

Hilton of Cadboll is undoubtedly the most intriguing of all the Pictish Stones and the reason is not hard to find. The pre-eminent figure on the Stone is that of the mysterious Lady Rider and although there has been much speculation about it's origin and meaning no interpretation of the Scene on the Stone can be considered tenable unless it provides a satisfactory and credible explanation for who the Lady Rider may be, why she is pictured as she is and how she may fit into the Scene as a whole.

Who is she? The first clue comes from Continental Europe where there are several sculptures of the Romano-Celtic Goddess Epona which bear a striking resemblance to that of the Lady Rider on the Stone. The one from the town of Kastel in Germany, now in the Rhineland Museum in Bonn, is typical of these. Epona is unquestionably a mythological entity and the point-for-point correspondence between this sculpture and that of the Lady Rider does, ***per se***, imbue the Scene on the Stone with a mythological dimension which is then a direct invitation to pursue a mythical interpretation for the Scene as a whole. A further indication of the mythological import of the Scene comes from the presence of the Mirror & Comb sculpted on the top left corner of the Stone.

Why is she pictured as she is? There are valid arguments which link 'Epona' to 'Rhiannon' and to 'Rigantona'. Rhiannon being the dominant character in the 'Tale of Pwyll and Rhiannon' in The Mabinogion and Rigantona being a very ancient name or description occurring in early Celtic Mythology. Thus the depicting of the Lady Rider as Epona subtly infers a relationship to Rhiannon which in turn supplies an essential link between the Stone and the Tale.

On the assumption that the Lady Rider is a

representation of Rhiannon the Tale can then provide an interpretation which accounts, not only for the Lady Rider, but also for each and every one of the other identifiable figures on the Stone and how they all fit in with the events and characters in The Tale.

2 The Stone 'Hilton of Cadboll' – (the sculpted Scene)
In the hunting scene at the bottom of the stone is a single stag beset by two hounds. Above the stag is a horseman riding a fine horse and holding a spear. To the right of the stag is another horseman, also holding a spear, but mounted on a smaller horse of a different type. In the top right hand corner are two minstrels and another hound. To the left of these, and more or less centre stage, is a Lady Rider mounted on a high-stepping horse, richly attired and wearing a headdress. She is seated *sideways* on the horse and holds something in her hands. The figure of the Lady Rider is superimposed on another figure of a Male Rider mounted on a horse which exactly matches hers in every respect – even stride for stride. In the top left hand corner are a mirror and a comb.

The Scene on the Stone
(Photo by kind permission of Prof. Miranda Aldhouse-Green)

3 The Tale of 'Pwyll and Rhiannon' (an outline of the initial episodes)

Arawn, a God of the Celtic Otherworld, and Pwyll, a Prince of Dyfed, are unbeknown to each other hunting in the same ForeSt Pwyll comes across a stag beset by a strange hound with shining white, silver-tipped fur and scarlet ears; he drives off this strange hound and sets his own hound at the stag. Arawn, the owner of the magical hound, appears on the scene and upbraids Pwyll for his discourtesy. As a penance Pwyll agrees to change identities with Arawn and, for one whole year, take his place as King of the Otherworld. This year passes pleasantly in a round of hunting, feasting and minstrelsy but at the end of it Pwyll is obliged to kill Hafgan, an enemy of Arawn. This he does successfully and having passed this final Test he returns to the normal world not only as Prince of Dyfed but also with the enhanced status of a 'Lord' of the Otherworld.

Later he is advised to go out from his Court and sit on a particular Mound from where it is promised he will see a wonder. The 'Wonder' duly appears in the form of a Lady Rider wearing rich robes of brocaded gold, topped with a headdress, and seated on a magnificent white horse; her horse, it seems, has magical talents for however fast Pwyll rides to meet her and however slowly the horse *appears* to move he can never get any nearer to them. At last, in desperation he calls out and implores the Lady to stop. She does so immediately – but at the same time rebukes him for not asking sooner- and so tiring his horse unnecessarily! The Lady Rider is 'Rhiannon' – a woman who, it transpires, also has supernatural powers. She has chosen Pwyll to be her earthly Consort and after some adventures and some misadventures, they are duly wed.

4 The Hypothesis

4.1 The scene depicted on The Stone can be separated into four basic component parts three of which can be arranged anti-clockwise from bottom-centre to top-right to top-left-centre in a chronological order which accords with the sequence of events in The Tale.

1. a hunting scene
2. a group of two minstrels and a hound
3. the figure of a Lady Rider superimposed on that of a Male Rider.
4. The fourth part (top-left) depicts what is said to be a representation of a mirror and a comb.

Other aspects of the sculpted figures are considered to be of significance. i.e. – (a) one of the horses is smaller and less impressive than the other three and – (b) the Lady Rider is depicted in a form identical in character to that of several sculptures depicting the Celtic Goddess Epona.

4.2. It is the purpose of this hypothesis to provide an 'interpretation' accounting for each of the animated figures on the Stone, as follows:

In the hunting scene at the bottom of the Stone the single stag (or deer) is beset by two hounds. One of these belongs to Arawn and the other to Pwyll. The rider above the stag is Arawn mounted as befits his divine status on a horse of some quality. Behind him and below him Pwyll, an ordinary mortal at that time, is astride the smaller horse. In the top right hand corner Pwyll's year of hunting, feasting and minstrelsy in the Otherworld is suggested by the figures of the hound and the two musicians playing wind instruments. To the left of these and more or less centre-stage is Rhiannon, richly attired, with a headdress, seated sideways on a horse and holding in her hands a symbol of the bounty she has to offer. The sculpture replicates some of those depicting Epona, a Romano-Celtic Goddess whose association with horses and the bringing of prosperity connect her, in some way, with Rhiannon. The figure of the Male Rider, upon which the figures of Rhiannon and her horse are superimposed, is Pwyll. He is riding a horse which exactly equals Rhiannon's, the superior nature of his new steed being indicative of the raised status bestowed on him as a result of his sojourn in the the Otherworld. His steed matches Rhiannon's stride-for-stride thus confirming that he has at last caught up with her and been accepted by her as her Consort in the 'normal' world. If so, then the Sculptures on the Stone illustrate, from beginning to end, the events encompassed within the first two Episodes of the First Branch of the collection of Tales known as the Mabinogion.

Epona
(Photo by kind permission of the National Museum of Scotland)

4.3 Although eminently plausible by itself alone the credibility of this interpretation is bolstered by independent evidence connecting both the Lady Rider and the Mirror & Comb to Epona, Rigantona and Rhiannon.

4.3.1 The connection between the Lady Rider and Epona is predicated on the similarity between the sculpture of the Lady Rider on the Stone and sculptures of Epona as epitomized by that from Kastel in Germany. I like to think that this connection is proved by the 'Duck Theorem' – i.e.

If it...........waddles.................... like a duck
If it...........swims........................like a duck
If it...........flies...........................like a duck
If it...........quacks.......................like a duck
If it...........has feathers.............like a duck
If it...........lays eggs...................like a duck
And it.......*looks*............................like a duck
Then it......**is**...............................a **DUCK**

Similarly, in the case of the Lady Rider and Epona

If she........rides a high-stepping horse................ like Epona
If the.........'horse' is a Mare.................................... like Epona's
If she.........is seated *sideways* on it......................... like Epona
If she.........is richly attired...................................... like Epona
If she.........is wearing a headdress......................... like Epona
If she........is holding something in her hands..... like Epona
And she....*looks*.. like Epona
Then she...**is**.. **EPONA**

Not so long ago people were sentenced to death and hanged on much less evidence than this!

It should be noted also that the character of Rhiannon as she appears in the Mabinogion shares three of the five main characteristics exhibited by the sculpture of the Lady Rider; i.e. she rides a fine *'white horse of large size'*, she is richly attired in *'a garment of shining gold'* and on meeting with Pwyll *'she threw back that part of her headdress which covered her face'*. Thus we have a well substantiated 5-line connection between the Lady Rider and Epona together with a slightly less well substantiated 3-line connection running between Epona, Rhiannon and the Lady Rider as is shown in the following 'circular double-duck' theorem which illustrates these connections from the Lady Rider to Epona, then from Epona to Rhiannon and finally from Rhiannon back to the Lady Rider.

richly attired.......... Lady Rider.. Epona.. Rhiannon.. Lady Rider...
wears a headdress... Lady Rider.. Epona.. Rhiannon.. Lady Rider...
rides a fine horse...... Lady Rider.. Epona.. Rhiannon.. Lady Rider...
seated *sideways*......... Lady Rider.. Epona...
something in hand.. Lady Rider.. Epona...

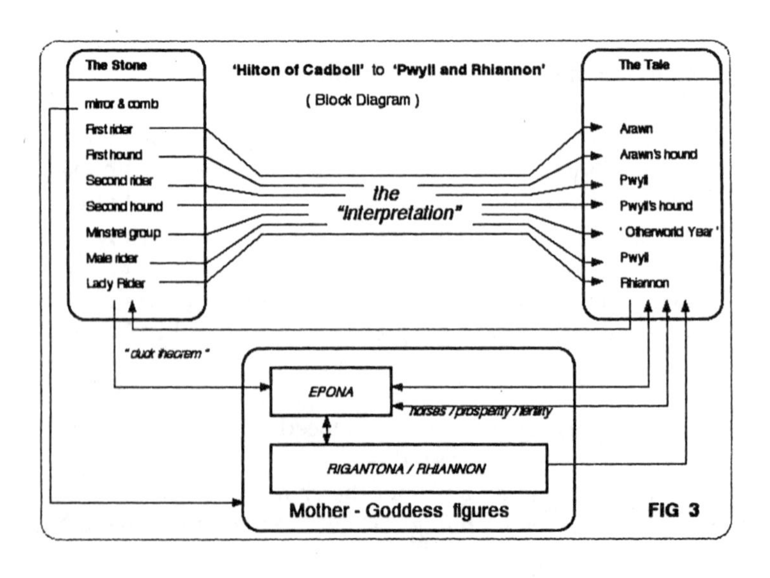

FIG 3

4.3.2 The connections between Epona, Rigantona and Rhiannon are supported by various linguistic and mythological studies which, whilst accepting that connections do exist, do not always agree with each other as to what exactly these connections could be. The mythological studies consider 'Rigantona' as a title meaning 'Great Divine Queen', possibly a reference to the original 'Earth Mother' or 'Mother Goddess' figures of very ancient times, and linguistically it is considered that Rhiannon is simply the name Rigantona translated into Welsh. What is more certain is that Epona, Rigantona and Rhiannon all have 'Mother Goddess' associations which link them together in some way. Epona and 'Rhiannon' (as in 'Pwyll & Rhiannon') are intimately linked to the Celtic Cult of the Horse and both are associated with attributions of fertility and the bringing of prosperity. These shared characteristics constitute a link between the two which is independent of the connection via 'Rigantona/Rhiannon'. Rhiannon, in the Mabinogion, is of course simply a Character in a Folk Tale but it seems that the essence of this Character is woven around the early beliefs surrounding Epona and Rigantona.

4.3.3 The overall relationships between 'Hilton of Cadboll', 'Pwyll and Rhiannon', 'Epona' and 'Rhiannon' are illustrated in the block diagram of FIG 3. It can be seen that the connection between The Stone and The Tale is not solely dependent on the link between the Lady Rider, Epona, and Rhiannon; it is also linked quite independently by the 'Interpretation' which equates the individual Figures on The Stone directly to the Characters in The Tale. Thus the Lady Rider is linked to Rhiannon not only through the Interpretation but also through Epona and it can be observed that these two links are mutually supportive in that the credibility of one adds credence to the other

5. Review

5.1 At the most superficial level it is possible to analyse the scene on the Stone and construct a very reasonable interpretation equating the figures on the Stone with characters and events in the Tale of Pwyll and Rhiannon.

5.2 More significantly, the striking correspondence (see the 'Duck Theorem') between the sculpture of the Lady Rider on the Stone and the similar sculptures of Epona in Continental Europe provides ***positive evidence*** of a link between the two.

5.3 This correspondence does, ***by itself alone***, imbue the whole of the Scene on the Stone with a mythical dimension which lends substance to the idea of a connection between it and the mythical Tale. This mythical dimension is further reinforced by the presence of the Mirror & Comb sculptures on the Stone and although the exact significance of these two symbols is obscure it seems to be generally accepted that they are somehow associated with 'mother goddess' figures such as Epona and Rhiannon. Thus their presence on the stone may be a direct pointer to the identity of the Lady Rider. It may also be relevant that Mermaids, who are magical creatures in their own right are sometimes thought to be have associations with 'mother goddesses' and are invariably pictured seated on a rock holding a mirror in one hand and combing their hair with the other.

5.4 Mythological studies support a link between Epona and Rigantona, whilst linguistic and etymological studies consider the name 'Rhiannon' to be simply the name 'Rigantona' as it was absorbed into the Welsh Language Taken together these studies complete an additional connection from the Lady Rider to Rhiannon via Epona and Rigantona, which adds independent reinforcement to the

Interpretation. According to some sources 'Rigantona', 'Rig Antona', or 'Rigani' is not the name of some mythological being but simply a title meaning 'Great High (or Divine) Queen' – possibly related to the original 'Earth Mother Goddess' of historic antiquity. Other sources specifically place Epona as the daughter of Rigantona and Teutares (the God Mars by another name). No one however seems to doubt the existence of a connection between Epona and Rigantona even though there is some argument as to what exactly that connection may be.

5.5 It is considered that the Stone was sculpted somewhere about the 9th century AD, some hundreds of years after Christianity had supplanted the earlier Gods and beliefs of the Picts. It is unlikely therefore that the sculptor intended his sculpture of the Lady Rider to represent the pagan Godess Epona, far more likely that he intended that the Lady Rider should be seen directly as the Folk character Rhiannon and not as either of the pagan deities Rigantona or Rhiannon or Epona.

5.6 That this *Pictish* Stone from the 8/9th century should have a connection to a *Welsh* Tale first written down in the 12/13th century but dating back to long before then, and that all the disparate aspects of, and entities present in, the Scene can be explained away in every detail by reference to what is one of the most ancient of all the Tales in the Mabinogion is, although remarkable, not altogether surprising when it is minded that the Picto-Britons to the north of the Forth-Clyde axis and their fellow Britons to the south of that line spoke dialects of the same P-Celtic language and *'shared the same political and cultural space, the same language and the same ethnicity'* (*Dr Thomas Owen Clancy*). In all probability they would also have shared the same ancestral Folk-Myths. The common language of the

Britons and Picto-Britons although sometimes described as 'Brythonic' or 'Pictish' is in todays world better recognised and understood when described as a form of Old Welsh and in the age of the Pictish Stones and the Mabinogion the terms 'British' and 'Welsh' were in fact synonymous.

There is also the connection made by the North British Chieftain, Cunedda, when he left North Britain (now 'Scotland') to establish the 'Kingdom' of Gwynedd in what is now North Wales. Did he and his followers take the mythology, including the Tale of Pwyll and Rhiannon, with them? Or was it already common knowledge to *all* Britons both North, South, East and West? Alternatively was the Tale brought to Pictland by the Britons of Northumberland who, it is now thought, are the ones who brought their stonemason skills to the task of sculpting Pictish Stones such as Hilton of Cadboll?

5.7 The Hypothesis so constructed is, so far, the only interpretation which is able to provide a convincing explanation, not only for the whole Scene, but also for each and every one of the individual sculptures upon it.

What does the Hypothesis, if true, tell us about the person (or persons) who sculpted the Scene on the Stone? He (or 'they') would have had a knowledge of the Tale of Pwyll and Rhiannon, he (or 'they') would have been familiar with the sculptures of the Goddess Epona and would also have had the confidence to know that by sculpting the Lady Rider in the style of Epona this would effectively convey a sense of the Lady Rider's relationship to Rhiannon. It is also possible to think of the Scene on the Stone is a sort of illustrated 'comic-strip' introduction not only to the Tale of Pwyll and Rhiannon but also to a whole collection of Mythical Tales of which only remnants are known to us today. It is surely no coincidence that the sculptures can be related to the *very first* Episodes of the *very first* Tale in the

Mabinogion and can therefore be seen to act as the prologue or introduction to all subsequent Tales.

What is or was the purpose of the Stone? The only thing the Hypothesis tells us is that the Scene on the Stone is an illustration of the Tale. It may be entirely fanciful therefore but those of a romantic disposition may find it possible to imagine an itinerant Shaman (storyteller) gathering his audience around the Stone and then, as the light fades over the Moray Firth, holding his audience enthralled as, using the Stone as an introduction, he launches himself into the whole saga of P-Celtic Mythology handed down from untold generations of dedicated Bards steeped in the Oral Tradition of his day and age?

Addendum – Madrun, Matrona, Rhiannon

The following quotations are taken from ***The Celtic Goddess*** (Claire French : Floris Books, Edinburgh 2001)

> **Page 74** – *'Until Reformation Times, Rhiannon / Modron was worshipped in Wales as St Madrun ['foster mother'] and in that role was represented as a woman on horseback, cradling a child in her arms and fleeing from some sort of conflagration – an image reminiscent of Mary with the Baby Jesus on the Flight from Egypt ...'*

> **Page 74** – *'The Welsh scholar W.J. Gruffydd was the first to recognize the fusion of Modron (Great Mother) with Rigantona (Great Queen) and Epona (Great Mare)'.*

> **Page 228** – *'The name 'Rigani' originally found only in Gaul, must have changed via 'Rigantona' to 'Rhiannon' in Britain. Very early her image must have merged with that of the Celtic horse goddess Epona as well as that of the pre-celtic Earth Mother Modron / Matrona to form a complex deity who has many parallels and similarities with the pre-hellenic barley goddess Demeter and the Roman Cardia or Ceres.*

The above extracts from the book by Claire French may add some further enlightenment to the mystery of The Stone. It is universally accepted that in the early years of Christianity it was a common ploy to build new Christian places of worship right on top of ancient Pagan sacred sites, this in order to at once obliterate any evidence of it's previous use whilst simultaneously taking into it's new purpose any remaining aura of a more ancient sanctity. Indeed there are those who think they went even further and subsumed the Pagan cult of the various Earth Mother Goddess figures into the context of the Christian Religion as the 'cult' of the Virgin Mary ('Holy Mary – Mother of Jesus' etc.). Thus it is no surprise when looking at the archaeological site at Hilton of Cadboll, in it's entirety, to see the ruins of a Christian Chapel within a few yards of where The Stone was originally sited and to learn that this was known as *Saint Mary's Chapel*. It is surely not too outrageous to suggest that this name resulted directly from the early Christians' deliberate attempt to portray part of the Scene on The Stone as a representation of the Holy Family on their Flight into Egypt and so name their chapel accordingly? Thereby very effectively overlaying all previous Pagan remembrances and endowing the Chapel with an ancient but somewhat artificial Christian provenance.

In Wales Saint Madrun is recorded in early writings as fleeing, together with her baby son Ceidio (later St Ceidio), from the 'flames of King Vortigern's last stand at Tre yr Ceiri'. St Ceidio himself is said to have founded a Church at Llangeidio in Wales before betaking himself and his mother to Cornwall. He had an association with horses which he must have inherited from his mother Madrun / Modron who in this respect displays her own association with Epona and Rhiannon and therefore also with the Lady Rider on The Stone.

Although Saint ***Madrun, Madrun, Modron, Madryn, Fadryn, Fadrun,*** or ***Materiana*** is well represented in Welsh place-names she remains a nebulous figure and it would be nice to know more about her!

Appendix B

Notes on Cunedda

Cunedda was a North British Chieftain of Manaw Gododdin, now Clackmannanshire, in central Scotland. Sometime around the end of the 4th century AD and the begining of the 5th century AD it is said that he, together with eight of his nine sons, betook themselves to northern Wales where they drove out the Irish 'Scottii' who were attempting to infiltrate that area in the wake of the Roman withdrawal from Britain. Having taken control of the region and given it the name Y Guneddion = 'Land of Cunedd', now known as Gwynedd, he allocated other lands to his various sons. Other parts of Wales are named after these sons and other members of his family. For example. Ceredigion is named after his son Ceredig and Merioneth is named after his grandson Meirion. His remaining sons Ysfael, Rhufon, Dunod, Afloeg, Einion Eyrth, Dogfael, and Edern also gave names to places in Wales but these names have not survived.

Reading.

In Search of the Picts – Elizabeth Sutherland

The Mabinogion – Lady Charlotte Guest

The Mabinogion – Gwyn Jones and Thomas Jones

Celtic Myths – Miranda Jane Green

Celtic Wales – Miranda Green & Ray Howell

Unpublished Paper – Professor Miranda Auldhouse Green

The Horse in Celtic Culture – Various Authors, University of Cardiff

Scotland's Story- Part 3 – Various Authors, Scottish Universities, Celtic Departments

The Triumph Tree – Thomas Owen Clancy

King Arthur and the Britons – in Wales and Scotland – W F Skene

The Celts – John Davies

The Celtic Goddess – Claire French